The Beach Boys FAQ

All That's Left to Know about America's Band

Jon Stebbins

Backbeat Books

An Imprint of Hal Leonard Corporation

Published in 2011 by Backbeat Books
An Imprint of Hal Leonard Corporation
7777 West Bluemound Road
Milwaukee, WI 53213

Trade Book Division Editorial Offices
33 Plymouth Street, Montclair, NJ 07042

All images are from the personal collection of the author unless otherwise noted. Permissions can be found on page 319, which constitutes an extension of this copyright page.

The FAQ series was conceived by Robert Rodriguez and developed with Stuart Shea.

Printed in the United States of America

Book design by Snow Creative Services

Library of Congress Cataloging-in-Publication Data

Stebbins, Jon.
    The Beach Boys FAQ : all that's left to know about America's band / Jon Stebbins.
        p. cm.
    Includes bibliographical references and index.
    ISBN 978-0-87930-987-9 (pbk.)
    1. Beach Boys. I. Title.
    ML421.B38S74 2011
    782.42166092'2—dc23
                                    2011026708

www.backbeatbooks.com

To my dad, because he made everything possible

Contents

Foreword

I remember loading our equipment from the alley into Western Recorders the day we recorded "Surfin' Safari" in April 1962. I was only 13 years old, and those Fender tube amps were heavy. Plus the outboard reverb units, our guitars, and Dennis's drums. By the time we got it all into the studio I was ready for a break at the snack station down the hall. There were vending machines with Cokes, and we could sneak a cigarette there. That studio always had famous people floating around. I recall seeing the Ronettes there. Frank Sinatra recorded there, too. For a kid like me it could all be a little distracting, although I did understand how important it was to record in a studio like that. I immediately felt like the studio environment was where I was meant to be.

Brian was so enthusiastic. Sometimes he'd get a little ahead of himself. Chuck Britz, and his assistant, got the equipment positioned, and the microphones placed. Once everything was set up and plugged in, we started setting levels. The room sounded great. We'd rehearsed the songs at home, so we were ready that day. The Beach Boys' style was already there. We had it down. Our heavily reverbed guitars gave the recording a little extra pop. It was a unique combination of stuff that created that snappy sound. The guitars, amps, room sound, type of microphones, and their placement. It all worked well. Dennis's drums, too: they had that snappy snare sound. When we put it all together with the voices it was magic.

When we left the studio, Brian was carrying the acetates. He couldn't wait to get them home and listen to them. It wasn't long before Capitol Records signed us, and then it all escalated very quickly. I was eating dinner with my parents when "Surfin' Safari" came on the radio. I got so excited. I stuck my face in my napkin and screamed! Carl was buying copies of *Billboard* magazine every week, and every week it was going higher in the charts. Carl would come running over and say, "It's got a bullet!" Then the next time he'd say, "It's a double-sided hit!" It was a big deal. Things were changing for us very quickly.

Since then a lot has happened to all of us. Two of us are gone and the rest of us are getting older, but we're still rocking. It's important to tell these stories now and make the information available to Beach Boys fans.

I had the experience of co-writing my own biography, *The Lost Beach Boy*, with Jon Stebbins in 2006. I know firsthand that Jon will do his best to tell the Beach Boys' story in an entertaining way, but he will also make sure the facts are right. I'm glad Jon is writing *The Beach Boys FAQ* book. I can't wait to get a copy and dig in. I know I'm going to learn some new things about my old band.

—*David Marks*

David Marks is a founding member of the Beach Boys and played guitar on the classics "Surfin' Safari," "409," "Surfer Girl," "Surfin' U.S.A.," "Shut Down," "Little Deuce Coupe," "In My Room," "Catch a Wave," "Be True To Your School," and many others. He grew up in a house that was located directly across the street from the Wilson home in Hawthorne, California

THE BEACH BOYS

CAPITOL RECORDING ARTISTS

For Your Entertainment Pleasure

DAVID MARKS	TEENAGE HOPS
RHTHYM GUITAR	TV, RADIO AND
Bus. OR 8-6054	STAGE APPEARANCES

Preface

Having read some of the other FAQ books I am excited to offer a similar treatment on the Beach Boys. With so much achievement, creativity, controversy, and drama woven through their 50-year history the Beach Boys offer incredibly fertile ground for the FAQ format. And with their wealth of contradictions, extreme highs and lows, artistic triumphs and personal volatility, it would seem natural that a lifelong Beach Boys obsessive such as me, who has seen and heard it all, would be the right person to tackle the job. Just understanding the incredible historical nuances, ever shifting public perceptions of the group, and always evolving factions within the group is a challenge. I've been managing fairly well as a Beach Boys historian for over a decade, but it's the four-decades long fan in me that constantly wants to dig deeper.

At their early peak in the summer of 1964, the Beach Boys were without a doubt America's number-one pop group.

A great rock-and-roll story is a magnet. Without a doubt, the Beach Boys story has one of the strongest pulls of all. With over 120,000,000 in record sales, the Beach Boys have certainly earned the title "America's Band." Their story is worthy of being analyzed, updated, and shared because there are few like it. Through my work I've been lucky enough to have the pleasure of telling various pieces of the Beach Boys story, sharing fresh perspectives and breaking new ground. Along the way I've constantly been editing the Beach Boys FAQ book that lives in my head. Thanks to Backbeat Books and the Hal Leonard Group for giving me the vehicle to give my head a good cleaning out.

Al Jardine pictured shortly after rejoining the group in 1963. Al helped found the Beach Boys in 1961, but then quit the group in its early months of existence. With the band in the midst of its rise to national fame, Al came back as a part-time sub for Brian Wilson in the spring of 1963. Al finally became a full-time Beach Boy again upon David Marks's departure in late 1963.

Bruce Johnston in 1967. Bruce became Bri Wilson's full-time replacement on stage star in 1965, and also proved to be a major asset to Beach Boys in the studio.

Acknowledgments

I'd like to thank the following people, all of whom greatly helped me during the long process of putting this book together.

Howie Edelson, who is my collaborator, sounding board, and close friend; he helps me every day, and makes me laugh more often than that.

Andrew G. Doe, whose knowledge of the Beach Boys is unsurpassed, and whose personal assistance and fantastic Website (Bellagio 10452) make doing my job so much easier.

Craig Slowinski, who is the best sessions researcher in the Beach Boys world.

Ian Rusten, who is the best gigs researcher in the Beach Boys world.

All the dudes and gals at the Smiley Smile message board. This book is filled with your heart and energy. Thanks for your help!

To my family—Nadia, Shannon, and Sophie—thank you for supporting me and loving me. You are the very best thing in this whole world.

To Caroline and Felix; thanks for the support, the love, and the fun.

To my sisters Carla and Tina, you two are the ones who got me started on this path. Thanks for the great records and for having such excellent taste in music!

A big thanks to everyone below for all the good things you do.

Bernadette Malavarca, Marybeth Keating, Robert Lecker, Robert Rodriguez, Carole Dreier, Alan Boyd, Mark Linett, Ed Roach, Domenic Priore, Danny Rothenberg, David Beard, John Hanlon, James Guercio, Carrie Marks, Peter Reum, Gregg Jakobson, Don Williams, Joost van Gisbergen, Billy Hinsche, Jeffrey Foskett, Phil Cooper, Nelson Bragg, Probyn Gregory, Darian Sahanaja, Jez Graham, Stevie Kalinich, Barbara Wilson, Carole Bloom, Scott Wilson, Michael Wilson, Carl B. Wilson, Gage Wilson, Chris Wilson, Jennifer Wilson, Justyn Wilson, Jonah Wilson, Carnie Wilson, Wendy Wilson, Matt Jardine, Adam Jardine, Margaret Dowdle-Head, Dan Addington, Susan Lang, Paula Bondi-Springer, Trisha Campo, Betty Collignon, Marilyn Wilson Rutherford, Daniel Rutherford, Elliot Kendall, Lance Robison, Chris Woods, Perry Cox, Glen Starkey, Brian Chidester, Peter Carlin, Matt O'Casey, Richie Unterberger, Mark Dillon, Gene Sculatti,

Dale and Mary Fahnhorst, Bob and Kathy McCleskey, Tom Concannon, Teri Tith, the Calhoun Sisters, Tom Alford, Victoria Evanoff, Mike Alford, Greg and Kathleen Edwards, Reefers Rollers—and Brian Wilson, Dennis Wilson, Carl Wilson, Mike Love, Al Jardine, David Marks, Bruce Johnston, Blondie Chaplin, and Ricky Fataar.

The Beach Boys
FAQ

And Now . . . from Hawthorne, California (and Inglewood, Brentwood, and Durbin) . . . the Fabulous Beach Boys!

The Beach Boys consisted of six founding members, and three additional "official" members who joined subsequently. They are as follows . . .

Brian Wilson

(Brian Douglas Wilson, born June 20, 1942) Brian is the creative force behind the Beach Boys' most acclaimed work. He wrote the music, and some of the lyrics, to a string of hits that are among the most frequently played and best remembered in the history of popular music. His harmony arrangements have been called the ultimate vocal sound in '60s rock music. As a producer and musical arranger, Brian pioneered the use of the studio as an instrument of progression in pop music, along the way creating his masterpiece LP *Pet Sounds*—which altered the rock landscape and influenced everyone, including the Beatles. He then topped that by masterminding an avant-garde pocket symphony into three minutes of pop perfection with the iconic hit single "Good Vibrations." Brian's participation as a performing Beach Boy was always inconsistent at best, as he prefers the studio to the stage. His mental problems have plagued him since the earliest days of the

The *Surfin' Safari* photo shoot at Paradise Cove in Malibu, summer, 1962. The five Pendleton-clad boys with an old pickup truck became an iconic image that resonated from coast to coast.   *Photo courtesy of Phil Rotella*

group. He has been institutionalized more than once, and placed under 24-hour therapy for many years of his life. He last appeared with the Beach Boys in 1996, and currently tours and records as a solo act. Brian has contributed vocals, keyboards, and bass to the band's records and performances.

Dennis Wilson

(Dennis Carl Wilson, born December 4, 1944; died December 28, 1983) Dennis was the physical personification of the Beach Boys' sun-and-fun image. He lived fast and died young. Dennis was the quintessential embodiment of the carefree California wild child, and many consider him to have been Brian Wilson's fundamental muse. He was the original band's only serious surfer, and brought that lyrical idea to the group, who then sold it to the world. He also held the distinction of being the Beach Boys' sex symbol and girl magnet. As a drummer, his technique was primitive, but his approach was incredibly energetic and powerful, often giving the group's concerts their focal point. Dennis unexpectedly evolved into the second great composer of emotionally gripping music in the Beach Boys family, and became their first acclaimed solo artist with his classic 1977 LP *Pacific Ocean Blue.* His musical productivity stalled as his life was short-circuited by severe alcoholism and substance addiction. At the time of his death from drowning in 1983, he was barred from appearing with the Beach Boys and was homeless. Dennis's musical role in the Beach Boys band was on vocals, drums, and keyboards.

Carl Wilson

(Carl Dean Wilson, born December 21, 1946; died February 6, 1998) Carl may have possessed the greatest voice in rock's greatest vocal group. He sang lead on some of the Beach Boys' absolute timeless classics, including "God Only Knows" and "Good Vibrations." Carl also provided much of the signature Fender guitar sound on the band's hit records, and is considered one of rock's early influential guitarists. The youngest of the three Wilson brothers, Carl was essentially the band's leader for nearly three decades of its existence. He played his last Beach Boys concert in 1997, and died of cancer the following year. Carl's role in the Beach Boys' band was on vocals, lead guitar, and occasional keyboards.

Mike Love

(Michael Edward Love, born March 15, 1941) Mike is the often-controversial frontman and longest-serving member of the Beach Boys. He is the first cousin of the Wilson brothers, the Beach Boys' primary lyricist, and lead singer on the majority of the Beach Boys' hits. Mike's lyrics are some of the best known in rock history, and run the gamut from sophomoric to incredibly artful. His ability to directly connect and communicate playfully with listeners has been compared to the equally successful writings of Chuck Berry. Mike has also proved his ability to move beyond the Berry style with timeless lyric sets like "The Warmth of the Sun" and "Good Vibrations." He continues to be the only founding member of the Beach Boys still touring in the band called the Beach Boys. He has been at it for 50 years. Mike's role in the Beach Boys band is that of singer (lead and bass) and occasional saxophonist.

Alan Jardine

(Alan Charles Jardine, born September 3, 1942) Al was a high-school classmate of Brian Wilson and an essential element in the genesis of the Beach
Boys. Al's voice is ever-present within the complex harmonic structures
of the Beach Boys' music. He also occasionally shined as a lead singer, as
demonstrated on the number-one hit "Help Me, Rhonda." Al's ability to
uncannily reproduce the sound of Brian Wilson's voice made him an invalu-
able asset due to Brian's spotty attendance record at Beach Boys concerts
and recording sessions. Al was also the least flamboyant personality in the
band. He never took drugs, and preferred folk music to rock and roll. He was
terminated from the Beach Boys in 1998 due to a conflict with Mike Love. He
continues performing as a solo artist and in Beach Boys spinoff groups. Al's
role in the Beach Boys band was on vocals, rhythm guitar, and bass.

David Marks

(David Lee Marks, born August 22, 1948) David was the Wilsons' neighbor
and the youngest member of the original Beach Boys, joining the band at
age 13. He performed on the group's first six hit singles for Capitol Records
and their first four gold-selling LPs. David's founding-member status has
often been overlooked by rock historians due to the fact that he was not on
the Beach Boys' first indie single, "Surfin," recorded in 1961 by the Wilsons,
Love, and Jardine. However, a fair examination of the Beach Boys' genesis
reveals that in 1958, David and Carl Wilson began developing the dual-guitar
vocabulary that permeated the early Beach Boys hits. Marks walked away
from the band in late 1963 just as the group's initial fame was solidifying
due to a conflict between his parents and Beach Boys father/manager Murry
Wilson. He rejoined the band in 1997, and quit again in 1999 due to health
concerns. He again joined the Beach Boys on a 2008 tour of the British Isles
as a special guest. David is the best pure musician among the original Beach
Boys. For many years he was the only group member to travel freely between
each of the lawsuit-consumed Beach Boys factions. David's role in the Beach
Boys band is on rhythm and lead guitar, and occasional vocals.

Bruce Johnston

(Benjamin Baldwin, born June 27, 1942) (Adopted name Bruce Arthur
Johnston) Bruce joined the Beach Boys in 1965, and, aside from one
extended absence (1972 to 1978), has been a Beach Boy ever since. He gave
the band another great voice for Brian's harmony arrangements as well as

flexibility as a musician and a permanent replacement for Brian in concert. Bruce was a successful record producer and composer long before he joined the Beach Boys, and his partnership with producer Terry Melcher attained modest commercial success. Bruce eventually hit the jackpot by winning a Grammy in 1975 for penning the Barry Manilow hit "I Write the Songs." He had less success producing two LPs for the Beach Boys in 1978 and 1979, and was maligned for steering them toward disco. Today he continues touring with Mike Love in the current-day Beach Boys. Bruce's role in the Beach Boys band is on vocals, keyboards, and bass.

Blondie Chaplin

(Terrence William Chaplin, born July 7, 1951) A native of South Africa, Blondie joined the Beach Boys in 1972. He is best remembered as lead vocalist on the classic Brian Wilson tune "Sail On Sailor." His tenure was cut short in late 1973 after a backstage fight with then-manager Steve Love. He has since become part of the Rolling Stones' touring band. Blondie's contributions to the Beach Boys band were on vocals, guitar, and bass.

Ricky Fataar

(Born September 5, 1952) Ricky, a bandmate of Blondie Chaplin's in the group the Flame, also joined the Beach Boys in 1972. He became the Beach Boys' primary drummer until his departure in late 1974, when Dennis Wilson finally recovered from a serious 1971 hand injury. He went on to play the character Stig O'Hara in the Beatles parody group the Rutles, and is currently a member of Bonnie Raitt's band. Ricky's role in the Beach Boys band was on drums, steel guitar, and occasional vocals.

The 1972 Beach Boys (l–r): Carl, Al, Ricky Fataar, Dennis, Blondie Chaplin, and Mike. By this time, Brian had initiated his deeply reclusive phase, rarely participating in anything involving the Beach Boys.

2

Sideman Surfin'

A Who's Who of Beachboydom

G len Campbell, Captain & Tennille, Jan and Dean, John Stamos, and others have been wrongly credited as being former *members* of the Beach Boys; however, each of them *have* toured with and worked with the group in one capacity or another. The incredibly long list of collaborators, sidemen, and special guests who have been a part of the Beach Boys story includes names as diverse as Charles Manson, Annette Funicello, Leon Russell, Julio Iglesias, and the Fat Boys. This is an overview of the many famous and not-so-famous musicians that were almost . . . kind of . . . but not really Beach Boys.

Glen Campbell

"Which Country Music Entertainer of the Year and Hall of Fame legend was formerly a member of the Beach Boys?" Glen is the standard answer to the ubiquitous trivia question. The problem with this riddle is that Campbell was never *really* an official member of the Beach Boys. On December 6, 1964, when Brian Wilson retreated from touring due to mental stress, Glen Campbell temporarily replaced him on stage, and the legendary myth of Glen as Beach Boy began. But the truth is that the Beach Boys have used more than a few fill-in performers through the years. Dennis Wilson had a live replacement as early as February 1963, when drummer Mark Groseclose subbed for him owing to a leg injury sustained in a serious car crash. And in the years since, there have been a number of temporary stand-ins for frontline Beach Boys, with Campbell just being the most famous of them. Campbell did serve as session guitarist on a number of well-known Beach Boys tracks; and in early 1965, Campbell *was* offered a slot as an official Beach Boy. That same year, Brian Wilson wrote and produced a fantastic vocal showcase for him with the single "Guess I'm Dumb." However, Campbell had designs on a solo career and never accepted the permanent

Beach Boys slot, and by April 1965 Bruce Johnston had grabbed the role of official sixth Beach Boy. Within a few years, Campbell was riding high on the pop charts with signature tunes like "Gentle on My Mind" and "Wichita Linemen," and hosting his own weekly television show.

Jan and Dean

Sometimes casual observers of pop culture think of the Beach Boys and Jan and Dean as the same thing. There have even been those who confuse the singing duo as members of the Beach Boys group. Not true, never was. The late Jan Berry *was* a huge creative influence on Brian Wilson, and vice-versa. In the early 1960s, the bands performed together in concert with the Beach Boys sometimes providing the instrumental backing for Jan and Dean's set. Brian co-wrote and contributed vocals to a number of Jan and Dean songs, including the number-one hit "Surf City" in 1963. Jan's partner Dean Torrence contributed a chirpy falsetto vocal to the Beach Boys' brainwasher of a single "Barbara Ann" in 1965, and designed dodgy cover art for a couple of their LPs in the '70s. After nearly dying in a horrific 1966 car crash and suffering permanent brain damage and partial paralysis as a result, Jan Berry's ability to create and perform music was never the same. But he kept fighting his way back, and eventually reunited with Dean Torrence in the late 1970s. The Jan and Dean/Beach Boys cross-pollination resumed when the bands toured together again in 1978 under an avalanche of permed hair, Hawaiian shirts, and cocaine. Jan Berry passed away in 2004 at age 62. Jan and Dean and the Beach Boys . . . good friends and collaborators . . . but not bandmates.

Captain & Tennille

Daryl "Captain" Dragon and his wife Toni Tennille are known worldwide as 1970s pop icons for maddeningly catchy hits like "Love Will Keep Us Together." They also both toured as members of the Beach Boys' live band and performed on some of their records. Daryl Dragon, in particular, was deeply involved with the Beach Boys during the years 1968 through 1973. He is the son of American conductor, composer, and arranger Carmen Dragon, and is a classically trained pianist. His knowledge of orchestral arrangements proved useful in his collaborations with Dennis Wilson on songs like the incredibly lush "Cuddle Up," released in 1972. Dragon was reportedly offered a slot as an official Beach Boy at one point, but declined.

Billy Hinsche

Billy was perhaps the closest of all to being an official Beach Boy who wasn't. He was asked to join the fold in 1969, but remained loyal to his own hit group Dino, Desi & Billy, and to his collegiate studies at UCLA. Hinsche already had a family connection to the Beach Boys, as his sister Annie had married Carl Wilson in February 1966. Billy was a staple of the Beach Boys touring band as a keyboardist, guitarist, and backing vocalist from the 1970s through the 1990s. Today he continues as a board member of the charitable Carl Wilson Foundation and as Al Jardine's musical director. Billy was never an official Beach Boy, but nobody came closer than him.

Gary Usher

Usher was Brian Wilson's first significant outside collaborator, and an early influence on the Beach Boys' recorded output. He co-wrote several Beach Boys classics, including "In My Room" and "Lonely Sea." His friendship with Brian was cut short due to Murry Wilson's insistence that Usher was a bad influence. Due to his own problems with Murry, an angry Dennis Wilson briefly flirted with bolting from the Beach Boys and joining Usher in a new group called the Four Speeds. Dennis moved in with him and played drums on two Usher-penned singles in 1962. Despite the tension, Dennis remained a Beach Boy, and Usher went on to produce and perform on records by the Super Stocks, the Hondells, and several other Beach Boys sound-alikes. He again collaborated with Brian in the late 1980s, but this time it was Brian's guru therapist Dr. Eugene Landy who got between Brian and Gary and killed the creative buzz. Usher passed away in 1990.

Roger Christian

Christian was one of Brian Wilson's early collaborators, and contributed lyrics to several Beach Boys classics including "Don't Worry Baby," "Little Deuce Coupe," and "Shut Down." The former KHJ radio "Boss Jock" suffered from chronic depression, and committed suicide in 1991.

Van Dyke Parks

Parks was Brian Wilson's most eclectic collaborator, writing artistically ambitious lyrics for the aborted *Smile* project as well as the single "Heroes and Villains." Parks's lyrics are without a doubt the most esoteric in the Beach

Boys' canon. He split from the Beach Boys' sphere in 1967, amid tensions with Mike Love and due to the increasingly weird scene building around Brian. He returned on occasion in future years to aid the receding creative fortunes of his friend Brian. The pair renewed their collaborative spirit in 1995 when Brian added lead vocals to Parks's *Orange Crate Art* project, and Parks returned the favor by assisting on Brian's 2004 resurrection of *Smile*, as well as his 2008 release *That Lucky Old Sun*.

Tony Asher

Asher seems to be the forgotten man in the Beach Boys saga. As Brian Wilson's primary collaborator and lyricist for *Pet Sounds*, which is arguably the greatest pop/rock LP in music history, his is a relatively unknown name. A former advertising executive, Tony isn't really a music-business type. However, if you are going to be a one-trick pony, co-writing "God Only Knows" and "Wouldn't It Be Nice" is as good a trick as one could possibly hope for.

Ron Swallow

Originally a close friend, driver, and road manager for the Beach Boys, Swallow also played percussion on several Beach Boys sessions, including an appearance on the *Pet Sounds* LP. He is seen in the background on several Beach Boys record covers and in some early publicity photos.

Louie Marotta

The Wilsons' neighbor, and the Beach Boys' first roadie and entourage member. Louie borrowed his sister's surfboard so the Beach Boys could use it for their now-iconic publicity shots. He remained a resident of the old Hawthorne neighborhood into the 2000s, often regaling curious visiting fans with stories about growing up with the Beach Boys. Louie died in 2004, just before the group's California State Landmark was erected near his home.

The Honeys

Brian's first wife Marilyn Rovell, her sister Diane, and their cousin Ginger Blake formed a feisty group and called themselves the Honeys in reference to the "Surfin' Safari" lyric . . . "some honeys will be comin' along." Brian wrote and produced their recorded output, which was at times excellent but

Hal Blaine was the studio drummer on a number of Beach Boys hits like "Good Vibrations" and "California Girls." However, the notion that he replaced Dennis Wilson as drummer on nearly all of the Beach Boys' classic recordings is untrue.

never commercially successful. Marilyn and Diane both contributed to many Beach Boys recordings and sessions in a number of roles, not to mention inspiring some of Brian's best compositions. He reportedly had romantic involvement with sister-in-law Diane, while simultaneously managing to remain married to Marilyn for nearly 15 years. In 1972, the sisters recorded as a duo under the name Spring. Their lone LP, coproduced by Brian, was again excellent and again a commercial failure.

The Sunrays

Known as the Renegades until Murry Wilson took over as their manager in 1965, Murry saw them as a path to redemption after being fired by the Beach Boys the previous year, and he quickly changed their name to the Sunrays. Their personnel consisted of the talented drummer, vocalist, and songwriter Rick Henn, and the late, great guitarist and raconteur Eddy Medora, plus Marty DiGiovanni, Vince Hozier, and Byron Case. Their single "I Live for the Sun" was huge in L.A. and Australia, but didn't make the U.S. national Top Fifty. Murry doted on them and did his best to bring them success, but their rise to the top never happened.

Dave and the Marksmen

When David Marks left the Beach Boys in October 1963, he had already been rehearsing his own band on the side for months. By early 1964 they'd become the first rock act signed to A&M Records. Unfortunately, a vengeful Murry Wilson informed deejays that if they played any Dave and the Marksmen records, he'd cut them off from receiving any Beach Boys exclusives, promotional goodies, and other wheel-greasing perks. KFWB and KHJ deejay Roger Christian confirmed this later in his life. After having no success on A&M, the Marksmen signed with Warner Bros. in fall 1964 and released their best single, an amazing British Invasion–meets–Phil Spector production titled "I Wanna Cry," which was written and produced by 16-year-old David. He again received zero attention from radio. The Marksmen disbanded in 1965.

Annette Funicello

In 1964, the Beach Boys backed Annette on the title song to the Disney movie *The Monkey's Uncle*. Some have surmised that the Beach Boys were somehow involved in the string of "beach party" movies that Annette and Frankie Avalon churned out, and they are right in that Brian co-wrote several songs with Gary Usher that were part of the surf-sploitation assembly line.

John Maus

Carl Wilson and David Marks learned how to play rock-and-roll-style guitar from Maus beginning in 1958. His mentorship of the two teen guitarists had a significant influence on the early Beach Boys sound. In 1965, Maus changed his name to John Walker and became one third of the hugely successful vocal group the Walker Brothers, whose hits "The Sun Ain't Gonna Shine Anymore" and "Make It Easy On Yourself" both reached number one on the British singles chart. Maus passed away in May 2011.

Hal Blaine

Blaine was among the first top session musicians to play on a Beach Boys recording when he played drums on the track "Our Car Club" on the Beach Boys' third LP in 1963. His brilliant drumming is present on many Beach Boys classics, including "Help Me, Rhonda," "California Girls," and "Good Vibrations." Somehow a myth has grown that credits Blaine with being the studio drummer on practically all of the Beach Boys records and hits. Although Hal Blaine contributed mightily to a good many of their sessions as both a drummer and percussionist, the same can be said for Dennis Wilson, whose contributions as a studio drummer for the Beach Boys have been vastly underreported and underappreciated due to the massive credit heaped on Blaine.

Mark Groseclose

When Dennis Wilson broke his leg in early 1963 while smashing his mother's car into crinkly bits, the Beach Boys called upon Hawthorne High classmate Mark Groseclose to take over on drums. Dennis eventually healed, and Mark returned to his own group, the Jaguars. As his Beach Boys days became numbered, David Marks, who had taken a liking to Mark, took over the Jaguars and changed their name to Dave and the Marksmen.

Terry Melcher

A hugely successful record producer and scenester, Terry Melcher was a close friend of and collaborator with the Beach Boys, being especially close to Bruce Johnston and Dennis Wilson. His professional relationship with Johnston resulted in several notable singles as "Bruce & Terry," as well as the massive 1964 hit "Hey Little Cobra" under the Rip Chords banner. Terry was greatly influenced by Brian Wilson, and poured some of that influence into his pioneering work producing the Byrds and Paul Revere and the Raiders. His friendship with Dennis Wilson connected him to future convicted murderer Charles Manson and his followers, who, in 1969, turned Melcher's former Cielo Drive home into one of history's most gruesome crime scenes.

Melcher maintained his Beach Boys connection throughout his life, and co-wrote their 1988 number-one hit "Kokomo." Melcher died of cancer in 2004.

Charles Manson

When Manson met Dennis Wilson in 1968, he was already a convicted felon and notorious grifter. However, Charlie was better known around L.A. as a singer/songwriter and freaky philosopher. Dennis took a liking to Manson and his harem of hippie waifs, and for a time he allowed them to live in his Sunset Boulevard home. Manson impressed Dennis with his trippy songs and oddball outlook, which motivated Dennis to introduce Charlie to Terry Melcher and brother Brian with an eye towards recording. Things went south when Manson's violent side surfaced in the studio, causing everyone in the Beach Boys organization to shun and run. However, Charlie could never be completely scrubbed from the Beach Boys story, because they'd already recorded and released one of his songs! Titled "Cease to Exist," Dennis polished it up, changed the title to "Never Learn Not to Love," and took the writing credit. The Beach Boys released it as a B-side to their 1968 single "Bluebirds Over the Mountain." Whoops, bad idea. Manson and his followers went on a killing rampage in August 1969 that will forever be among the most horrific and sensational crimes in U.S. history. In the wake of the murders and with the press totally

Cult leader and convicted murderer Charles Manson was also a composer of Beach Boys music. Several of his songs were demoed by Brian, Carl, and Dennis in Brian's home studio, with one actually making it onto a Beach Boys album in 1969.

focused on Charlie, his demo of "Cease to Exist" was unearthed, and of course it pointed directly to Dennis Wilson and the Beach Boys. The company line of "we didn't know he was going to become a mass murderer" has done nothing to lessen the public's obsession with the Wilson/Manson connection.

The Moon

In 1968, David Marks was part of an unheralded but excellent psychedelic band named the Moon. With keyboardist Matthew Moore functioning as the group's main songwriter and lead vocalist, and drummer Larry Brown handling the production, David concentrated on lead guitar and added harmony and occasional lead vocals. The Moon signed a production deal with Mike Curb and released two underrated psych/pop albums on Imperial Records. Neither dented the charts; and by 1969, the Moon had broken apart.

Leon Russell

Russell, a veteran session musician who worked with Phil Spector among others, played piano on his first Beach Boys recording in early 1964 on the track "Why Do Fools Fall in Love." He subsequently played on a number of their sessions over the next two years. In 1971, as Russell's star rose and he held court at his Church Recording Studio on Third Street in Tulsa, Oklahoma with luminaries like George Harrison, Bob Dylan, and Eric Clapton in attendance, another guitar player named David Marks visited the scene—causing Russell to drop everything and inquire relentlessly about his old boss Brian Wilson.

Jack Rieley

A former Beach Boys manager and lyricist, Rieley presided over the image-altering period when the Beach Boys became increasingly accepted by the *Rolling Stone* magazine–approved counterculture. He sang lead vocal on "A Day in the Life of a Tree" and convinced the band to move their families and studio to Amsterdam to record their 1972 album *Holland,* a move that in hindsight was viewed as frivolous, if not unproductive. Rieley left the band under a cloud of suspicion, but is viewed by historians and Beach Boys fans as an important element of their early-1970s renaissance.

Chicago

In 1974, Dennis Wilson, Carl Wilson, and Al Jardine contributed lovely and ethereal harmony vocals to the Jim Guercio–produced Chicago hit single "Wishing You Were Here." This was essentially the closest thing to a Beach Boys radio hit in six years. Guercio encouraged a further Chicago/Beach Boys collaborative concept when the two groups co-headlined a wildly successful concert tour in 1975. The two groups toured together again in the '90s with less fanfare. The legendary 1975 "Beachago" affair was recorded for a possible live album, but to this date no official release has surfaced.

James Guercio

The prolific record producer, label head, studio owner, band manager, filmmaker, and business entrepreneur is, first and foremost, a musician. Guercio was an early guitarist for the Mothers of Invention and a bassist and musical director for Chad & Jeremy. He also played bass in the Beach Boys' touring group in 1974 and 1975. Besides that, he co-managed the Beach Boys for a stint, did some production work for them, and signed them to his CBS-affiliated Caribou record label in 1978. He'd previously signed Dennis Wilson as a solo artist two years earlier, and subsequently signed Carl Wilson to a two-album solo deal. Guercio is best known for producing an incredible string of hits for the group Chicago, as well as winning an Album of the Year Grammy in 1969 for producing Blood, Sweat & Tears.

Nik Venet

Producer and A&R man Nikolas Kostantinos Venetoulis joined Capitol Records at age 21 and had immediate success producing hits by the Lettermen, among others. His career-defining moment came in 1962, when Nik insisted on signing the Beach Boys, despite trepidation from the execs around him. Venet was actually credited as producer on the first two Beach Boys LPs, but while he bickered with Murry Wilson for control of the group, Brian Wilson stepped in and did the actual producing. Venet had a long career working with an endless stream of notables, including Nat King Cole, Chet Baker, Sam Cooke, Wayne Newton, Ravi Shankar, Bobby Darin, Jim Croce, Linda Ronstadt, and Frank Zappa. Nik died of lymphoma in 1998 at age 61.

Eugene Landy

Dr. Landy is often credited as both saving and ruining Brian Wilson, and sometimes in the same breath. A controversial therapist known for unorthodox 24-hour, 7-day-a-week methods, Landy took control of Brian's life in 1982, removing him from substances, friends, family, and for the most part, his band. Landy eventually became Brian's manager, writing partner, coproducer, financial partner, and beneficiary. He was charged in court with exploiting Wilson for profit; and, in 1992, was legally barred from any further contact with Brian. In an interview more than a decade later, Brian insisted he "missed" Landy and would like to see him again, but before that could happen Dr. Landy died of lung cancer in 2006.

Jeffrey Foskett

Jeff joined the Beach Boys touring band in 1981, and played with them on and off until 1990. He sang and played guitar on the studio recording of the massive 1988 hit "Kokomo," and was given a platinum-record award for it along with the Beach Boys. He went on to become a key member of Brian Wilson's band, and has essentially served as Brian's right-hand man on his solo tours since 1999.

Mike Meros

The late Mike Meros became the Beach Boys touring group's official keyboard wizard in 1979. A musician's musician, Meros thrived in the position of Beach Boys keyboardist extraordinaire until July 4, 2001, when he was unexpectedly and unceremoniously terminated. Mike passed away from heart failure the day after Christmas in 2007.

Ed Carter

In 1965, when Glen Campbell was wavering and Bruce Johnston hadn't yet bit on an official Beach Boys job, Bruce's friend Ed Carter was one name that surfaced as a possible Brian Wilson replacement. Carter finally joined the Beach Boys touring group as a guitarist/bassist in 1969. He was employed by the Beach Boys on and off until the 1990s. Ed also contributed some memorable musicianship to the Beach Boys in the studio, including standout guitar work on "Bluebirds Over the Mountain," "Disney Girls," and the Dennis Wilson solo track "You and I."

Carli Munoz

Puerto Rican–born Carlos Munoz initially played congas in the Beach Boys live band starting in 1971. The gifted Latin jazz–influenced musician quickly evolved into the group's primary organist and occasional pianist. He played live with the Beach Boys until 1979. Munoz also collaborated with Dennis Wilson on his solo studio project *Bambu*, composing the acclaimed songs "It's Not Too Late" and "Constant Companion."

Bobby Figueroa

Bobby auditioned for a position as the Beach Boys touring percussionist and part-time drummer in 1974 on the recommendation of his "cousin" Carli Munoz. After thinking he'd been passed over and in the process of loading his drums back into his car, Dennis Wilson approached him in the parking lot and offered him the job. Bobby kept it for over 15 years.

Mike Kowalski

Mike joined the Beach Boys 1968 tour as an extra percussionist. Over the next 15 years, he participated as an occasional Beach Boys fill-in drummer until taking a permanent role in 1983 that lasted until 2007.

Adrian Baker

Baker joined the touring Beach Boys band in 1981 as a falsetto voice to replicate Brian's parts. He has since left and rejoined the group several times, with his last stint ending in 2004.

John Stamos

Some have incorrectly added the soap heartthrob turned sitcom heartthrob turned middle-aged heartthrob to the list of official Beach Boys. Stamos has often appeared with the Beach Boys in concert and on television as a special guest percussionist and, of course, de facto heartthrob. He was featured prominently in their 1988 "Kokomo" video, and he covered Dennis Wilson's classic ballad "Forever" and performed it on his cheesy *Full House* TV series. He also produced the critically lambasted TV miniseries *The Beach Boys: An American Family*. But despite the fact that he keeps returning to the Beach

Boys scene like an incurable rash, John Stamos has never been an official member of the troupe.

The Fat Boys

In 1987, the Brooklyn-based hip-hop trio paired with the Beach Boys to record a cover of the Surfaris classic "Wipe Out." Reportedly Brian Wilson was the sole member of the Beach Boys who actually sang on the recording. Nevertheless, the single reached #12 on the *Billboard* singles chart and #10 on the R&B chart, giving the Beach Boys their biggest hit in over a decade.

Status Quo

The veteran British rock band, most famous in the States for their 1968 mind-numbing psychedelic hit "Pictures of Matchstick Men," were joined by the Beach Boys in 1996 on a rollicking cover of "Fun, Fun, Fun." The single became a Top Thirty U.K. hit.

Wilson Phillips

Brian's daughters Carnie and Wendy formed a vocal troupe with Chynna Phillips, the daughter of Papa John Phillips, and in 1990 they had massive commercial success. With three number-one singles and a debut album that sold 10,000,000 copies worldwide, Wilson Phillips spent two years at the top before disbanding. A 2004 reunion brought nothing close to the glory they'd enjoyed more than a decade earlier.

Session Musicians

The Beach Boys benefited from a wealth of fabulous session musicians who contributed mightily to their recorded output. The following is a selected list of many of those talented performers: Hal Blaine, Jimmy Bond, Glen Campbell, Frankie Capp, Al Casey, Roy Caton, Joe Chemay, Jerry Cole, Al de Lory, Steve Douglas, Carl Fortina, Jim Gordon, Jim Horn, James Jamerson, Plas Johnson, Carol Kaye, Barney Kessel, Larry Knechtel, Maureen Love, Jay Migliori, Tommy Morgan, Earl Palmer, Bill Pittman, Ray Pohlman, Don Randi, Billy Riley, Lyle Ritz, Howard Roberts, Leon Russell, Sid Sharp, Billy Strange, Paul Tanner, Tommy Tedesco, Ed Tuleja, and Julius Wechter.

Current and Former Touring Beach Boys Sidemen

Mike Love and Bruce Johnston continue to tour under the Beach Boys banner with a talented group of support musicians including John Cowsill, Tim Bonhomme, Randell Kirsch, Scott Totten, and Mike's son Christian Love. Other past touring-band members and studio support musicians include Gary Griffin, Charles Lloyd, Richie Cannata, Chris Farmer, Elmo Peeler, Ron Brown, Joel Peskin, Sal Marquez, Robert Kenyatta, Sterling Smith, Daryl Dragon, Toni Tennille, Dennis Dragon, Doug Dragon, Putter Smith, Joe Chemay, Phillip Bardowell, Ron Altbach, and Al's son Matt Jardine.

The Wondermints

The L.A. underground pop band caught Brian Wilson's ear in 1999, and three of its members—Darian Sahanaja, Nick Walusko, and Mike D'Amico—became staples of the Brian Wilson Band. Auxiliary Wondermint Probyn Gregory also joined the Brian Wilson fold. D'Amico has subsequently been on and off as drummer and percussionist for Wilson, while the other three have remained relatively steady in their participation in Brian's solo endeavors.

Other Brian Wilson Band Members

Brian was initially assisted by Chicago-based *Imagination* producer Joe Thomas in assembling a touring band in 1999. Although Joe himself only stayed for a handful of dates, several Thomas-affiliated musicians hooked on permanently with Brian, including Scott Bennett, Paul Mertens, and Taylor Mills. Aside from the Wondermints members and the Thomas/Chicago contingent, Brian's band has also benefited from the participation of Nelson Bragg, Todd Sucherman, Brett Simons, Bob Lizik, and Jim Hines, among others.

Other Collaborators and Notable Friends

David Anderle (artist, producer); David Beard (journalist); Curt Boettcher (arranger); Alan Boyd (archivist); Chuck Britz (recording engineer); Trisha Campo (studio manager); Peter Carlin (author); Steve Desper (recording engineer); Andrew G. Doe (historian); Dick Duryea (promoter, road manager); Howie Edelson (journalist); Brad Elliott (historian); Nick Grillo (manager); John Hanlon (recording engineer, guitarist); Frank Holmes (graphic artist); Danny Hutton (supplier, vocalist); Gregg Jakobson (lyricist); Stephen Kalinich (lyricist); Steve Korthoff (cousin, assistant); David Leaf (author, filmmaker); Earl Leaf (journalist); Steve Levine (producer); Mark Linett (recording engineer); Mark London (graphic artist); Stan Love (personal trainer, bodyguard); Steve Love (manager); Earle Mankey (recording engineer, guitarist); Elmer Marks (road manager); Stephen Moffitt (recording engineer); Dorinda Morgan (publisher); Hite Morgan (publisher, producer); Rick Nelson (tour manager); Bob Norberg (collaborator, vocalist); Andy Paley (collaborator); Jon Parks (road manager); Domenic Priore (author, historian); Peter Reum (historian); Ed Roach (photographer); Ian Rusten (historian); David Sandler (producer); Jerry Schilling (manager); Loren Schwartz (associate); Stanley Shapiro (lyricist); Craig Slowinski (historian); Derek Taylor (publicist); Fred Vail (promoter); Michael Vosse (assistant); Timothy White (author); Paul Williams (journalist); and Gary Winfrey (collaborator).

Marriages and Children

The Beach Boys as a whole have had many marriages, and have fathered and adopted many children. As a result, they enjoy a wealth of family.

Brian Wilson

First marriage—Marilyn Rovell, 1964–79 (two children: Carnie and Wendy)
Second marriage—Melinda Ledbetter, 1995 (five adopted children: Daria, Delanie, Dylan, Dash, and Dakota).

Dennis Wilson

First marriage—Carole Freedman, 1965–1967 (two children: Scott (who was Carole's son and was adopted by Dennis), and Jennifer)
Second marriage—Barbara Charren, 1970–1974 (two children: Michael and Carl)
Third and fourth marriage—Karen Lamm, 1976–1977, 1978
Fourth marriage—Shawn Love, 1983 (one child: Gage)
(sons Chris and Ryan, daughter Denni born out of wedlock)

BEACH BOYS
& THEIR WIVES

HEAD BEACH BOY Brian Wilson was married to his long-time steady, Marilyn, two years ago, December 7, 1964. Brian never kept his marriage a secret. The rest of the Beach Boys, who had (before or since Brian's marriage) taken themselves brides, decided to keep their weddings a secret.

However, as it always happens, rumors began to spread and secrets began to be exposed. Finally, the Beach Boys decided to no longer keep their marriages hidden from their many fans. Here are the facts:

Beach Boy **Al Jardine** was the first to marry when he wed his Linda at St. Michael's Episcopal Church in El Segundo, Calif., on February 4, 1964. The Jardines' first baby is due any minute — they picked out about two dozen names. Al wants a boy; Linda wants a girl.

Youngest Beach Boy **Carl Wilson** had been secretly dating Annie Hinsche (Billy's older sister) for almost a year when they decided they could wait no longer, so they got married at the Los Angeles Registry on February 3, 1966. No children are expected and Annie and Carl would like to wait two years before starting a family.

Daredevil Beach Boy **Dennis Wilson** has been married to his wife, Carol, since July 29, 1965. Carol has a four-year-old son, Scott, from a former marriage. Recently, Dennis legally adopted Scott. Dennis and Carol expect another child this coming March or April.

That leaves handsome, rich **Bruce Johnston** the only single Beach Boy. Here is a picture of Bruce with his mother, Irene, in the den of their Los Angeles home. Bruce plans to stay *available* for a long, long time!

Mike Love met a beautiful dancer in Las Vegas a little over a year ago. After a whirlwind courtship, he took Suzanne to be his wedded wife on October 15, 1965. Their first baby is due in January, 1967.

Mike and Dennis tried to hide the fact that they were married from their fans in the mid-'60s, only to have several teen magazines suddenly out them. This feature shows the Beach Boys finally publicly sharing the details of their marriages circa 1966.

Carl Wilson

First marriage—Annie Hinsche, 1966–1980 (two children: Jonah and Justyn)
Second marriage—Gina Martin, 1987

Mike Love

First marriage—Frances St. Martin, 1961–1963 (two children: Melinda and Teresa)
Second marriage—Suzanne Belcher, 1965–1968 (two children: Hayleigh and Christian)
Third marriage—Tamara Fitch, 1972–1977 (one child: Summer)
Fourth marriage—Cathy Martinez, 1981–1982
Fifth marriage—Jacqueline Piesen, 1994 (two children: Brian and Ambha)
(son Michael born out of wedlock)

Al Jardine

First marriage—Linda Sperry, 1964–1983 (two children: Matthew and Adam)
Second marriage—Mary Ann Helmandollar, 1984 (two children: Drew and Robert)

David Marks

Carrie Haight, 1999
(daughter Jennifer born out of wedlock)

Bruce Johnston

Harriet Diamond, 1976—currently separated (four children: Max, Ozzie, Justin, Ryan)

3

Catch a Wave

Genesis and the Creation of a Sound

From their humble working-class beginnings in Hawthorne, California, to their massive fame as worldwide stars, the Beach Boys' climb to the top is one of the most compelling in show-business history. It began unassumingly with three brothers learning to harmonize together while riding in the backseat of their father's car. It became more when their father made it his life's mission to convince his sons to sing from the heart no matter what. The combination of spiritually earnest sibling chemistry and a frighteningly aggressive parental drive created a beautiful but damaged core that was absolutely central to the Beach Boys' evolution.

The home of Murry and Audree Wilson at 3701 West 119th Street was a house where music was not only consumed and enjoyed, but a place where it was nurtured and developed. The garage of the modest two-bedroom home had been remodeled into a den completely devoted to the family's musical endeavors. Murry Wilson made his living working in a low-level job at an aviation research firm and later by leasing, cleaning, and repairing industrial machine equipment. Along the way he experienced the horror of losing an eye in a freak on-the-job accident. Despite that life-altering setback, Murry continued to work hard and provide for his family. Perhaps more importantly, in his spare time he also continued to pursue his dream of being a hit songwriter.

Murry actually experienced a fleeting glimpse of success when the Lawrence Welk Orchestra performed his tune "Two-Step Side-Step" on Welk's popular radio show in 1952. The song was subsequently recorded and released on 78 RPM by multiple artists, but fell short of becoming a chart hit. The occurrence of Murry briefly gaining traction as a composer was probably due more to his perseverance, and abilities as a self-promoter, than his talent.

Murry's wife Audree was very musical as well. She made a point of teaching basic boogie-woogie style piano chording to all three of her sons. While both parents possessed keyboard skills and could vocalize in two-part harmony, Audree was the more patient teacher of her sons. However, it was

Murry who spent freely to insure the family had what it needed in terms of instruments and equipment. The Wilson music room was outfitted with a great Hammond organ, a well-tuned upright piano, and a good-quality hi-fi record player. The sanctuary of the Wilson music room became oldest son Brian's first laboratory for his budding sonic experimentations. It wasn't long before he proved conclusively that his parents were virtually talentless in comparison to him.

Brian's younger brothers Dennis and Carl were years behind Brian in their musical ability, but both were undoubtedly musically gifted as well. Brian spent the majority of his days obsessively learning the complex vocal arrangements of groups like the Four Freshmen and the Hi-Lo's. Brian's routine was to listen to short passages on the family record player, and then lift the needle, walk to the piano, and emulate the note pattern first with the keyboard, then with his voice. This became something of a hypnotic ritual, with Brian's focus so deep that it burned a permanent recall into his ear for stacking harmony. Arranging numerous and complex interlocking harmony notes from memory is a skill that few possessed, but one that Brian excelled at.

By the late 1950s, Brian already had the ability to arrange harmony vocals for four and even five voices. It was just a matter of finding enough singers for him to work with. Dennis, rough and wild, rarely hung around the house long enough to learn much, and was usually busy surfing and chasing girls. But Brian had a solid partner in Mike Love, who possessed the family chemistry due to the fact that his mother, Glee, and Brian's mother Audree were sisters. Mike also had a unique texture to his voice that Brian would use to great effect in the future. Brian and Mike already had years of joint singing history since their families often mingled during holiday gatherings and conducted regular Wilson/Love sing-alongs.

Carl was more interested in developing his guitar skills than vocalizing, but he also idolized Brian. He gamely learned and sang the harmony parts that

Even as a child, Dennis Wilson was known around his Hawthorne, California, neighborhood as "Dennis the Menace." His wild and rebellious streak often resulted in severe punishment from his father, but his free-wheeling lifestyle also pointed the Beach Boys toward their embrace of the emerging surfing culture.

Brian insisted upon while simultaneously progressing as a guitarist. Carl's guitar partner was his neighbor David Marks. Although two years younger than Carl, and a full six years younger than Brian and Mike, Marks was a tenacious learner when it came to the guitar. In 1959, David introduced Carl to his friend John Maus, who was their first and perhaps most crucial mentor. From Maus the duo learned the standard Chuck Berry–style lead riffs and rhythm chording that would soon give the Beach Boys a solid rock foundation for Brian to overlay his harmonies. Maus also undoubtedly passed on the influence of his own mentor, Ritchie Valens, to David and Carl. Other artists who heavily influenced David and Carl's playing style (and by extension, that of the Beach Boys) include Duane Eddy, Dick Dale, and the Ventures. Records by these musicians were constantly spinning in the Marks home.

Although David Marks undoubtedly participated in the group's genesis, even learning and rehearsing some of Brian's earliest original compositions, Marks was temporarily bypassed when a tentative group was finally formed in the summer of 1961. The main reason is that David was only 12 years old, and his voice was not reliable. Brian's former high-school classmate and football teammate Alan Jardine possessed the type of sweet, clear voice that Brian coveted. Al also played folk guitar and stand-up bass, but preferred the Kingston Trio to rock and roll. With Brian, Mike, Al, and Carl singing together, an excellent four-part vocal harmony could be achieved. Dennis wasn't initially thought of as an option, but Audree insisted he be part of any potential group. Brian begrudgingly agreed; and, to his surprise, Dennis's sandpaper vocal texture added a unique quality to the overall blend. The developing sound definitely grabbed Murry's attention.

Surfers Rule Thanks to Dennis

In August 1961, with only a few numbers rehearsed, the band auditioned for Murry's friend Hite Morgan, who was a well-connected Los Angeles music publisher. Al had auditioned his own folk trio for Morgan just weeks earlier, and Hite was somewhat bemused when Al returned with a completely different set of partners. Morgan wasn't exactly thrilled with what he heard from either group . . . that is, until Dennis blurted out the lie that Brian had written a new song about the sport of surfing. Morgan perked up and wanted to hear it right away. Brian said it needed some work, and a plan was made to come back for a second audition. Brian's statement that the song needed some work was a gigantic understatement as there *was* no song about surfing. But Dennis's instinct proved beyond prescient, and Brian and Mike went right to work on a new tune titled "Surfin."

The legendary and probably somewhat mythical tale of the band renting instruments with money left behind for food and emergencies by a vacationing Murry and Audree on Labor Day 1961 has been told and retold to death. It seems the story became an extremely tidy way to sum up the group's more complicated genesis after they had become famous and needed to constantly recount their formation to the press. What *is* absolutely true is that the group, which was now calling itself the Pendletones, began rehearsing "Surfin" in the Wilsons' music room that September. By Labor Day they had it down so well that Murry was impressed enough to commit to being their manager. He arranged a demonstration of "Surfin" for Morgan at his home, and the result was an extremely positive reaction from both Hite and his wife Dorinda. Brian and Mike were signed to a songwriting and publishing contract the same day, and a recording date for the group was scheduled at World Pacific Studios.

On October 3, 1961, the band recorded "Surfin," "Luau," and "Lavender" with the lineup of Mike (vocals), Brian (vocals, percussion), Dennis (vocals), Carl (guitar, vocals), and Al (stand-up bass, vocals). The single "Surfin," backed with "Luau," would be released on the independent Candix label. What surprised the group most about the release was the print that had been typeset onto the record's label. Instead of labeling the artist as the Pendletones, the single's label read "the Beach Boys." In a moment of off-the-cuff genius, record promoter Russ Reagan suggested the name change to Candix A&R man Joe Sarceno. Without the group's knowledge, Hite Morgan approved the switch. The group debuted on record as the Beach Boys in late November 1961, and it stuck.

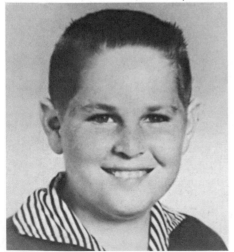

As a youngster Carl Wilson was very shy compared to his brothers, but he eventually developed into the most reliable and consistent leader in the Beach Boys band.

"Surfin" features Brian's fairly primitive harmony arrangement, with Mike singing both the signature doo-wop style bass line and the lead vocal. The musical bed is barely there, with Carl strumming an unplugged Kay hollowbody electric guitar, Brian tapping a snare drum with his index finger, and Al plucking a stand-up bass rented by his mother Virginia. It wasn't exactly a scintillating debut. However, the lyric about surfing being the only life, and cruising along and listening to the surf reports on the radio, was something absolutely unique in 1961. To this point "surf music" consisted solely of instrumental guitar, with Dick Dale being the unchallenged king of the genre. Now the Beach Boys were articulating the search for surf lyrically, and with group harmonies to boot. The flipside of the single was titled "Luau" and was a fun but lightweight tune written by the Morgans' son Bruce. It featured lead vocal lines alternated between Mike, Brian, and Dennis with the same acoustic-folk-style instrumental backing as "Surfin." The Beach Boys' signature sound wasn't quite there yet, but this was an interesting first step.

Upon its release, "Surfin" was not an instant hit. However, its perfectly current subject matter gave it a distinct advantage on Southern California radio. This was helped along when the Wilsons and their friends showered

Brian, Carl, and David in early 1963. Brian's ability to combine sweet harmony vocal arrangements with Carl and David's edgy surf-guitar style gave the Beach Boys a unique sound.

David Marks was only ten years old when he began to show promise as a guitarist. Before his fifteenth birthday, he'd already played guitar on several major hits. (Photo courtesy of David Marks)

local radio station KFWB with call-in votes when "Surfin" was slotted against several other new releases in an on-air popularity contest. "Surfin" collected the most listener requests, and was added to the regular rotation as a result. By the end of December, "Surfin" appeared in KFWB's Top Forty survey, and was on its way to being a Southern California radio hit.

Although the Beach Boys had a record, they weren't really a band yet. No photos have ever surfaced of this Beach Boys lineup, making it the murkiest period of their history. One would think that a group with a record out and seeking gigs would immediately have publicity photos shot and distributed, but this was seemingly not the case. It isn't exactly clear what lineup took the stage when they debuted their live act by playing two songs at the intermission of a Dick Dale show at the Rendezvous Ballroom in Newport Beach on December 23, 1961. Al claims he was playing stand-up bass that night, and Carl the Kay guitar through a small amplifier. Dennis had become the drummer by default, and that was okay by him. Mike was comfortable as the lead singer, but Brian was a square peg. He suffered from stage fright and was apparently left to either play piano (if there was one) or stand alongside Mike at a microphone. What everyone remembers is that the audience reaction was negative. Many surfers perceived the Beach Boys as a gimmick, and in Dick Dale's kingdom they were not exactly welcome.

About a week later, the group played again, this time in Long Beach at a Ritchie Valens memorial concert on New Year's Eve. There were a few more gigs performed with the mystery lineup, and little evidence to verify just how it presented itself. In February, the boys went back to World Pacific Studios and recorded some new Brian Wilson material. The session produced early versions of "Surfin' Safari," "Surfer Girl," and "Beach Boys Stomp." The results were ragged and the overall sound wasn't good, but the material showed promise. Al Jardine became disillusioned with the electric rock-and-roll direction for which Carl was lobbying. He was more interested in acoustic folk music. Al hadn't enjoyed the Beach Boys' shaky live performances either, and apparently this recording session was the last straw for him. He let the others know he was leaving the group to concentrate on his school studies at El Camino Junior College with the knowledge that the Beach Boys hadn't really gelled yet, and that maybe they never would.

Brian didn't seem to be solely committed to the Beach Boys as a group concept either. Within weeks he was back at World Pacific with Audree, Carl, Al, and a friend named Val Poliuto recording more of his original material, none of it having anything to do with the Beach Boys. When the material was released, the one-day grouping was listed as "Kenny and the Cadets." Brian saw himself developing in the vein of his idol Phil Spector. He wanted to be a writer/arranger/producer with his fingers in multiple acts, skillfully throwing sessions together, inventing an artist's name to label the material with, and hopefully making hit records from these acts. That was his dream. Being in a band was okay, but really too confining, and too exposed for Brian's sensibilities. However, fate had a different plan for Brian.

The Shift—The Beach Boys Get Electric

While Al was bailing out, and Brian was trying to avoid the confines of a specific band, "Surfin" was becoming a hit. By February 1962, it had risen to #5 on the KFWB chart in Los Angeles and had entered the U.S. *Billboard* national Hot 100 singles chart. There was suddenly growing demand for the Beach Boys as a live act. Carl lobbied Brian for the addition of David Marks on guitar. The Wilson brothers only had to walk across the street to make sure it was okay with Dave's parents for the now 13-year-old guitar slinger to join the act and help them promote their hit record. David was in. The addition of Marks immediately changed the group's sound into something more electric and rocking. Brian bought himself an electric Fender Precision bass, while Carl and David bought matching sunburst Fender Stratocasters. Murry paid for a set of Gretsch sparkle-finish drums for Dennis, who began to display a natural ability for energetic drumming. Mike volunteered to add some basic saxophone to a few of the songs. Publicity photos were taken. Business cards were printed. Things were beginning to solidify.

The single "Surfin" peaked on the *Billboard* national chart at #75 in March 1962. This coincided with some major business problems at Candix Records, who were not dealing with their surprise hit very well. A gap between retailers demand, distributors' orders, and payment of pressing-plant bills caused the single's chart life to cave in all at once at the end of March. Candix went belly-up in May. The Beach Boys would only receive about $900 in royalties for a record that blew everyone's expectations away and sold surprisingly well. This was their first taste of how making hit records didn't necessarily equal getting paid. It was at this point that Murry Wilson took firm control of the situation as Beach Boys business manager and music publisher. In fact, Murry became much more than that. He was the band's loudest cheerleader, and their harshest critic. He was their choreographer, coproducer, road manager, publicist, and absolute drill sergeant. He had his hand in everything relating to the band, and would eventually quit his day job and focus 100 percent of his attention on the Beach Boys and their business.

On April 19, the Beach Boys recorded a three-song demo at United Western Studios in Hollywood with Chuck Britz at the recording console. The version of "Surfin' Safari" recorded that day was a massive improvement over the World Pacific version recorded just two months earlier. Brian's harmonic arrangement shined brightly, Carl and Dave's guitars blazed away, and Dennis's drums rocked in a thrilling surf style. The boys also captured another high-energy garage rocker titled "409" that sang the praises of the big-block Chevrolet drag car. A precedent had been set. The Beach Boys were claiming both surfing and hot-rods as thematic territory, and the mixture of the two was another stroke of unwitting genius.

LET'S **STOMP** ALL NITE
WITH THE
BEACH BOYS
POPULAR RECORDING ARTISTS
'SURFIN' LATEST HIT RECORD
NEWEST HIT TO COME
FRI. **MAY 4** 1962
8 to 12:00 p.m.
INGLEWOOD WOMEN'S CLUB
325 NORTH HILLCREST, INGLEWOOD
TWO LONG BLOCKS EAST OF MARKET ST. AT FLORENCE
FREE SOFT DRINKS FOR THIRSTY STOMPERS

This early concert poster shows the Beach Boys were still promoting their 1961 debut single "Surfin" in spring 1962. The recording session for their first major hit, "Surfin' Safari," had occurred only a few weeks before this show, and that single wouldn't see release until the following month.

At the United Western demo session, Mike Love handled the lead vocal on both up-tempo tunes, and his sharp nasal voice helped give the group immediate distinction in their sound. However, the third song displayed something altogether different that was equally distinct. Gary Usher and Brian collaborated on a gorgeous and tender ballad titled "Lonely Sea" that featured a plaintive lead vocal from Brian and flourishes of group harmony topped with Brian's amazing pitch-perfect falsetto. Brian added a spoken narrative before the song's dramatic fade, which features Mike's deep bass vocal with Brian, Dennis, and Carl nailing the family blend. As a group, these three tracks nicely demonstrated that Brian and the Beach Boys' time had arrived. But how many record execs would recognize the sound of change roaring down the music-business highway?

Murry's first order of business was to use the newly cut demo to land a real record contract for the band. His relentless and aggressive tactics were at first met with total disinterest by nearly all of the major labels in L.A. Murry later recounted how he spent hours "cooling his heels" in various record-company reception areas only to be ignored, blown off, turned down, and chased away. Finally, during the first week of May, as a result of the urging of Murry's friend Don Podolor, a meeting with Capitol Records A&R man Nik Venet was secured. There was no sign of indifference this time as Venet was simply knocked out by what he heard on Murry's demo tape. Venet immediately notified several other veteran Capitol executives that he had stumbled upon something special, but none of them quite understood why Nik was so excited about the Beach Boys. Venet remained convinced that this was the sound of the future, and he purchased the demos from Murry on the spot. He quickly arranged to have the Beach Boys signed to a Capitol Records contract.

In June, the label released the single "Surfin' Safari" backed with "409" as the group's Capitol Records debut. These were the same exact versions of the songs as heard on the demo tape. Venet was so sure of the band's hit potential that instead of bringing them into the legendary Capitol studios to rerecord the songs with their respected staff of producers and engineers, he wanted Brian and the group's magic pressed directly onto vinyl just as he heard it in his office the day Murry walked in the door. Venet's instinct proved right on the money.

As the Beach Boys gigged around California and polished their act, "Surfin' Safari" began a slow climb up the charts. By August it had broken out in several non-California markets; by September it had entered the *Billboard* Top Forty; and by mid-October it was sitting at a lofty #14. The Beach Boys had a bona-fide hit record. Surprisingly, in certain landlocked areas of the U.S., it was the flipside "409" that received major airplay and generated healthy sales. It too rose on the national charts, hitting #76 the same month that the A-side peaked. Capitol was thrilled and prepared for the debut Beach Boys LP to be released.

The group was ordered to record the material in Capitol's cavernous basement studios, which Brian immediately disliked. The Capitol Studios were fine for orchestral music, and had served Frank Sinatra and Nat King Cole well, but Brian liked a livelier and less isolated sound. The Capitol facility had no such acoustic vibe. The other issue was that Venet and Murry each considered themselves producers, and both used their leverage to influence the proceedings. Although Venet got the credit on the album sleeve, Brian did much of the production work himself, but with Murry in his ear the entire time. As a consequence, the results were not stellar.

The LP, titled *Surfin' Safari*, featured a great-looking cover photo that has since become an iconic pop-culture image. In the picture, the boys are sitting in an old pickup truck that is decorated with palm leaves. Venet rented the jalopy specifically for the cover shoot from a Hollywood beatnik named Calypso Joe. The truck was driven onto the sand at Malibu's Paradise Cove and pointed towards the surf. The Beach Boys, dressed in their de rigueur Pendleton shirts, piled into the truck. Mike and Brian sat on top with surfboard in hand, Dave perched on the hood pointing towards the surf, Dennis was at the wheel, and Carl peered from the truck's wooden bed. The image perfectly captured the exciting pursuit of freedom and the celebration of Southern California culture as heard in the Beach Boys' sound.

The *Surfin' Safari* LP did well sales-wise, entering the *Billboard* Top Forty in December 1962 and hitting a peak position of #32 in January 1963. It began a string of years of unbroken LP success for the group as the youth market flexed its consumer muscle and rapidly changed the industry. But *Surfin' Safari* is among the weakest Beach Boys LPs artistically. It is the sound of amateurs trying to find their creative voice, and a label not quite sure how to help them along. The "Surfin' Safari"/"409" single was a perfect template for everyone to follow, but that direction was temporarily lost, and by comparison the choice of additional material for the LP didn't measure up. Somehow the great "Lonely Sea" was left off of the LP. Instead, silly novelty songs like "Chug-a-Lug" and "Cuckoo Clock" dominated the lineup. A sped-up version of "Surfin" was thrown in, as were a couple of cover tunes. The only LP track that truly projected the desired surf mojo was a cool instrumental titled "Moon Dawg" that was written by musician Derry Weaver, who'd previously recorded the tune with a group called the Gamblers that had included future Beach Boy Bruce Johnston.

The choice for the band's second single was a Wilson/Usher tune titled "Ten Little Indians," taken from the LP. It clearly didn't possess the magic of the first single, and didn't perform as well with deejays and customers; it crested at #49 in January 1963. Truthfully the Beach Boys were just beginning to get their feet wet as a performing entity. The first LP wasn't given much support from them as a live act. They were only just starting to book shows outside of California. The group was definitely in demand up and down the West Coast, but now the time had come to test their drawing power in U.S. markets to the East, and overseas. Spring 1963 would see the first extensive tour, as the band ventured into the Midwest in late April and early May, and across the Pacific to Hawaii in June. Simultaneously, Brian Wilson began his pattern of avoiding the road. He missed at least part of the Midwest swing and the entire Hawaii visit, preferring to stay home and record non–Beach Boys acts like the Honeys. Ironically, Brian's concert-tour replacement on bass and vocals would be none other than Al Jardine.

"Surfin' U.S.A."—The Beach Boys' Big Bang

Nineteen sixty-three was the year the Beach Boys became a national phenomenon, and it was the group's next release that did the trick. When Capitol asked for a third single, Brian insisted the band avoid the Capitol studios and return to United Western and engineer Chuck Britz for the session. The group was already familiar with Brian's piano demo of the song they were about to record. It turned out to be a perfect fit, as the band immediately nailed the Chuck Berry–style rock-and-roll progression that Brian titled "Surfin' U.S.A." The song's lyrics projected a compelling imagery of escapism and wanderlust that was essential to the surfing experience. Carl came up with a quick and shimmering guitar intro that was basically a

RADIO - ACTIVE

KAFY

"FABULOUS 55"

Bakersfield's OFFICIAL Top Tune Survey

APRIL 12, 1963 — APRIL 19, 1963

This Week		Last Week
1.	SURFIN' U.S.A./SHUTDOWN .... THE BEACHBOYS	1
2.	I WILL FOLLOW HIM .... LITTLE PEGGY MARCH	23
3.	PUFF .... PETER/PAUL/MARY	2
4.	DON'T SAY NOTHIN' BAD .... THE COOKIES	3
5.	DON'T MENTION MY NAME ... THE SHEPPARD SISTERS	7
6.	CAN'T GET USED TO LOSING YOU .... ANDY WILLIAMS	6
7.	END OF THE WORLD .... SKEETER DAVIS	4
8.	WATERMELON MAN .... MONGO SANTAMARIA	5
9.	THE REVEREND MR. BLACK .... THE KINGSTON TRIO	11
10.	STING RAY .... THE ROUTERS	9
11.	HE'S SO FINE .... THE CHIFFONS	8
12.	THE BOUNCE .... THE OLYMPICS	10
13.	SANDRA .... THE VOLUMES	12
14.	LITTLE LATIN LUPE LU .... THE RIGHTEOUS BROTHERS	22
15.	FOOLISH LITTLE GIRL .... THE SHIRELLES	20
16.	CHARMS .... BOBBY VEE	24
17.	GRANNY'S PAD .... THE VICEROYS	25
18.	HERE I STAND .... THE RIP CHORDS	30
19.	HE'S A BAD BOY .... CAROLE KING	13
20.	RONNIE, CALL ME .... SHELLEY FABARES	16
21.	BABY WORKOUT .... JACKIE WILSON	26
22.	OUR DAY WILL COME ... RUBY AND THE ROMANTICS	15
23.	MR. BASS MAN .... JOHNNY CYMBAL	17
24.	LIKE I DO .... MAUREEN EVANS	18
25.	I'M MOVIN' ON .... MATT LUCAS	31
26.	WHAT ARE BOYS MADE OF .... THE PERCELLS	32
27.	HELLO STRANGER .... BARBARA LEWIS	*
28.	ANOTHER SATURDAY NIGHT .... SAM COOKE	*
29.	TWO KINDS OF TEARDROPS .... DEL SHANNON	21
30.	MY HEART CAN'T TAKE IT NO MORE ... THE SUPREMES	40
31.	ON BROADWAY .... THE DRIFTERS	29
32.	BONY MORONIE .... THE APPALACHIANS	33
33.	YOU CAN'T SIT DOWN .... THE DOVELLS	*
34.	YOUNG AND IN LOVE ... DICK AND DEE DEE	21
35.	LITTLE BAND OF GOLD .... JAMES GILREATH	27
36.	DO THE BIRD .... DEE DEE SHARP	37
37.	MECCA/TEARDROP BY TEARDROP ..... GENE PITNEY	27
38.	BOSS STRIKES BACK .... THE RUMBLERS	28
39.	TOM CAT .... ROOFTOP SINGERS	*
40.	PATTY BABY .... FREDDY CANNON	*

As the single "Surfin' U.S.A." rocketed to the top of the charts in Bakersfield, California in April 1963, it was also just entering the national Top Forty. For the next several months it dominated the rock-and-roll radio airwaves, finally peaking at number three on the *Billboard* national singles chart.

riff borrowed from Duane Eddy's song "Movin' and Groovin'." David Marks added a biting rhythm-guitar tone that drove the song from within. Mike's vocal was playful and direct, while Brian's falsetto and the group harmony lifted the song into blissful territory that hadn't really been heard before in rock. Brian's overdubbed organ solo was the cherry on top of a surfing sundae that went down very sweetly with the American public.

"Surfin' U.S.A." became a massive hit. It dominated U.S. radio during the spring and summer of 1963, and stayed in the national Top Forty for four months. The single peaked at #3 in late May. The accompanying LP, also titled *Surfin' U.S.A.*, might have been an even bigger success than the single. Outside of Elvis Presley, and to a lesser degree Rick Nelson, there had never really been a rock-and-roll LP with this kind of impact on the music business. The early sixties folk boom led by Capitol Records artists the Kingston Trio, and the great Peter, Paul and Mary, had clearly displayed the buying power of the college-age and young-adult market. But the Beach Boys drew their audience from a much younger demographic. They were, without a doubt, a teen phenomenon, and the *Surfin' U.S.A.* album blew all of its teen competition away.

(l–r): Mike, promoter Fred Vail, David, unknown, Dennis, Carl, and Al backstage after a concert in 1963. Al had come back to fill-in for Brian at some concerts, and for a few months the studio Beach Boys numbered six members.

Photo courtesy of Fred Vail

The *Surfin' U.S.A.* LP remained in the *Billboard* Top Twenty for an astonishing five months. The teen consumer that had previously been active in the 45 RPM singles market saw the Beach Boys expand their influence into album sales, and in a big way. In fact, it was the Beach Boys' retail power that paved the way in America for the coming British Invasion. *Surfin' U.S.A.* album sales displayed impressive strength and longevity as the LP hovered in the Top Ten for over two months and finally peaked at #2 in July 1963, only being kept from the top position by adult-pop crooner Andy Williams, who was in the midst of his TV-celebrity superstardom. Williams kept the parents happy—but the Beach Boys had the kids.

One reason the *Surfin' U.S.A.* album had such a universal effect is that it truly embraced the California surfer image and sound, which in turn seduced the teen imagination. The LP's lineup was basically a marginally polished representation of the Beach Boys current live set. The gritty guitar interplay of Carl and David is exactly the same material and textures they had been working on together for years. Dennis's drumming gave the songs a primitive and unbridled joy that was unique to him. Mike as usual was clear and direct, and his singing always sounded young. But the key was Brian and his ability to sprinkle beautiful vocal arrangements on top of what was a somewhat edgy garage-rock sound. The juxtaposition of nasty and nice is what made it different and what made it work.

The B-side of the "Surfin' U.S.A." single, titled "Shut Down," was another one of the LP's highlights. Written by Brian and L.A. disc jockey Roger Christian, it graphically recounted a drag race between a fuel-injected Corvette and a super-stock Mopar. Mike Love contributed the lead vocal and added a bleating saxophone part, while the rest of the band cooked a slick-smoking groove that somehow sounded like burning rubber and fast track times. "Shut Down" gave the Beach Boys a solid double-sided hit by reaching #23 on the pop singles chart, mainly due to its sensational hot-rod sound, which was exciting and authentic. The rest of the LP mainly focused on the synergy of electric-guitar prowess and surf imagery. Unlike the first LP, which at times seemed timid and half-baked, the *Surfin' U.S.A.* album made a strong and complete statement from beginning to end. The ingredient that lifted that statement to a higher aesthetic plane were the few Brian Wilson falsetto gems like "Farmer's Daughter," "Lana," and the gorgeous "Lonely Sea," which added genuine melodic depth to the tough surroundings.

By year's end, the Beach Boys were performing to sold-out arenas filled with screaming fans, and they were a household name. One negative would be Chuck Berry's demand for credit due to the similarity their song "Surfin' U.S.A." held to his own "Sweet Little Sixteen." For Brian and the Beach Boys, this was a minor annoyance; the group had now risen to an elite plateau of fame and success. The only meaningful downside came from within, as David Marks would leave in October due to increasing tension between himself, his parents, and Murry. This insured Al's return to a full-time role, and also forced Brian's reluctant adherence to touring duty. From here it would all get bigger; and, with the impending arrival of the Beatles, it would certainly become more pressure packed for Brian. Whether or not it registered inside the bubble of fame they had just entered, for that brief time between summer 1963 and the early weeks of 1964, the Beach Boys undoubtedly had become America's number-one rock-and-roll band.

Meet the Beach Boys: 1 song writer, 1 arranger, 5 singers, 2 guitarists, 1 drummer, and 2 students.

They started surfing music. With a record called "Surfin' Safari." And they started hot rod music. With "Shut Down."

The Beach Boys have had one great hit after another. Wild songs like "Be True To Your School" and "Little Deuce Coupe." Quiet ballads like "Surfer Girl" and "In My Room."

When you know the Beach Boys, this success isn't surprising. Because they like the kind of music you like. And because they are five talented and hard working guys. Brian writes and arranges most of their songs himself. And sings the lead along with Mike. Carl and Dave play guitar any way you want...rockin' or dreamy or anything in between. And Dennis sings... while he raps out the beat on the drums.

With every album, the Beach Boys put their tremendous talent and versatility on display.

Listen to the Beach Boys on Capitol, and you'll hear what we mean.

For a start, listen to these newest Beach Boys albums:

By the end of 1963, the Beach Boys already had four hit albums under their belts. Even though David Marks had left the band three months earlier, Capitol Records was not yet mentioning his replacement, Alan Jardine, in this January 1964 advertisement.

4

If Everybody Had an Ocean

The Truth About the Beach Boys and Surfing

In the early 1960s, the real surfers of Southern California labeled the Beach Boys as poseurs, sellouts, and worse. From day one it was an uneasy relationship between the dudes and chicks that rode the waves and the rock group from Hawthorne that became rich singing about them. But despite the local grumbling along the California coast, the Beach Boys helped create a national obsession with surfing that solidified into a permanent cultural force. For better or worse, they gave the sport a huge voice on radio and record, and that voice spoke to thousands upon thousands of listeners and in turn influenced the world's perception of surfing. For some, that resulted in pure fantasy about the surfing life. For others, it meant actually grabbing a board and getting involved. But for the surfers who were already there, it meant the commercialization and overpopulation of something sacred.

It all started with Dennis Wilson. The middle Wilson brother was more outgoing than his siblings. He was a roughneck, or a "hood" compared to athletic and artistic Brian, and quiet and friendly Carl. His two brothers usually steered clear of trouble, but Dennis saw no reason to avoid trouble; instead he met it head on. He actually liked to fight. This was mainly due to the fact that taking on anyone else was a picnic compared to the beatings he'd been receiving from his father Murry since he was a toddler. Dennis was fearless, he was wired for danger, and he was constantly looking for action. The L.A. beach scene was a natural home for him. Pretty girls in bikinis and a never-ending party were a nice way to avoid the reality of failing grades and an angry father. The wild and crazy surfers were ready-made peers for a teenager with Dennis's semi-delinquent sensibility. So he hung around the beach, and he learned to surf.

Dennis was never a great surfer, but he was good enough. He was muscular and an excellent swimmer. As a youngster he managed to find acceptance and respect among the other surfers. He could handle the medium-sized waves around the Manhattan Beach pier, and those slightly to the north at Dockweiler Beach near Playa Del Rey. There were occasions when he'd bum a ride up to Malibu, where the real local action was peaking. For Dennis it was as much about the social scene as it was about the sport. Surfing was exciting and sometimes dangerous. He loved the thrill. But he also loved the rebellious attitudes of the surfers. Dennis might not have been a world-class board rider, but he was undoubtedly a world-class rebel. For a guy who bedded women, crashed cars, got into fights, smoked, drank, and was kicked out of high school *and* his own home more than once, he was right at home with the delinquent fringe characters that pervaded the surf culture. The cult of surfers around Southern California was a loosely knit gang of misfits and nonconformists. Dennis Wilson was the only member of the Beach Boys who became truly accepted by that gang.

In summer 1961, when Dennis passed the "Surfin" thematic baton to Brian and Mike Love, he had no idea that he'd lit a fuse connected to a cultural bomb. The cult of surfing was already under commercial siege because of movies like *Gidget* starring Sandra Dee, and other romantic media accounts of Malibu's wave-obsessed youngsters. That surfing community was once a relatively small group drawn to Malibu's perfect right-breaking wave, but due to ongoing media glorification new surfers and wannabes were now multiplying by hundreds there each week. California's love affair with surfing was increasingly under the Hollywood spotlight. Up and down the coast the word spread among veteran surfers that ho-dads, greasers, squares, and poseurs were to be shunned. Within a couple of years, the "beach party" movie franchise starring Annette Funicello and Frankie Avalon would engulf whatever remnants of self-defense that the locals could muster. In the midst of all of this the Beach Boys became . . . *The Number-One Surfing Group in the Country* . . . according to Capitol Records, and the local surfers in Southern California didn't exactly appreciate it.

A Surfin' Casanova

It became part of the Beach Boys' standard press release and bio blurbage to highlight the fact that Dennis was a "real" surfer, *and* a lady's man. And according to the lore, while he was catching waves and cuddling up with honeys, the rest of them preferred to just "relax" on the beach. Brian in particular had no interest in surfing. Carl was a non-athlete. David was more comfortable on a skateboard than a surfboard. Al went out with Dennis once to learn, but was disgusted when he realized they were surfing exactly where L.A.'s sewage was emptying into the South Bay. Mike claimed that he surfed a little; and Bruce was a surfer early on, and apparently still does ride the waves regularly.

Regardless of how much or how little surfing any of the others actually did, Dennis was the only Beach Boy who somehow gained a reputation as an actual surfer. This is mainly due to the fact that he was a known surfer before the Beach Boys hit. He also gets credit for being the one who suggested that they sing about the sport. The fact that this suggestion morphed into something bigger than anyone could have imagined undoubtedly is part of why the Dennis-as-surfer lore continued to grow. Dennis's profile as a real surfer did give the Beach Boys a modest amount of credibility, and the group used it for cover for many years. In a way, they still do.

Although the surfing community's opinion of the Beach Boys as a whole was skeptical at best, Dennis was a personal friend of many of California's most notable surfing legends. Dennis knew Miki Dora, Gregg Noll, Gypsy Boots, Mike Doyle, Terry "Tubesteak" Tracy, Corky Carroll, and many of the other names that permeate Southern California surf lore. In fact, when rebel surfer Dora ended up in Vacaville State Prison due to fallout from his grifting ways, he dropped Dennis's name to ensure his safety among the inmates there. Dennis was the common thread between himself and fellow California Medical Facility inmate Charles Manson, who apparently had

(l–r): Dennis, David, Carl, Mike, and Brian in one of their iconic 1962 surfing-related images. Even though Dennis was the only serious surfer in the band, the Beach Boys would forever be associated with the sport due to Brian and Mike's brilliance at communicating the excitement and fun of surfing via song.

tremendous clout among the prison population. According to Dora, his association with Dennis (and by extension, Manson) removed some serious heat from his back while incarcerated at Vacaville in 1982.

The fact remains that none of the Beach Boys, including Dennis, were top-notch surfers, and only some of them had any surfing experience at all. Dennis started out riding a long board, but by his thirties he was mainly a knee boarder. Brian remained opposed to any contact with the ocean, only giving in when John Belushi and Dan Aykroyd wrote a comedy sketch around the reclusive genius finally catching a wave for the Beach Boys' classic 1976 NBC television special. The results were hilarious to view: hapless Brian lying on a board backwards in his bathrobe. But Brian wasn't laughing . . . he only described it as "scary." Despite Brian's conflicted relationship with the ocean, and Dennis's solidarity with the surfing community, and that community's suspicious perception of the Beach Boys as an entity . . . the boys from Hawthorne will always be associated with surf, surfers, and surfing. It's an endless wave that the Beach Boys will ride forever.

Stoked!

The following is a selected list of songs about surfing recorded by the Beach Boys.

"Surfin"—Dennis gave Brian and Mike the idea, and the group had an instant identity.

"Surfin' Safari"—The band's first national Top Twenty hit, it's all about camaraderie and fun.

"Surfin' U.S.A."—The quintessential surfing vocal song. Chuck Berry got paid too.

"Noble Surfer"—A righteous surfing dude celebrated in song.

"Surf City"—Jan and Dean had the hit, but Brian co-wrote it and sang the high part.

"Surfer Girl"—Brian makes surfing music romantic and pretty.

"Catch a Wave"—A punk-rock groove and a harp, and yet another surfing anthem.

"Surfer's Rule"—Dennis sings about the surfer clique. Four Seasons, you better believe it.

"Hawaii"—I don't know what town you're from, but Hawaii has better waves.

"Don't Back Down"—The last great Beach Boys surfing song. You gotta be a little nuts.

"Do It Again"—The first Beach Boys song that trades on nostalgia. This time it works.

"It's OK"—A nice return to a surfing-related theme. Fun is in, it's no sin.

SURFER GIRL

Words and Music by BRIAN WILSON

06288
09999

PRICE
75c
U S A

GUILD MUSIC COMPANY

Brian has stated that "Surfer Girl" was one of his very first compositions. The 1940s Disney classic "When You Wish Upon A Star" was his inspiration for the melody. Brian added its surfing-related lyrics years after he'd written the music.

5

I'm Bugged at My Old Man

Murry Wilson—Showbiz Dad

He was the ultimate show-business parent. He was generous and strict, forgiving and censorious, loving and violent, successful and tragic. Murry Wilson was the enigmatic father of Brian, Dennis, and Carl Wilson. He was also the Beach Boys' first manager. Murry instilled a deep spiritual connection to music that his sons absorbed completely. He devoted himself to the Beach Boys' budding career, and willed them to a major record contract. Murry was also an abusive parent and a ruthless, jealous tyrant who ultimately swindled his boys and their bandmates out of millions of dollars of earnings. He left his sons psychologically damaged for life, and died a lonely broken man.

Murry Gage Wilson was born on July 2, 1917 in Hutchinson, Kansas. His family moved to Southern California when Murry was five years old. Things weren't exactly golden during Murry's formative years as the Great Depression engulfed the nation. Like most men of his generation, Murry displayed a formidable work ethic and a hard-edged tenacity. He not only worked hard to earn money, but he worked even harder, probably too hard, in demanding the respect of his sons. There was a severely controlling side to him that never gave in, and never backed down. He was manipulative and highly judgmental.

His sons, especially the oldest, Brian, and middle son Dennis, would spend much of their adult lives unsuccessfully trying to cope with the crushing emotional baggage their father left them holding. Brian's near-total hearing loss in his right ear has also been attributed to a possible beating from Murry; Brian himself has made this claim, and has also denied it. Regardless of which specific scars Murry left and which he did not, his sons were damaged goods, and he was the father who molded them.

But without Murry there would have been no Beach Boys. And most likely without his double-edged ways, there would be no ingenious body

Beach Boys dad and manager Murry Wilson with Capitol Records executive Nik Venet. Murry made it his mission to land the Beach Boys a major recording contract, and with Venet's help his wish came true in the summer of 1962.

of work created by Brian and his brothers. His mantra was "sing from the heart," and Brian, Dennis, and Carl thus became three of the all-time greatest at projecting sincerity and sensitivity in their music. This was Murry's gift to the world through his sons, and it resonated deeply with a generation of listeners that he would never really understand.

What's It All About?

Murry was a man whose rigid, moralistic bowtie aesthetic aligned well with early-1950s America. Although both Murry and Audree were registered Democrats, Murry at his core was a very conservative man. As the Beach Boys came of age he found himself swept into a rock-and-roll tornado roaring towards a 1960s cultural upheaval that ultimately had no place for him. At first he grabbed the Beach Boys managerial reigns with zeal. It was Murry who pounded the pavement, knocked on and knocked down doors, and demanded that the Beach Boys be contracted to a major record label. Once Capitol Records surrendered and signed the group, the only buyer's remorse that surfaced was due to the fact that they'd now have to cope with Murry. As his positive edge became less relevant once the band had achieved some success, his negative edge incurred political damage on an almost-daily basis. Murry was as unpopular behind the scenes as the band was popular with its teen fan base.

A power struggle occurred between Murry and David Marks's parents over management issues in late summer 1963. Dave's mom Jo Ann Marks recalled that even though the band was becoming hugely successful, Murry "took the fun out of everything." He fined the boys for not smiling on stage and for cussing off stage. Eventually 15-year-old David's earnings for grueling concert tours were completely cut off by Murry. When the Marks challenged this nonpayment by threatening to pull David from the band, Murry said, "Go ahead, make my day." David himself had had enough of the tension and was already rehearsing his own band, the Marksmen, on the side. He told Carl and his folks he wanted to quit the Beach Boys. David played his last gig in October 1963, but it wasn't exactly a clean break.

With Al Jardine already in the wings functioning as Brian's occasional concert replacement, and as an auxiliary studio contributor, there were essentially six Beach Boys in the months prior to David's departure. But only the Wilsons, Mike, and David were under contract. Murry took advantage of the musical chairs by getting a naïve David to sign a termination agreement backdated to August 1963. This meaningless piece of paper had no legal bearing on the original Capitol contract that gave David 20 percent of the Beach Boys record royalties through 1967. But David just wanted out. He was given no settlement; and to this day received only a fraction of the royalties the original contract called for.

David Marks lost out on millions while the Wilsons became rich. However, Al Jardine, who became Dave's official replacement, was not awarded David's full royalty share for a decade. Al was instead paid by Murry as a sideman, while David's 20 percent was absorbed under the table. As the hits piled up, this unaccounted share generated a fortune. Where did it go?

Well, in case anybody investigated, it didn't matter anyway. In 1971, when 22-year-old David was awarded a $15,000 payout due to an accounting settlement from the Beach Boys late-1960s lawsuit against Capitol Records for (of all things) unpaid royalties, the group helped cover Murry's and Capitol's butt regarding David. When David showed up to collect his check, he was told by the Beach Boys he had to sign for it. But instead, unbeknownst to him at the time, what he had actually done was sign away any rights to challenging the legality of his 1963 termination agreement . . . which was definitely illegal. Thanks for the memories.

Murry's overbearing managerial ways would finally find their limit with Brian in 1964. That spring Murry was suddenly fired as the acting Beach Boys manager. Ironically, it happened during the recording session for what would become the Beach Boys first number-one chart single, "I Get Around." Murry apparently berated Dennis's vocal performance a little too strenuously and a little too loudly for Brian's already-damaged ears. Murry was then physically pushed against a wall by an enraged Brian, and given his marching orders. Murry's reaction was to crawl into bed for several months and sink into a self-absorbed depression.

Getcha Back—The Wrath of Murry

Once he emerged, it was only a matter of time until his inevitable revenge was planned and executed. Murry fiercely maintained his grip on the Beach Boys' publishing catalog, Sea of Tunes, and kept his fingers in the revenue-stream pie. He simultaneously spewed a constant stream of manipulations and guilt trips into his son's lives over the next several years. One of Murry's most blatant attempts to show up his sons was by producing a Beach Boys sound-alike group named the Sunrays in 1965. It was a vain and unsuccessful attempt to compete on the charts with his own offspring, who by then had transcended the lightweight fluff that Murry perceived as their niche.

There are those who remember Murry in a better light, including early concert promoter Fred Vail, who continues to insist that Murry was an honorable man and a good father doing the best that he could. There are certainly many examples of Murry's generosity, and even humility, that seem 180 degrees opposed to his bad reputation. But regardless of the controversial taint that Murry injected into the Beach Boys story, he was without a doubt essential to their success in countless fundamental and crucial ways.

Ultimately Murry Wilson found himself living out his last years as a virtual outcast from the music business and his family. His final vindictive and incredibly shortsighted act was to go against Brian's wishes in 1969 and sell the Sea of Tunes publishing catalog for the paltry sum of $700,000. Within a relatively short time, this same catalog of timeless Beach Boys original songs would be valued at well over $30,000,000.

Murry died of a heart attack on June 4, 1973. He was 55 years old. Brian and Dennis did not attend his funeral.

A Brief Chronology of the Beach Boys' Managers

From the time Murry Wilson was fired in April 1964 to early 1966, Cummings and Currant, who also happened to be Murry's tax accountants, managed the Beach Boys. Cummings and Currant were responsible for the Beach Boys' finances, while Brian and Carl handled the balance of the band's management chores. In the spring of 1966 the band moved from Cummings and Currant to Julius Lefkowitz & Company, whose agent Nick Grillo handled the Beach Boys account. Grillo was quickly invited to become their personal manager. Grillo lasted until April 1972, and was replaced by Jack Rieley, who had already been in control of the Beach Boys' management duties since early 1971. Rieley was fired by mid-1973, and replaced by Steve Love (Mike's brother). Jim Guercio essentially took over the Beach Boys' management through most of 1974 and 1975. Steve Love again stepped in as Beach Boys manager from spring 1976, until March 31, 1977, when his contract was not renewed. Carl's friend Henry Lazarus managed the band until the summer of 1977, when a potentially lucrative European tour had to be cancelled because Lazarus had not filed the proper paperwork. Once again, Steve Love returned to the management post, and was fired in early 1978 following a monumentally troubled Australian tour. Tom Hulett and Jerry Schilling became the Beach Boys' management team into the mid-1980s. Today the duties fall to the president of Brother Records Incorporated, the Beach Boys' corporate entity, who is Carl's former assistant Elliott Lott.

6

We've Been Having Fun All Summer Long

The Beach Boys' Golden Years, 1963–1965

B eginning with the Beach Boys third LP, 1963's *Surfer Girl*, one very important change was apparent in the album credits. For the first time it read: "Produced by Brian Wilson." Brian had probably already contributed the majority of the production ideas at every Beach Boys recording session prior to *Surfer Girl*, and Murry undoubtedly had thrown in his two cents. But it was Capitol's Nik Venet who was given the official producer's credit on the first two Beach Boys LPs. If a committee had produced the Beach Boys at first, there was no equivocation starting in the summer of 1963. Brian was now in charge.

The result was a string of eight classic LPs over a two-year span that defined and elevated the surf/pop genre to its seemingly ingrained status within the American culture. The words and music on these records reflect an embrace and a celebration of something so distinctly American that it becomes difficult to describe it as anything other than "the Beach Boys." Those words undoubtedly evoke a certain feeling. It's more than a band name. It is an undeniable energy that lives in the hearts of the fans who've embraced the beauty and fun in these albums.

Why were they so good? Why did they connect so perfectly with the kids and the times? Why did they seem so archaic so quickly after their release, and then so sweetly nostalgic so quickly after that? I can say that the basic answer to all of these questions is that these records are without cynicism. They are young, innocent, human, hopeful, and wonderfully naïve. These records project an America that is, for the most part, long gone, but still there are traces. There are these songs, and there are girls, and beaches, and cars, and sunny days. If you want to know what it was really like to come of age in California under blue skies and good times, this is the soundtrack. This is the feeling.

Surfer Girl

Released in September 1963, this is Brian's coming-out party as a producer. The LP is built around the previously released double-sided smash hit single "Surfer Girl"/"Little Deuce Coupe." Brian was beginning to add more textures to the Beach Boys sound, doubling their voices more often, and adding more piano and more percussion to the records. He brings a harpist (Maureen Love) into the sessions for two tracks, and even adds a string section to one song, "The Surfer Moon." Some flexibility is gained because of the part-time return of Alan Jardine, who had been absent on all of the Beach Boys records made since their first single, "Surfin." With Carl and David Marks covering guitars, Jardine became the bassist on several of the album's songs, freeing Brian to play piano on basic tracks. "In My Room," "Catch a Wave," and "Hawaii" feature all six Beach Boys: Brian, Dennis, Carl, Mike, David, and Al.

Little Deuce Coupe

Some count this as the first concept album by a major rock band. The concept was fast cars. This LP is a bit of a strange one in that it was released a mere three weeks after the *Surfer Girl* LP. Four of the album's songs were borrowed from previous Beach Boys LPs, so it really only contained eight new songs. But the quality was high, and the album was a major hit, reaching #4. Again, six Beach Boys are used on many of the tracks, as David Marks would not leave the Beach Boys until after this album was mastered and ready for release. Standout tracks include "Be True To Your School" and "Spirit of America." The album's cover, featuring a heavily chromed hot rod, has since become an album-art classic.

Shut Down Volume 2

Released amid the explosion of Beatlemania in March 1964, this LP didn't chart as high as the previous three Beach Boys LPs, reaching only #13 on the *Billboard* album chart. Despite not peaking higher, this record remained a strong seller over a long period of time and easily went RIAA Gold. The Beach Boys are pictured on the cover standing behind Dennis's '63 Corvette

Stingray and Carl's '64 Pontiac Grand Prix. It is the first Beach Boys LP to not feature David Marks on the cover, and the first featuring Al Jardine as the official fifth Beach Boy.

The album begins with the great "Fun, Fun, Fun," which was a major radio hit that topped out at #5 on the singles chart. Perhaps the album's best track is the iconic "Don't Worry Baby," which features not only one of Brian's greatest melodies and best lead vocals, but also an amazing harmony vocal backing sung primarily by the three Wilson brothers. As with all of the previous Beach Boys albums, *Shut Down Volume 2* features the Beach Boys themselves not only singing, but playing nearly all of the instruments as well. The one clear exception is a cover of the Frankie Lymon classic "Why Do Fools Fall In Love," featuring Brian's first use of the Wrecking Crew as full replacements for the Beach Boys as musicians.

All Summer Long

In many ways this is the quintessential Beach Boys album. *Pet Sounds* is more sophisticated, *Sunflower* is a greater team effort, *Endless Summer* sold more copies, but *All Summer Long* is the definition of what made the Beach Boys great. Released in the summer of 1964, it sparkles with harmonic magic, and it exudes an irresistible zest for fun. The songs offer a sweetly framed window into the lives and feelings of California boys and girls. The album captures its place and time so perfectly that with every listen you are transported there again.

All Summer Long shows a continuing maturation of the Beach Boys sound. Again, more textures and

Somehow Brian and his lyricist Roger Christian took this tune about a drag race and turned it into one of the most beautiful pop songs ever recorded. One of the main reasons "Don't Worry Baby" resonated so deeply was due to its gorgeous harmonies sung by the three Wilson brothers.

complexity in the arrangements are integrated. The Beach Boys themselves still play the majority of the instruments heard on the tracks, but saxophones, piccolo, marimba, and timbales are among the added seasoning. The album begins with the megahit single "I Get Around," which reached the number-one position on the *Billboard* chart on July 4, 1964. "I Get Around" features one of the most progressive musical and vocal arrangements of its time. There was a shiny space-age quality to the song's overall sound. Exciting sax and percussion flourishes accent the beat, and a killer Carl Wilson guitar solo propels the song forward like a rocket. The lyrics written by Mike Love have gained an iconic familiarity that perfectly communicates the somewhat hedonistic concerns of the teen cruising culture.

Following the sonic onslaught of "I Get Around," the album continues with an unforgettable string of classic Brian Wilson songs. The wistful title track is somehow instantly nostalgic, and recounts the pure fun that filled those carefree days of summer. "Hushabye" is a cover of a doo-wop oldie that the Beach Boys completely make their own with one of the most beautiful and dramatic group harmony performances ever. "Little Honda" is joyous garage rock, with the Beach Boys, as a band, rocking out to one of Brian's catchiest songs, and one of Mike's best lead vocals. The melancholy "We'll Run Away" could be Brian's most underrated ballad, and his heartfelt lead vocal is one of his greatest. The hook-filled "Wendy" could have been a giant hit single. It is both progressive-sounding musically, and a throwback to the '50s with its "we went together for so long" sentiment. "Girls on the Beach" shows off Brian's incredible vocal-arranging skill, with complex group blends and multiple key changes. Dennis's brief solo vocal in the middle section is one of the album's most soulful moments. "Don't Back Down" provides one last burst of bravado extolling the insane thrill of surfing giant waves.

All Summer Long was a hugely successful album, reaching #4 on the charts, but even more impressive was the fact that it remained in the U.S. Top Forty for over nine months. Another factor that solidified its classic status was the wonderful cover, which absolutely shimmers with the aura of summer and fun. To see the boys and their girls, enjoying the beach and each other, and actually having fun all summer long, somehow made the music better. There is an undeniable fleeting quality that is projected, and it's a bittersweet sensation. As Dennis writes on the back cover, "It won't last forever . . . but the memories will." It didn't, and they did.

Beach Boys Concert

With *All Summer Long* still selling huge numbers, the Beach Boys unleashed another megahit album in October 1964. *Beach Boys Concert* did a beautiful

1964's exciting *Beach Boys Concert* album was the group's first number-one LP. It was maligned in later years for having two "fake" live tracks among its 13 songs. Although there were some postproduction additions to several of its tracks, *Beach Boys Concert* featured a majority of songs that are pure live recordings, which in 1964 was a rarity in the rock realm.

job of projecting the flash and excitement of a Beach Boys live performance. American teenagers absolutely ate it up. It became the first Beach Boys LP to rise to the number-one position on the album chart. It stayed at number one through the whole month of December, and became the hottest music-related Christmas gift during the Year of the Beatles. The Beach Boys also released a proper Christmas album that November featuring mostly holiday standards with a few originals thrown in. It sold well, but received minimal interest from teens compared to the white-hot *Beach Boys Concert* LP. The twin success of *All Summer Long* and *Beach Boys Concert* elevated the Beach Boys to such a lofty position of popularity that from here there really was no place to go but down.

Beach Boys Concert has been assailed in retrospect because some of it is not live. Two tracks, "Fun, Fun, Fun" and "I Get Around," are slightly altered studio tracks with crowd noise added. A few of the other tracks had some postproduction enhancements to make them more palatable. But there is plenty of "live" on this record, and it came at a time when even the Beatles were not brave enough to release a live album. This was really the first commercially successful live concert album by a rock group. The reason why is because it is a great album, and a great concept, and it came in a great package.

Aside from the two previously mentioned "fake" live songs, most of what you hear on *Beach Boys Concert* is real. Recorded at two separate shows at the Sacramento Memorial Coliseum, the audience energy is electric and the performances are excellent. There are several great cover songs that the Beach Boys never recorded in the studio, like "Little Old Lady from Pasadena" and "Monster Mash." Two outstanding tracks—and it should be noted that both are completely live recordings with no studio trickery—are "Graduation Day" and "Let's Go Trippin'." The former is a wonderful vocal performance showing just how good the Beach Boys harmony vocals were in the live setting. The instrumental cover of Dick Dale's "Let's Go Trippin'" just blazes away with pure surf-guitar energy. It ignites the audience in way that is truly thrilling to hear, and proves that the Beach Boys could really rock.

Again a wonderful album cover beautifully enhances the sounds within. A deluxe gatefold package with a multipage photo booklet provides numerous shots of the band performing. Their appeal as performers translates nicely through these photos. The group's iconic striped shirts and gleaming white Fender guitars project an image that is both youthful and professional. Dennis stands out with his surfer-meets-Beatles hair and his movie-star face. The entire package of *Beach Boys Concert* was unlike anything available in its time. It somehow perfectly exuded the excitement and fun that only 1960s rock concerts had to offer. A night out seeing your favorite band was undoubtedly a thrilling experience, and *Beach Boys Concert* allowed you take that thrill home and enjoy it whenever you wanted.

The Beach Boys Today!

This is the crossroads of commerciality and artistic expression. Among the handful of bestselling Beach Boys LPs ever, *The Beach Boys Today!* is also one of their most artistically impressive. Brian's production skills were now reaching full flower, while the group's sound maintained an absolutely accessible quality. Released in March 1965, *The Beach Boys Today!* sold only marginally less than its two hugely successful predecessors. It reached #4 on the LP chart and maintained its bestseller status throughout most of the year. It was an extremely high-quality affair that included three hit singles and many classic album tracks. Brian's increased use of session musicians meant more polish in his productions, although Carl still played guitar on nearly every track, and Brian (keyboards), Dennis (drums), and Al (bass and guitar) played on a good many of them.

The album begins with Dennis Wilson's energetic vocal showcase "Do You Wanna Dance?" Brian's production on this Bobby Freeman cover is both Phil Spector–like and punk-rock influenced. It's simultaneously lush and raw. Another big hit is "When I Grow Up (To Be a Man)," which is a lovely whirlwind of harpsichord and harmonies, featuring one of Dennis's best studio drum performances. The original version of "Help Me, Ronda" (with a differently spelled name) is here and its good, but Brian's decision to rerecord it for single release was a wise one. "Dance, Dance, Dance" is a flat-out rocker with a great Carl guitar line, and was yet another hit single that had already reached the U.S. Top Ten the previous December.

Side Two features Brian and Mike's gorgeous "Please Let Me Wonder," which shows the emerging complexity in Brian's arrangements. "I'm So Young" yet again proves that when the Beach Boys covered a song by another artist they usually improved upon the original. Perhaps the pinnacle of balladry, surrounded by impeccable examples, is "Kiss Me, Baby." It's one of the Beach Boys' most romantic and emotional songs. "Kiss Me, Baby" is also a mammoth artistic achievement. There is something so penetrating about this recording that it can make the hairs on your neck stand up, or even bring tears. The level of quality that Brian and the Beach Boys could produce in bunches is astounding, and this song is more proof of that. "Kiss Me, Baby" would be a career achievement that any musical artist would be proud of, but for the Beach Boys it was just another album track on another album of great ones.

One more *Beach Boys Today!* track that should be paid special notice is "In the Back of My Mind." Brian, squarely in the midst of emerging mental-health problems, having just decided to forego live appearances with the Beach Boys, placed this revealing cry for help as the last song on the album.

Sung by Dennis, "In the Back of My Mind" communicates a gnawing fear that even though he's blessed with everything, something might go wrong. Brian orchestrated the track in a way that predicts the *Pet Sounds* format, and the song's semi-psychedelic string fade is certainly ahead of its time.

The album's cover certainly looks as if the Beach Boys are basking in the glow of fame. It shows the five smiling boys in collegiate-style sweaters looking happy and golden. But in a way the cover photo also projected an

By the time the Beach Boys released their 1965 LP *The Beach Boys Today!* their string of consecutive hit albums had reached eight. Although each release had shown considerable artistic progression, *The Beach Boys Today!* was the group's biggest leap forward in sophistication by a considerable margin.

embarrassingly square image compared to contemporary images of the Beatles, Stones, and Byrds, who were the group's main competition. Still, the overriding impact of *The Beach Boys Today!* comes from the music in its grooves. It nicely shows off the current sound of a talented and successful band, and one that was still getting better.

Summer Days (and Summer Nights!!)

Yet another classic collection of original songs from the Beach Boys, *Summer Days (And Summer Nights!!)* in some ways is a less ambitious record than *The Beach Boys Today!* Its high points are equally great; there just aren't as many of them. The album was another big seller, peaking at an impressive #2 in late summer 1965. However, compared to its three predecessors, it did not have a particularly long stay on the charts.

Summer Days (And Summer Nights!!) sees the Beach Boys once again numbering six members as Bruce Johnston comes aboard. His smooth vocal presence gives the Beach Boys blend a sweeter sound, and gives Brian more to work with. Bruce also adds some excellent keyboards to a few of the tracks, as he, Brian, Carl, Dennis, and Al all make instrumental contributions to the album, though not as many as prior LPs due to a greater reliance on session musicians. One great track that features the Beach Boys as musicians is "Girl Don't Tell Me," which certainly could have been a hit if released as a single. On this song, the boys absolutely nail the Beatles jangle-pop feel, with Carl delivering a sensational lead vocal. Another classic included on the LP is the hit-single version of "Help Me, Rhonda," which reached number one that summer. Brian's dynamic production vastly improved the song over the *Beach Boys Today!* version, and Al Jardine's lead vocal is stellar.

The standout track here is the single "California Girls." A #3 hit in September 1965, it features one of Brian's most inventive musical moments. The song's dramatic introduction is truly majestic; and according to Brian it was written under the influence of LSD. Mike Love's lyrics to this song have become some of the most recognizable in pop history, and his lead vocal is tremendously appealing. The track features members of the Wrecking Crew delivering the music for one of Brian's most beloved productions. Brian managed to include yet another gem with his beautiful "Let Him Run Wild," which stylistically points the way towards the upcoming *Pet Sounds*.

In a way, *Summer Days (And Summer Nights!!)* is the last all-original Beach Boys album to evoke summer as its primary theme. The cover shows Brian, Dennis, Carl, and Mike on a sailboat, enjoying a sunny day out on the Pacific. The fact that Al and Bruce are not pictured means little as the Beach Boys by this time had become an entity that didn't rely on individual faces as

Upon its release in summer 1964, the song "I Get Around" was one of the most unique and progressive-sounding rock productions of its time. It also became the Beach Boys' first number-one single, and remains one of the most popular records of their long career.

much as an aura. They were the boys of summer . . . smiling, sunny, brothers of the sun. There would be future compilations trading on the nostalgia of past times, but this LP, in the context of its time, was one last golden embrace of sun and fun from the masters of the genre.

Beach Boys' Party!

With the mid-'60s folk-rock boom sweeping the U.S., Brian came up with a pioneering idea to record an acoustic, or unplugged, style album. No other major rock group had done it prior to the November 1965 release of *Beach Boys' Party!* To enhance the casual atmosphere projected by a stripped-down musical delivery, Brian decided to create a party vibe as part of the production. Friends and family came to the studio and were recorded mingling, eating, drinking, laughing, and commenting, and these sounds were then mixed in as a backdrop to the somewhat loose musical performances.

The result is a kind of Beach Boys hootenanny LP that actually became commercially successful, topping out at #6 on the LP charts on the first day of 1966. To hear the group crank out off-the-cuff sounding renditions of Lennon and McCartney, Bob Dylan, and Phil Spector tunes among others is mildly enjoyable. They also seem to be making fun of themselves while performing a rough medley of "Little Deuce Coupe"/"I Get Around." Overall the attitude is less than serious, and it should be, considering the title of the LP is *Beach Boys' Party!*

Despite the tongue-in-cheek-presentation of the majority of the tunes, there are a few standout moments. Brian's performance of the Crystals' classic "There's No Other Like My Baby" is fantastic. Perhaps even better is Dennis's moving lead vocal on the John Lennon ballad "You've Got to Hide Your Love Away." The most recognizable track on the album is the surprise international hit single "Barbara Ann," which has a guest vocal appearance by Dean Torrence of Jan and Dean, and which hit #2 on the U.S. singles chart and #3 in the U.K. "Barbara Ann" has become one of the Beach Boys' most recognizable songs, equally dividing fans between those who love it and those who hate it. To some it represents the Beach Boys in a way that is all simplicity and fun; to others it is a throwaway novelty tune, and a weak one at that.

Beach Boys' Party! was packaged in one of the group's most beautiful album covers. A bright orange background nicely surrounds an array of gorgeous color photos of the boys hanging out in party mode. The wives and girlfriends of each Beach Boy are also pictured in the assortment of shots. *Beach Boys' Party!* is the last gasp of relative innocence from the Beach Boys. From here it all became more serious and more troubled. On the creative horizon there were great things to be achieved, but with them came new pressures and many cultural curveballs. The Beach Boys had experienced an incredible run of success between early 1963 and late 1965, and *Beach Boys' Party!* symbolizes the end of a golden era.

7

The American Beatles

Why the Beach Boys Were the Closest Thing to the Fab Four

Many people consider the Beach Boys to be the closest thing America had to the Beatles. However, their popularity in the U.K. actually came closer to Beatlemania than it ever did in the States. When *Pet Sounds* was near the top of the U.K. charts and the Beach Boys were touring Britain in 1966, there was a palpable clamor surrounding the group. They had usurped the Beatles in the vaunted *New Musical Express* Readers' Poll, the first time any group had done that since 1962. By December, "Good Vibrations" had become the group's biggest U.K. single, and the British press and fans were definitely projecting something close to Beach Boys-mania.

Back in late 1963, when the Beach Boys were virtually unknown in the U.K. but had risen to the level of national stars in the United States, they had no idea what was about to invade their comfortable American teen niche. The Beatles' legendary appearance on *The Ed Sullivan Show* in February 1964 unleashed a wave so large that nearly every other American artist was crushed by it. The Beach Boys managed to ride it out, mainly due to the sheer quality of Brian Wilson's songs. The single they released in the absolute eye of the Beatles hurricane, the teen anthem "Fun, Fun, Fun," only made it to #5. That may have been less than the stellar tune deserved, but it was good enough to keep the group in the nation's popularity mix during a brutal Beatles chart barrage that seemed to choke nearly everything else out. By August, the Beach Boys had not only survived, but were thriving with the number-one single in the U.S., "I Get Around." That single also hit the Top Ten in Britain. During the Christmas season of 1964, the year of Beatlemania, it was the *Beach Boys Concert* LP that was the number-one album on the U.S. *Billboard* LP charts.

The Fab Five?

It was during this late-1964 period that the Beach Boys came their closest to experiencing "mania"-style adulation in the U.S. Their concerts were usually sold out, and they featured throngs of screaming girls who at times

arl, Al, Dennis, Mike and Brian go sightseeing in Berlin.

Brian takes a "movie" of the Beach Boys.

The Beach Boys had a hit in Europe with "I Get Around" when they visited England, France, and Germany in late 1964. But it wouldn't be until 1966 when U.K. fans truly went manic for the California quintet.

drowned out the band's music. A great example of this fan-generated elec-tricity is the Beach Boys' performance during the great concert film known as *The T.A.M.I. Show*. This late-1964 set filmed at the Santa Monica Civic Auditorium shows how rabid the group's followers could be. Dennis Wilson is clearly the focus of most of the screaming from the females in the crowd. And it's his animal magnetism and wild charisma that gives the Beach Boys' live presentation a Beatles-like magic. Brian and the others drew their share of screams as well, but as Brian himself later admitted, the front line would be regularly knocked aside by girls rushing the stage to get closer to Dennis.

Nineteen sixty-five was another huge year for the Beach Boys, with multiple hit records and massively successful tours. But it became apparent that although their fame grew, they'd never equal the iconic status that the Beatles held. The Fab Four would forever be known as America's and the world's favorite rock group, with Britain's Rolling Stones being the only 1960s band that gave them a serious run for their money worldwide. The Beach Boys would always be rated a few rungs or more down the popularity ladder, particularly in America. This circumstance must have been troubling for them, considering that *they* were the American pioneers when it came to self-contained rock groups who sang, wrote, and performed their music. It was also the Beach Boys who gave Capitol Records their template for promot-ing and distributing rock albums to the U.S. teen market, a genre that had previously been a mostly singles industry. This template was conveniently adapted and used to push the Beatles into the album-sales stratosphere.

Meanwhile, as time passed, the Beach Boys found that the British concert audiences and record-buying public were their most loyal fans. It was the British who first recognized *Pet Sounds* as the great masterpiece that it was, while in the U.S. it remained underrated for many years. And even in the late 1960s, when the Beach Boys domestic popularity had faded and they hadn't cracked the U.S. Top Ten in years, the British gave them a number-one single with the song "Do It Again." And when they released the wonder-ful *Sunflower* LP in 1970 to a resounding thud in the U.S., where it peaked at number 151 on the LP charts . . . the British music critics gave it a thumbs-up as it eased into the U.K. Top Thirty. With this in mind, when the Beach Boys are referred to as the "American Beatles," it seems that the term has some truth to it from perspectives on *both* sides of the Atlantic Ocean.

The Beachles—Cross-Pollination and Covers

"Girl Don't Tell Me"—The Beach Boys definitely channeled a little bit of "Ticket to Ride" during this song.

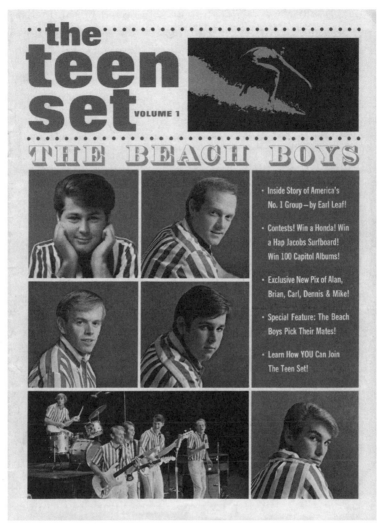

Most 1964 teen magazines feature the Beatles on their cover. However, the Beach Boys dominated this issue of *Teen Set* magazine, published at the peak of the British Invasion.

Beach Boys' Party!—On this 1965 LP, the Beach Boys covered three Beatles songs unplugged style: "I Should Have Known Better," "Tell Me Why," and "You've Got to Hide Your Love Away." The latter was used as a concert showcase for Dennis in 1966.

"Here, There and Everywhere"—Paul McCartney has admitted that the Beatles were trying for a Beach Boy–inflected harmony sound on this 1966 song.

"Penny Lane"—McCartney was hugely influenced by the Beach Boys *Pet Sounds*, and it shows unmistakably on this 1967 classic, which has a decidedly "God Only Knows" bass feel, not to mention flutes, piccolos, flugelhorn, and high harmonies.

"Vegetables" (or "Vega-Tables")—In 1967, Paul reportedly dropped in on a *Smile* session while Brian was recording this song. Apparently Paul chewed on some celery or sat on a radish or something while tape was rolling.

"Back in the U.S.S.R."—McCartney has described this as a Beach Boys "parody," and it certainly harkens to the "California Girls" style of name-checking geographic areas and their girls. Mike Love has claimed he actually offered input when Paul was writing this while both were in Rishikesh, India studying with Maharishi Mahesh Yogi. The Beach Boys covered the song live in the 1980s with Ringo Starr joining them, and have made at least one unreleased attempt at a studio version of the song.

"Rock and Roll Music"—Many rock fans assumed the Beach Boys were covering the Beatles with their 1976 hit "Rock and Roll Music," not realizing the Beatles late-1964 version of the song was a Chuck Berry cover. Things became more confusing when Capitol Records released a Beatles compilation LP titled *Rock 'n' Roll Music* in June 1976, just as the Beach Boys single was becoming a hit.

"Imagine"—Mike Love absolutely massacred this beloved song during a few early-'80s Beach Boys concerts.

"A Friend Like You"—Paul McCartney sang a co-lead vocal on this song from Brian's *Gettin' In Over My Head* solo CD, released in 2004.

"Walk With You"—This track from Ringo's 2010 CD *Y Not* has added vocals from Paul McCartney, and interestingly a Van Dyke Parks lyric. McCartney has long admired Parks's *Smile*-era work with Brian, but he had to wait until Ringo collaborated with him to sing one of his songs.

8

Brian Wilson Is the Beach Boys

The Truth About the Studio Beach Boys, the Wrecking Crew, and Who Really Played on the Records

Conventional writings in rock-journalism circles have long stated that, following their earliest records, Brian Wilson independently replaced the Beach Boys as musicians in the studio. Brian's celebrated use of Phil Spector's core of seasoned L.A. studio veterans, known to some as the Wrecking Crew, revolutionized the Beach Boys' sound, and influenced the entire record business. However, a closer examination of the facts has shown this "replacement theory" to be a partial myth.

Dennis Wilson once famously stated, "Brian Wilson is the Beach Boys," and the rest of the group were his messengers. "He's everything, we're nothing." As with most Dennis Wilson quotes, this one contains some truth, some exaggeration, some bite, and some humility. No doubt that Brian was the Beach Boys' sun, and the others were the unique planets in *his* solar system. The quote may have been Dennis's stealthy way of needling credit-grabbing Mike Love. But Dennis was also truthfully admitting that *none* of the others, including himself, could ever match Brian's creative gift, and that they were *all* lucky to have had Brian lead them to fame and fortune.

As Brian evolved as an arranger and producer, the studio became his laboratory, and the Beach Boys' recording sessions became his concentrated experiments. Each one broke new ground and gave Brian the momentum and the confidence to take things a step further. His creative growth, and by extension the group's, was astonishing. Compare the basic raw garage sound of "409," recorded in mid-1962, to the arrangement wizardry of "I Get Around," recorded in mid-1964. That kind of growth in just two years is nothing short of stunning. And Brian was only getting warmed up. Within another two years he'd make the once-futuristic-sounding "I Get Around" seem absolutely archaic with the ultra-rich productions within *Pet Sounds* and the envelope-pushing single "Good Vibrations." Brian may have burnt out at a relatively early age, but what he accomplished by age 25 will forever stand as one of, if not the greatest, streaks of brilliance by any artist of his time.

So yes, Brian Wilson is the Beach Boys in the sense that it was his creativity and genius vision that led the group to glory. But genius does not exist in a vacuum. True genius usually has an awesome support system. Brian's support system, though at times dysfunctional, and at times a barrier, was in its own way as brilliant as he was. From Murry's fearless drive, to Dennis's instinct and charisma, to Carl's steadiness and one-of-a kind voice, to Mike's innate ability to connect with his lyrics, Brian had an incredible gang.

And did I mention those voices? Well, I did mention Carl's; his was one of the greatest vocal gifts in pop history. Mike's voice was distinct, and made the Beach Boys immediately identifiable. Al's voice was rich, versatile, and most importantly could mimic Brian's. Dennis's vocals had that sandpaper texture that made everything seem more sensual and honest. Bruce's precise, clear, and sugary sound was the perfect opposite of Dennis. And Brian's falsetto could raise goose bumps and bring tears. It could also make everything seem a little happier and a little sunnier. Put them all together with Brian's savant-like ability to create interweaving and interlocking parts, and what you had was the prettiest, most sophisticated, most euphoria-inducing sound to ever be emitted from the lips of human beings.

The Beach Boys' vocal sound at its best is nothing short of pure pop bliss. If aliens ever land on Earth and we need to impress them quickly, just shoot a little "Our Prayer" their way and they'll immediately understand everything worthwhile about the human race. Brian found the good or the God within us all, the indescribable spiritual chord that connects us. But he wasn't alone in his discovery. He created the genius body of work along with his brothers, his cousin, and his friends. Brian Wilson is the Beach Boys, but Brian Wilson isn't Brian Wilson without them.

Remember This ... the Beach Boys Were Musicians

Since their vocals were peerless, it's easy to think of the Beach Boys as predominantly a vocal group. But let's touch upon on those great instrumental tracks underneath the vocals. They were genius, too. Conventional wisdom has told us for decades that after the early days of garage rock and surf jams, the Beach Boys became a vocals-only entity. Respected journalists have insisted for years that following their first couple of hits, Brian hired the best musicians in L.A. to play the instruments on Beach Boys recordings. He'd arrange, record, produce, and then at the last minute the other guys would add their vocals, and voila . . . another Beach Boys release hit the record racks. This is largely a myth, but one with a nuanced vein of truth.

First off, the group's initial four LPs—*Surfin' Safari*, *Surfin' U.S.A.*, *Surfer Girl*, and *Little Deuce Coupe*—are virtually self-contained efforts. Those LPs, and the singles derived from them, feature Brian on bass and keyboards; Carl Wilson and David Marks on guitar; Dennis Wilson on drums; and, beginning with the third LP *Surfer Girl*, Al Jardine augments the lineup primarily as a bassist on the tracks which feature Brian on keyboards. Mike Love also plays very minimal saxophone on a handful of early tracks. This is the lineup that performs on nearly every track prior to 1964. All of the lazy clip-job journalism, anecdotal quips, and revisionist propaganda that insist session musicians were dominating these early tunes is complete hogwash, and has been thoroughly debunked. As respected experts depend less on shaky memories and the incorrect writings of years past, and actually study the session tapes and all the related evidence, year by year it becomes clearer that the Beach Boys themselves were the players on these records.

There were a few anomalies to the usual core Beach Boys instrumental lineup. Carl, not Dennis, was the drummer on the first LP's instrumental "Moon Dawg," which also probably features guitarist Derry Weaver in a modest supporting role. Dennis was apparently either augmented by, or replaced by, a session drummer named Frank DeVito on the single "Surfin' U.S.A." The first appearance of drummer extraordinaire Hal Blaine on a Beach Boys track is during the sessions for the their third LP *Surfer Girl*, on the song "Our Car Club," Hal also plays timbales along with Dennis's drums on the track "Hawaii." Mike Love's sister Maureen adds harp flourishes to "In My Room" and "Catch a Wave." On the same LP, on the song "The Surfer Moon," Brian used session players and a string section. That track was originally intended for non–Beach Boys use, but Brian reconsidered and had the group add vocals to it for the LP. On the previously mentioned "Our Car Club," and on a couple of tracks on the Beach Boys fourth LP, *Little Deuce Coupe*, Brian added the saxophone work of Steve Douglas and Jay Migliori to augment the Beach Boys' sound. Other than the few exceptions above, the Beach Boys play all of the instruments heard on their first four albums, and their first five singles.

The myth-defying fact that the Beach Boys largely played their own instruments in the studio does not end after album four. In fact, on their next two studio LPs, released in 1964, *Shut Down Volume 2* and *All Summer Long*, the Beach Boys again played the vast majority of the instruments. On two LPs released in 1965, *Beach Boys Today!* and *Summer Days (and Summer Nights)*, Brian significantly increased his use of studio professionals; but still the Beach Boys continued to play the instruments on many of the key tracks

Brian on bass and David on guitar at the Capitol Records studios in 1962. The Beach Boys, who have wrongly been written off as a band who were replaced by studio professionals on their hit recordings, actually played most of the instruments on the majority of their bestselling records.

and single releases. The very first Beach Boys LP to feature session players on nearly every track was Brian's 1966 masterpiece *Pet Sounds*. He continued with this session-player-dominated recording method through the initial stages of his ill-fated *Smile* project into early 1967. And that's the real truth. Beginning in 1963, session players augmented the Beach Boys, at first barely, and then increasingly, until 1966—when session players took over almost completely for about a year. After that, it's a mixed bag, with outside musicians generally being used in moderation to embellish or refine tracks as necessary. But if you need a thumbnail guide to the truth about who played on the Beach Boys' records during their golden age, try this one . . .

What follows is a select list of songs that feature one or more of the Beach Boys—. Brian, Dennis, Carl, Mike, Al, David, or Bruce—playing instruments on a track.

The Beach Boys as Musicians, 1962–1965

"Surfin"—Brian (snare drum), Carl (guitar), Al (upright bass)
"Surfin' Safari"—Brian (bass), Dennis (drums), Carl (guitar), David (guitar)
"409"—Brian (bass), Dennis (drums), Carl (guitar), David (guitar)
"Ten Little Indians"—Brian (bass), Dennis (drums), Carl (guitar), David (guitar), Mike (saxophone)

"Surfin' U.S.A."—Brian (bass, organ), Carl (guitar), David (guitar), track is augmented by Frank DeVito (drums)

"Shut Down"—Brian (bass), Dennis (drums), Carl (guitar), David (guitar), Mike (saxophone)

"Farmer's Daughter"—Brian (bass), Dennis (drums), Carl (guitar), David (guitar)

"Stoked"—Brian (bass), Dennis (drums), Carl (guitar), David (guitar)

"Lonely Sea"—Brian (bass), Dennis (drums), Carl (guitar), David (guitar)

"Noble Surfer"—Brian (bass, keyboard), Dennis (drums), Carl (guitar), David (guitar)

"Lana"—Brian (bass, keyboards), Dennis (drums), Carl (guitar), David (guitar)

"Surf Jam"—Brian (bass), Dennis (drums), Carl (guitar), David (guitar), Mike (saxophone)

"Let's Go Trippin'"—Brian (bass), Dennis (drums), Carl (guitar), David (guitar), Mike (saxophone)

"Surfer Girl"—Brian (bass), Dennis (drums), Carl (guitar), David (guitar)

"Catch a Wave"—Brian (keyboards, percussion), Dennis (drums), Carl (guitar), David (guitar), Al (bass), track is augmented by Maureen Love (harp)

"Little Deuce Coupe"—Brian (bass, piano), Dennis (drums), Carl (guitar), David (guitar)

"In My Room"—Brian (bass, organ), Dennis (drums, percussion), Carl (guitar), David (guitar), track is augmented by Maureen Love (harp)

"Hawaii"—Brian (piano), Dennis (drums), Carl (guitar), David (guitar), Al (bass), track is augmented by Hal Blaine (timbales)

"Our Car Club"—Brian (bass), Carl (guitar), David (guitar), track is augmented by Hal Blaine (drums), Steve Douglas (saxophone), Jay Migliori (saxophone)

"Your Summer Dream"—Brian (bass), Dennis (drums), Carl (guitar), David (guitar)

"Little Saint Nick"—Brian (piano, celesta), Dennis (drums), Carl (guitar, sleigh bells), David (guitar), Al (bass, glockenspiel)

"Fun, Fun, Fun"—Brian (keyboards), Dennis (drums), Carl (guitars), Al (bass), track is augmented by Hal Blaine (additional drums), Ray Pohlman (additional bass)

"The Warmth of the Sun"—Brian (bass), Dennis (drums), Carl (guitar), track is augmented by Hal Blaine (percussion), Steve Douglas (saxophone), Jay Migliori (saxophone)

"Don't Worry Baby"—Brian (piano), Dennis (drums), Carl (guitars), Al (bass)

"This Car of Mine"—Brian (piano), Dennis (drums), Carl (guitar), Al (bass)

"In the Parking Lot"—Brian (piano), Dennis (drums), Carl (guitar), Al (bass)

"Pom, Pom Play Girl"—Brian (bass), Carl (guitars), Dennis (drums, tympani), Mike (saxophone)

"I Get Around"—Brian (keyboards), Dennis (drums), Carl (guitars), Al (bass), track is augmented by Hal Blaine (timbales), Ray Pohlman (additional bass), Steve Douglas (saxophone), Jay Migliori (saxophone)

"All Summer Long"—Brian (marimba), Dennis (drums), Carl (guitars), Al (bass), track is augmented by Steve Douglas (saxophone), Jay Migliori (piccolo)

"Hushabye"—Brian (piano), Dennis (drums), Carl (guitar), Al (bass)

"Little Honda"—Brian (keyboards), Dennis (drums), Carl (guitars), Al (guitar and bass)

"Wendy"—Brian (keyboards), Dennis (drums), Carl (guitars), Al (guitar and bass)

"Girls on the Beach"—Brian (piano, chimes), Dennis (drums), Carl (guitar), Al (bass)

"Do You Remember?"—Brian (piano), Dennis (drums), Carl (guitars), Al (bass), track is augmented by Steve Douglas (saxophone), Jay Migliori (saxophone)

"Don't Back Down"—Brian (keyboards), Dennis (drums), Carl (guitars), Al (bass), track is augmented by Hal Blaine (additional drums), Ray Pohlman (additional bass)

"Dance, Dance, Dance"—Brian (bass), Dennis (drums), Carl (guitar), Al (guitar), track is augmented by session players

"Do You Wanna Dance?"—Brian (piano), Carl (lead guitar), all other instruments performed by session players

"Good to My Baby"—Brian (piano), Carl (guitar), all other instruments performed by session players

"Don't Hurt My Little Sister"—Brian (piano), Carl (lead guitar), Al (bass), Dennis (tambourine), track is augmented by session players

"When I Grow Up (To Be a Man)"—Brian (keyboards), Dennis (drums), Carl (guitars), Al (bass)

"Help Me, Ronda"—Carl (guitar), all other instruments performed by session players

"Please Let Me Wonder"—Brian (organ), Carl (guitars), Dennis (percussion), all other instruments performed by session players

"I'm So Young"—Brian (organ), Dennis (drums), Carl (guitars), Al (bass)

"Kiss Me, Baby"—Brian (piano), Carl (guitars), all other instruments performed by session players

"She Knows Me Too Well"—Brian (piano), Dennis (drums), Carl (guitars), Al (bass)

"In the Back of My Mind"—Carl (lead guitar), all other instruments performed by session players

"Help Me, Rhonda" (single version)—Brian (piano), Carl (guitars), Dennis (tambourine), all other instruments performed by session players

"The Girl From New York City"—Carl (lead guitar), Al (guitar), Bruce (piano), all other instruments performed by session players

"Then I Kissed Her"—Brian (piano, bass), Dennis (drums), Carl (guitars), Bruce (organ)

"Salt Lake City"—Carl (guitar), all other instruments performed by session players

"Girl Don't Tell Me"—Brian (bass), Dennis (drums), Carl (guitars), Bruce (celesta)

"California Girls"—Carl (guitar), all other instruments performed by session players

"You're So Good to Me"—Brian (piano), Dennis (drums), Carl (guitars), Al (guitar, bass), Bruce (organ)

(Special thanks to Craig Slowinski for his research on the above sessions.)

9

God Only Knows

Pet Sounds—The Greatest Pop/Rock Album of All Time

Paul McCartney and George Martin have both stated that the Beach Boys 1966 album *Pet Sounds* was a major influence on the Beatles' efforts on their 1967 masterpiece *Sergeant Pepper's Lonely Hearts Club Band*. Countless historians and artists have credited *Pet Sounds* as the greatest pop album ever. And yet, it wasn't considered a success in its time, and some feel it led directly to the Beach Boys demise as a top-tier act.

For years, Brian Wilson had been flirting with uniquely orchestrated production techniques that challenged the normal boundaries of the pop/rock format. He upped the ante by closing *The Beach Boys Today!* LP in 1965 with a song titled "In the Back of My Mind" that proved to be a harbinger of things to come. The song featured extremely introspective lyrics sung by Dennis, but it was the musical arrangement and backing track that stood out. It moved beyond Brian's previous flirtations with progressive sound, and took it into a realm that was a classical/jazz/pop hybrid with flashes of surf/psych seasoning. In late 1965, Brian heard the Beatles LP *Rubber Soul* and was impressed with the high quality of songs throughout the album. The idea of an LP as a total statement as opposed to a collection of separate songs appealed to him. Brian took it upon himself to record an album of his best work from beginning to end.

As rock music quickly matured in the mid-'60s, its lyrical content often struck a more serious tone. Bob Dylan, John Lennon, and others were giving rock a deeper and more meaningful thematic thrust. Brian too wanted his songs to reflect the changes that were happening within him and without him. He found an unlikely source for articulating this evolution in ad man Tony Asher. Brian's usual lyricist Mike Love would be temporarily bypassed for the vast majority of the album. Asher's collaboration with Brian insured that *Pet Sounds* projected the raw adult emotion that Brian hoped to communicate. With little collaboration with Love, and little use of the Beach

Boys as musicians, *Pet Sounds* was clearly the least band-influenced record the Beach Boys ever made. It was instead a window directly into Brian's feelings and creative soul. The results were both beautiful and difficult.

The assertion that *Pet Sounds* was a commercial failure upon its release in May 1966 is a bit of an overstatement. Let's just say it didn't quite meet the standard the Beach Boys were used to. The band's previous five LPs had charted at #4, #1, #4, #2, and #6 respectively in the U.S., while *Pet Sounds* only made it to #10. The outer reaches of the national Top Ten certainly isn't bad, but not exactly where one would expect the peak position of a record critically praised as their greatest ever to land. *Pet Sounds* does hold the distinction as the only Beach Boys LP to produce four Top Forty singles, with "Sloop John B," "Caroline, No," "Wouldn't It Be Nice," and its B-side "God Only Knows" all becoming radio hits. But at least some of the execs at Capitol Records, and some of the group's fans, thought the Beach Boys had compromised their sunny good-time image by releasing an album filled with introspection and melancholy.

Don't Fuck With the Formula

To hedge their bet, Capitol rushed out a Beach Boys greatest-hits LP packed with oldies directly on the heels of *Pet Sounds*. The fact that *Best of the Beach Boys* charted higher and outsold *Pet Sounds* wasn't exactly a confidence booster for Brian. There was, without a doubt, a less-than-celebratory air in the U.S. surrounding the release of *Pet Sounds*. It found itself perceived as a kind of square peg: too serious for some, not rocking enough for others, and so subtly sophisticated that most Americans wouldn't even begin to understand it for many years. It was, and still is, seen by many as the delineation point when the Beach Boys became something less than wildly popular.

It must be emphasized that this was not the case in Great Britain. In fact, *Pet Sounds* and its aftermath were the absolute pinnacle of the Beach Boys' popularity in the U.K. There, the album was fanatically embraced and hit a lofty #2 on the album chart. The British music press, many of the most notable British musicians, and the British record-buying public reacted to *Pet Sounds* with a genuine devotion. And as the Beach Boys' popularity rose and solidified in Britain, it ebbed in America. In the U.S. *Pet Sounds* was not certified RIAA Gold until the year 2000, at which time it was given a platinum certification as well. Once the Beach Boys and Capitol Records got over the fact that it was a somewhat disappointing seller in 1966, they began to understand that *Pet Sounds* was like a marathon runner, not a sprinter.

I'm Waiting for the Day

Each subsequent rerelease and reissue of the album has helped keep the legend of *Pet Sounds* alive in the public's collective mind. Reprise Records took over the rights from Capitol when the Beach Boys signed there in 1970, and at first confusingly decided to couple a reissue of *Pet Sounds* with the 1972 Beach Boys LP *Carl and the Passions—"So Tough"* as a double-LP set. Reprise reissued *Pet Sounds* again in 1974, this time in a more tasteful manner, with a reworked cover. Capitol then regained the rights and reissued it on vinyl in 1980. *Pet Sounds* made its debut on CD in Japan in 1986, and in the U.S. in 1990. Multiple CD and vinyl reissues followed worldwide as *Pet Sounds* became one of the most repackaged and reissued records of all time.

Capitol went all in with their deluxe *Pet Sounds Sessions* box set in 1997. The 4-CD package contained alternate mixes, instrumental tracks, vocals-only tracks, and edited highlights from the recording sessions, as well as extensive liner notes. It was nominated for a Grammy. This set included the first stereo mix of the LP, created by Mark Linett. A stereo *Pet Sounds* proved to be a revelation for many Beach Boys fans that never connected with Brian's original ultra-dense mono mix. This was another factor in expanding

(l–r): Carl, Al, Dennis, Mike, and Bruce in 1966. While Brian stayed in L.A. creating the beautiful *Pet Sounds* tracks, the other Beach Boys toured Japan. Upon their return they added their vocals to Brian's moody masterpiece.

the appreciation and accessibility of Brian's work. Capitol continued its never-ending *Pet Sounds* revival campaign with a fortieth-anniversary edition issued on CD and vinyl in 2006. Today *Pet Sounds* is not only considered an awesome artistic achievement, but one that over time has proved to be commercially viable as well.

Despite its late-bloomer status as a top seller, the *Pet Sounds* album's undeniable historical significance has absolutely nothing to do with sales figures, awards, and chart positions. It is the one-of-a kind musical experience that the record offers its listener that sets the album apart from just about anything else. It could be the most intimate grand production ever, the saddest hopeful sentiment of all time, the most comforting confession of loss, and the most beautiful pain ever communicated by an artist. It's a complicated yet humble record, and an extremely sophisticated but naïve one as well. The themes explored by Brian, and the album's primary lyricist Tony Asher, share a journey of bittersweet love and innocence lost. There are intensely somber moments like the songs "I Just Wasn't Made For These Times" and "Caroline, No." Despite its romantic lyrical thrust, "Don't Talk (Put Your Head On My Shoulder)" has an excruciating quality, with its foreboding strings gnawing away under the surface. There seems to be a constant shadow of doubt that overwhelms any lasting sense of well-being or peace of mind.

Dennis saw his vocal role reduced in the Beach Boys blend once Bruce Johnston established himself in the studio. But behind the scenes, Dennis was becoming more proficient on the keyboards and beginning to compose his own music. Brian would be both his mentor and his biggest influence.

Even some of the lighter moments on *Pet Sounds* are weighted with longing, regret, fear, and confusion. But somehow it's all presented in a way that is sonically gorgeous and vocally welcoming. Brian Wilson himself dominates the collection with his soul-baring lead vocals. And considering he wrote, arranged, and produced the album, *Pet Sounds* may be close enough to a Brian Wilson solo LP to have called it that. But he didn't. The other Beach Boys all make worthwhile contributions that elevate the experience and further articulate Brian's vision. Carl Wilson's angelic lead vocal on "God Only Knows" is an iconic moment in the history of pop. Mike's lead section on "Sloop John B" is nothing short of perfection. Al, Bruce, and Dennis each add vocal lines and harmony performances that help give *Pet Sounds* its incredibly varied and rich vocal texture.

The Crew Comes Through

Musically *Pet Sounds* is played almost entirely by studio professionals. Brian used his core of favorite L.A. session players to help him realize a highly sophisticated soundscape. *Pet Sounds* embraces pop, jazz, classical, exotica, and avant-garde elements using an extremely eclectic palate of instrument combinations and textures. It results in an overall style that melds nearly every modern genre into something absolutely original. Brian only used the Beach Boys as musicians on one *Pet Sounds* track. "That's Not Me" features Brian on keyboards and bass, Carl on guitar, and Dennis on drums, supporting Mike's distinct lead vocal. Its charming brotherly groove and surf-tinged vibe somehow blends perfectly with the other orchestrated and lushly produced *Pet Sounds* tracks. Even on his most studio-musician-dominated work, Brian proved he could still rely on his brothers to help him deliver something unique and timeless.

The one type of music that is mostly absent is the same one the Beach Boys had made a living playing up to this point. Although often described as one of the greatest rock records, *Pet Sounds* is anything but. There isn't much rocking here, and even less rolling. *Pet Sounds* is at times futuristic, progressive, and experimental. It's even slightly psychedelic—or at least impressionistic, but there's no boogie, no woogie, and the only blues are in the themes and in Brian's voice. The opener "Wouldn't It Be Nice" has what could be described as a rollicking feel, but with the dominant instruments in it being accordions, Brian defies any notion of genre safety.

Brian proved that a rock band, or a rock artist, could go somewhere entirely different, while still retaining elements of the signature sound that his group had crafted and owned for most of the 1960s. *Pet Sounds* indeed sounds Beach Boys, but as if they'd forsaken Fender guitars for vibraphones and violas, replaced Chuck Berry with Martin Denny, and channeled Nelson Riddle more than Phil Spector. But beyond influences and comparisons, it should be emphasized that *Pet Sounds* realizes the artistic maturation of Brian Wilson. In a sense he created his own genre with this album, and one that can only be labeled as *Pet Sounds* music, or better yet, Brian Wilson music. This wasn't necessarily his creative peak. He'd take it all a step further, but he'd never again hit his target as squarely as he did with *Pet Sounds*.

10

I Don't Know Where, But She Sends Me There

"Good Vibrations"—The Greatest Pop/Rock Single Ever

W hile immersed in the last weeks of recording his *Pet Sounds* project, Brian Wilson simultaneously launched himself into the challenge of making the greatest single of all time. It took an unheard of six months of on-and-off work to complete at a time when singles were usually recorded in a day or two. Brian used three different studios, seventeen recording sessions, a gang of session musicians, and multiple lyricists, all the while shuffling sections, creating and scrapping mixes and edits, and tweaking it all until he had it just right. At the time it was the most expensive and meticulously worked pop song ever recorded. The result was three minutes and thirty-five seconds of perfection. The single became an instant worldwide smash hit, and was perhaps the pinnacle of the Beach Boys' career.

Released in October 1966, "Good Vibrations" is an endlessly inventive, catchy but quirky love song, replete with sunshine, psychedelia, and Electro-Theremin, wrapped into a stunning bouquet of sonic bliss. It was also the last time the world truly connected with new Brian Wilson music. His constant probing of unexplored creative frontiers had led him toward a new approach in making records. Instead of recording a song as a freestanding and whole entity, Brian pioneered a modular system where individual pieces of music were recorded that fit together like a puzzle, sometimes in interchangeable ways. "Good Vibrations" was the debut of this philosophy in a totally committed way.

This Is the Way I Always Dreamed It Would Be

As a symphony has separate movements, "Good Vibrations," coined a "pocket symphony" by publicist Derek Taylor, has four completely different sections, with another two variations on those. It begins with an eclectic-sounding but somewhat typically structured verse/chorus, which cycles through twice. A gently welcoming lead vocal coaxes the verse forward over delicate organ stabs and incredibly artful bass figures. Lively drums lead to the chorus, which is propelled by driving cello, walking bass, and a wacky Electro-Theremin. The vocal hook featuring the title words sung by low lead voice is quickly joined by a glorious arrangement of harmonically interlocking voices. The chorus is exhilarating in its energy and complexity, but completely accessible to the ear.

The song then moves to a differently textured and paced section with tack piano, percussion, jaw harp, ethereal harmonies, and the lyric "I don't know where but she sends me there." This section might be called a bridge under normal circumstances, but the song's structure takes such an abstract route that traditional labels don't really apply. From there the mood suddenly darkens, and the song descends into a jarringly somber state with a church-style Hammond organ, which moves through its progression once with soft percussion only, and then is joined the second time through by the hopeful lyrical refrain: "Gotta keep those lovin' good, vibrations happenin' with her." The vocals fade as a friendly harmonica line joins the organ. A new, intense harmony stack suddenly bursts forth, and bang, a reprise of the chorus resumes only to stop again for a complex harmony round of "na, na, na's" and "ba, ba, ba's" and then a re-launch into the cello-driven chorus feel, this time with no vocals, which swiftly moves to a quick Electro-Theremin-dominated fade.

Somehow Brian manages to pull off all of this color and flash, light and dark, stop and go, and up and down in a seamless manner that never sounds off-balance or even slightly wrong. Instead it's a lovely adventure with a building momentum. There are a couple of moments along the way to pause and reflect before the song merges back into a joyous sprint to celebration and euphoria. Unlike the mostly melancholy *Pet Sounds*, the feeling projected by "Good Vibrations" is a decidedly happy one. As stated above, there are minor deviations into darkness and reflection, but the overwhelming impact of the song is nearly giddy positivity. Also, unlike *Pet Sounds*, the chorus of "Good Vibrations" projects a definite "rock and roll" energy and feel.

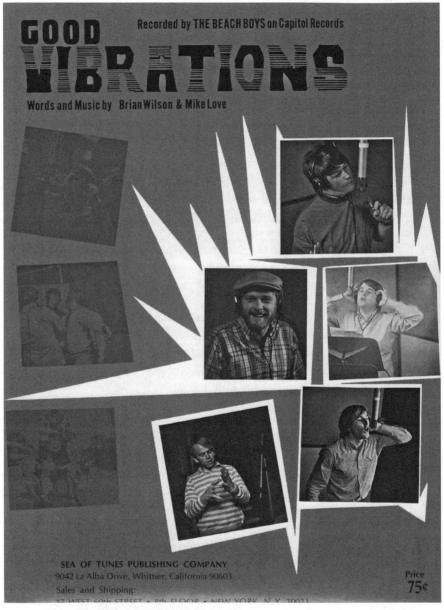

The fall 1966 single "Good Vibrations" was a massive worldwide hit, and for a brief moment it gave the Beach Boys a perfect balance between artistic credibility and commercial success. It was a unique blend of catchy pop music and trippy psychedelic production, something that the Beatles would also perfect in the months ahead.

Brian created nearly all of "Good Vibrations" with a group of his favorite studio musicians, and predominantly used the Beach Boys as featured vocalists, with Carl, Mike, and Brian all singing standout elements of the arrangement. Drummer Hal Blaine, bassist Ray Pohlman, harmonica player Tommy Morgan, Electro-Theremin artist Paul Tanner, and others perform the instrumental backing of the song admirably. The only other Beach Boy to contribute musically to "Good Vibrations" is Dennis Wilson, who plays the gentle Hammond organ progression during the song's slow section. It certainly adds an organic and moving element to the tune, knowing that a Wilson brother supplied perhaps the most spiritual-sounding moment of a track that will forever be celebrated as a true classic.

Dancing in the Night Unafraid

For the Beach Boys, "Good Vibrations" was a massively successful stroke. The psychedelic period of the 1960s was just dawning, and with "Good Vibrations" the Beach Boys vaulted nearly every other rock act in their delivery of a Flower Power classic. It was just strange enough to be hip, and just

As they had briefly in 1963, the Beach Boys again settled into a six-member lineup in 1965, with Brian being the non-performing Beach Boy. There seemed to be no rhyme or reason as to whether Brian or Bruce would appear in the group's publicity shots. This 1966 photo includes Brian.

progressive enough to be taken seriously, but still vibrant, happy, accessible Beach Boys-esque pop. This signature sound would be duplicated, cloned, commercialized, and re-fabricated in song, commercials, TV shows, movies, and elevators to the point of completely diluting the genius of the original. But "Good Vibrations" was probably the quintessential "sunshine pop" recording of the century. And in the context of the weeks when it steadily climbed the pop charts to number one on December 10, 1966, it was truly the most original single record on the radio. In a way, "Good Vibrations" seemed like a newly discovered universe.

The single's success was a temporary vindication for both Brian Wilson and Mike Love. Brian had taken some criticism over *Pet Sounds* for being too progressive or too far out. With "Good Vibrations" he went even farther out, but proved he could do so in a way that the public absolutely adored. Mike Love, who had been mostly bypassed as a lyricist on *Pet Sounds*, was given the job of replacing the lyrics Tony Asher and Brian had written for "Good Vibrations." Love not only proved he was up to the job, but he may have written one of the best lyric sets of his life, and supposedly he did it in less than 30 minutes.

There has long been an established tale of how Brian came upon the basic idea for the theme of "Good Vibrations." He consistently claimed that as a child his mother Audree used to tell him the reason dogs bark at some people and not others is they feel their vibrations, some good, some not good. This seems like a very plausible anecdote, and is probably true at its essence. However, it has also been discovered through later research that Brian's neighbor, Jo Ann Marks, was a noted psychic who was deeply involved in metaphysical and supernatural studies, and that as a young boy Brian showed a keen interest in her theories and her reading material. It is also established that Jo Ann often used the terms "good vibrations" or "bad vibrations" in conversation when an entity struck her that way. It may have been a combination of Audree's story about dogs' intuitive reactions, and the ideas and lingo of Jo Ann, which sparked Brian's use of the term in his song.

"Good Vibrations" is one of those rare artistic achievements that not only entertained and enlightened, but also caused lasting repercussions within the culture and society. How many times has someone used the term "vibes" in your life? We often say, "I'm getting a bad vibe" about something. "Good," as well. These terms have been ingrained into the vocabulary of our daily life, and they were not really there on a mass level until this song hit the radio. But it wasn't just the mystical theme of "Good Vibrations" that impacted the culture. It was a song that conclusively proved that rock music—even completely accessible and undeniably catchy rock music—could be a high form of art. It showed that a simple jingle could in effect be classic, classical, psychedelic, bubblegum, jazz-rock, and an incredibly complex production. What it did was not just push the boundaries . . . it obliterated them.

With future Beatles pop/psych epics like "Penny Lane"/"Strawberry Fields Forever" right around the corner, the days of "Good Vibrations" being perceived as a radical innovator were short. But the good feelings and inventiveness projected in Brian's "pocket symphony" would leave it standing for decades as one of the truly beloved '60s classics. And if you really think about it, analyze it, put it in its proper context and let it hit your ears as freshly as the day it was released . . . "Good Vibrations" probably *was* the greatest pop/rock single record of all time.

11

Your Favorite Vegetable

The Fantastically Freaky and Sad Legend of Smile

Smile, the 1967 Beach Boys LP, remains the greatest rock album that never was. It initiated the substance-addled train wreck that Brian Wilson became, and was perhaps the thing that haunted him most throughout his troubled years. It both made the Beach Boys irrelevant in their time and created a cult for Beach Boys music that will never die. The LSD-, amphetamine-, hashish-, and paranoia-fueled sessions that resulted in the strange and wonderful *Smile* music were the backdrop for some of Brian Wilson's most eccentric behavior.

Many of the *Smile* songs were written in a large sandbox that Brian had placed in his home, his grand piano resting upon the sand. A large tent was erected inside Brian's home as well, furnished with large pillows and psychedelic tapestries; in it, *Smile* strategy meetings took place and substances were consumed. Brian wanted to film everything during the creation of *Smile*; he wanted to perform and record comedy sketches; and he wanted to empty his swimming pool and conduct recording sessions at the bottom. Brian made arrangements to tape nature sounds, animal sounds, machine sounds, and water sounds, and he wanted to incorporate all of these into his music. Brian asked his studio musicians to wear firemen's hats while burning buckets of wood smoldered nearby. He ordered his first-rate horn section to blow into the wrong end of their instruments. Like a five-year-old child, Brian sprinted into the increasingly absurd *Smile* project in total wonder. He was both thrilled by what he discovered, and shocked to find a reality that eventually resulted in complete disillusionment. But despite the shambolic and inevitably disintegrating nature of the *Smile* project, it remains the best thing never released by the Beach Boys.

Smile has to be the most unusual record ever made, or almost made, in the context of its time and place. With the Beach Boys riding a giant wave of momentum created by the megahit "Good Vibrations," Brian suddenly

(l–r): Carl, Al, Bruce, Dennis, and Mike toured the U.K. in May 1967 while Brian's incredible *Smile* project was unraveling.

found himself with at least a small window of creative carte blanche. He quickly took it to the nth degree as the *Smile* sessions gained a full head of steam in late 1966. If his goal was to create the most avant-garde LP by a mainstream pop act in history, he came within inches of reaching the top of that mountain. But instead of planting his flag, he hesitated. The reasons why are as numerous and as mysterious as the myriad of bits and pieces of incredible music that make up the *Smile* puzzle. The bottom line . . . you should never look down when you are that high.

   Smile has been analyzed and dissected by legions of scholars, fans, and cultists for decades, and has been called everything from a Brian Wilson brain barbecue to the most brilliant and ambitious piece of musical art ever recorded. It could be both. Brian dove straight into the abstract with *Smile*.

It is more complex and diverse musically than anything the Beach Boys had previously or would ever release. Brian's collaboration with lyricist Van Dyke Parks ensured that the *Smile* themes and lyrics would not resemble anything previously put forth under the Beach Boys banner. Instead, Parks's sometimes stream-of-consciousness, alliteration-heavy style showed massive thematic depth as it artfully decorated Brian's acid-laced "Teenage Symphony to God."

Close Your Eyes and Lean Back

Smile songs range from abstruse reflections on the eradication of native cultures and the ensuing western expansion to deep spiritual pleas to God and to our own children for a better way. It's not exactly *All Summer Long*. The overriding feeling behind the *Smile* themes and sound is one of an incredible mind trip, and in many ways it's a bad trip. The project was originally titled *Dumb Angel* about an entity that tries its best to help others but constantly screws up everything it touches. It's been theorized that the inspiration behind that concept could have been Dennis, or America, or just mankind in general. The concept then evolved toward a type of humor album, from which the title *Smile* sprung. The title stuck, but much of the humor evaporated as many of the songs took on an unhinged and at times manic quality with foreboding gothic overtones.

Ultimately, the concept of *Smile* seemed to be a constantly undulating and ever-changing one. It was limitless creativity, but seemingly a process without end. Brian would compose, arrange, create, build, tweak, alter, erase, rebuild, retrofit, adjust, decorate, strip down, build up, polish, and then abandon elements of his project on a weekly basis. It was a kind of mad hatter's tea party, with amphetamine more than likely being the tea of choice. With a fragile vessel like Brian speeding through troubled waters, it was inevitable there would be an ultimate crash. The factors that brought it on are debatable and many.

One much-written-about theory is that the other Beach Boys killed *Smile* by criticizing Brian, who had become too advanced for them. This theory is built on the assumption that they did not understand or appreciate his genius. Any conclusion drawn from this point of view is overly simplistic and mostly wrong. As with any band, and with any family, there were some tensions between certain parties. Cousin Mike Love is usually singled out as the Beach Boy who had the most negative reactions toward the *Smile* approach. Logic would tell you that one of the main reasons for this is the resentment he felt for being shut out of the creative (and financial) process by no longer being Brian's primary lyricist. Mike reportedly had issues with the esoteric Van Dyke Parks lyric style, and according to Parks was not shy in letting this problem be known. Parks ultimately left the project, came back, and left again. According to some, the festering Mike Love negativity caused Parks to vacate, and opened one of the major cracks in the egg known as Brian Wilson.

However, Mike has subsequently stated that his main concern during that time is the fact that Brian was taking drugs, and that his cohorts during the *Smile* era were encouraging this. And it should be noted that Mike as usual added his excellent vocals to Brian's tracks despite any reservations about the project. Regardless of Mike's feelings about *Smile*, it is clear that Brian's brother Dennis was solidly supportive of the project. He stated emphatically to the press at the time that *Smile* was much better than the critically deified *Pet Sounds*. Carl participated in the *Smile* sessions more than any other Beach Boy. It would seem Carl's active support for the project was genuine as he, Dennis, and Al each contributed instrumentally to at least some of the studio-musician-dominated tracking sessions. There may have been differing factions within the Beach Boys: some who loved the music, some who were confused by it, some who disliked it. It's also possible that each member may have been torn within himself since *Smile* was such a huge departure from the previous Beach Boys' sound, and a major commercial risk. But to say the Beach Boys killed the project is laughable, as it clearly was Brian who was in charge, who tragically went off the rails, and who couldn't bring himself to finish it.

Lost in the Mystery

Mental stress may have been the main ingredient that took the deciding toll on Brian and his stillborn masterpiece. As the months rolled along and 1966 became 1967, Capitol Records increased their pressure on Brian to deliver product. They printed hundreds of thousands of *Smile* album-cover slicks in the hope that a Christmas or New Year's release was going to happen. They even took out print ads in magazines to announce the impending delivery of *Smile*. The problem with this is that Brian was unsure about the order in which the *Smile* components best fit together, and aside from that there was still more recording needed to complete it.

By mid-February, the Beatles had released the double-sided monster "Penny Lane"/"Strawberry Fields Forever." It was a pop/psych tour de force and was heralded as the most creative rock single ever. Lennon and McCartney had made the public forget about the once-progressive sounding "Good Vibrations" in an instant. In fact, it has been said that when Brian heard "Strawberry Fields Forever" on the radio while driving with his assistant Michael Vosse, he commented that the Beatles had "gotten there first." With *Smile* unfinished, Brian was still inches away from that imaginary creative mountaintop, and now he believed he had been overtaken by the Beatles, and had somehow lost his way.

Brian's immediate reaction was to concentrate on finishing the project's expected single "Heroes and Villains," for which recording had initiated months earlier. He hoped a massive chart hit similar to "Good Vibrations" could help him regain the momentum needed to complete *Smile*. But as with the other *Smile* music, "Heroes and Villains" was created in numerous sections or movements, bits and pieces, each one a small universe within itself, and each one giving Brian the option of fitting it together this way, or that way, or not at all. It was a deck of cards that was constantly being reshuffled and dealt, again and again, until the perfect hand, the perfect edit, and the artistic/commercial justification for *Smile* was in his grasp. He'd done it to perfection with "Good Vibrations" but he was not having the same success with "Heroes and Villains."

I Think I Know, I Mean, Uh, Yes ... But It's All Wrong

Something was wrong. Everything was wrong. In early 1967, Brian was shown a portrait of himself painted by his associate David Anderle. Brian felt the painting absolutely captured his essence, and somehow held some deeply symbolic or numerological key to his being. It scared the shit out of him.

By the end of March, Brian, who had outworked everyone around him for years, began cancelling recording sessions. Van Dyke Parks briefly returned to the project only to leave again due to Brian's increasingly bizarre behavior, which Parks

The highly inventive "Heroes and Villains" single turned out to be a symbol of both the fantastic potential and the derailed reality of *Smile*. It only reached number 12 on the *Billboard* charts, which was a major bummer for Brian—who had fretted over its creation for eight months.

described as "regressive." Brian wanted to stay home. He couldn't face the music. He began consulting psychics for advice in finding the perfect date to release his new single. The vibrations had to be just right. His confidence was beginning to cave. It went into freefall when the radio station on which Brian (and his psychic) chose to debut "Heroes and Villains" initially refused to play it.

By the time Brian and the Beach Boys had finally released "Heroes and Villains" to the public on the last day of July 1967, the world had already changed. More than two months earlier, the Beach Boys' publicist, Derek Taylor, had announced to the British press that the *Smile* project had been scrapped because Brian felt he was "in his jet age, building steamships." The Beach Boys simultaneously entered a protracted legal battle with Capitol Records over unpaid royalties and violation of their contract, and the relationship between band and label would never be the same. Meanwhile the Beatles released their much-heralded *Sergeant Pepper's Lonely Hearts Club Band* LP that crowned them for all-time as the absolute kings of the rock world. The Beach Boys countered by pulling out of the Monterey Pop Festival at the last moment. Monterey turned out to be an event that would forever be celebrated as *the* peak moment of the Summer of Love. It helped empower a new rock-and-roll hierarchy that would mostly view the Beach Boys as an embarrassing part of the past.

"Heroes and Villains" ended up being a minor hit by Beach Boys standards, reaching #12 on the singles chart and then fading fast. Brian's regression continued as he and the band quickly cobbled together an LP called *Smiley Smile*, which retained all of the absurdity and quirkiness of *Smile*, but none of the beauty, grandeur, or expansiveness. As Carl plainly stated, it was a bunt instead of a grand slam. In hindsight it is a uniquely original bunt, and even a classic in its intimate and quietly freaky way. But the expectations for the grand epic masterpiece *Smile* were so completely unmet by the underwhelming DIY production style of *Smiley Smile* that the latter was greeted with a universal yawn. It was, in effect, the sound of Brian Wilson coming down. This began Brian's transition from soaring in the pop stratosphere to lying in bed.

Heartbreak Searing

The great tragedy of *Smile* is that it was so good. Brian had created something so special that the thought of it being shelved is beyond painful. For the man who poured himself into it so completely and fretted over it so anxiously, the subject became toxic. The Beach Boys would exhume remnants and elements of the *Smile* tracks on future LPs, and often at Brian's displeasure.

They picked at the carcass of *Smile* to incrementally improve their releases for years. Though it was always a thrill to hear bits and pieces of the lost masterpiece, exposing small portions of *Smile* out of context and years past its time was a kind of blasphemy. The Beach Boys also used the legend of *Smile* as a bargaining chip when switching record labels, dangling it as a possible release, one which has yet to happen. But nonetheless, year by year, the cult of *Smile* slowly grows.

Brian didn't want to discuss it, and once claimed that he'd burned the tapes, adding another twist to the *Smile* myth. But it obviously wasn't true. By the dawn of the 1980s, a poor-quality cassette-tape recording of the *Smile* music was suddenly in circulation with non-insiders. The rumor was that Dennis Wilson himself had compiled the material as heard on the first *Smile* bootleg tapes. He'd made a few copies for his friends, who made a few copies for their friends, et cetera. The cat was out of the bag, and *Smile* bootlegs proliferated through the decade. In 1993, the Beach Boys allowed twelve *Smile* tracks in various stages of completion to be part of their thirtieth-anniversary box set. The music was pristine, but there was a disconnected feeling in the presentation, as only an uninvolved Brian knew how everything fit together (and perhaps even he didn't).

A mini-*Smile* industry sprouted, with books, films, dozens of bootlegs, reproduction artwork, T-shirts, and legions of cultists who argued over the real reasons *Smile* hadn't come out in 1967 and the keys to how it all fit together. Then, out of the blue, in May 2003 it was announced that Brian Wilson (a solo artist since 1998) would be performing *Smile* live with his backing band the following year. His astonished fan base nearly imploded in an orgasm of anticipation. Work on building a presentation of the music that flowed well for performance was mainly the responsibility of backing-band member and *Smile* aficionado Darian Sahanaja. He undoubtedly received helpful pointers from Brian, as well as Van Dyke Parks, but Darian was the person who pulled it all together. There were some minor additions of melody lines and lyrics, which resulted in the completion of pieces that had remained unfinished since 1967. But for the most part, it was just a matter of putting together Brian's abandoned puzzle.

It's A New Day

On February 20, 2004, Brian and his loyal band took the stage at Royal Festival Hall in London and played and sang the *Smile* music in three movements. Fans from all over the world who had converged for this moment were giddy over the result and stood and cheered endlessly. The endeavor was so successful that Brian and band entered the studio to record the newly constructed *Smile* set, complete with strings and horns. In September 2004, *Brian Wilson Presents Smile* was released to the public. The album charted at #13 in the U.S. and #7 in the U.K. Critics fell all over themselves declaring the new *Smile* a major vindication of Brian's vision. Brian was awarded a Grammy Award, his first, for Best Rock Instrumental Performance for the *Smile* track that perhaps had haunted him the most, "Mrs. O'Leary's Cow." Those close to Brian revealed his inner satisfaction with finally healing the old scar left by the 1967 *Smile* debacle.

But once the dust cleared and the hype died down, many fans of *Smile* concluded that *Brian Wilson Presents Smile* was only a facsimile, and a fair-to-good reproduction of the 1967 Beach Boys' *Smile*. All of the circulating bootlegs and the legitimately released *Smile* tracks showed that the original Beach Boys recordings were clearly superior to the 2004 version. The biggest difference was the fact that the Beach Boys' voices had an immeasurable quality that could never be matched. There is also an organic and one-of-a-kind aura that infuses the original backing tracks that makes the latter-day version seem sterile in comparison. The 2004 recording was great in that it showed that, when pieced together in a coherent flow, *Smile* completely worked as a musical statement. In fact, it was a surprisingly compact and efficient-sounding collection of songs. It was brilliant, bizarre, and Brian Wilson at his best. But the 2004 version is in no way the Beach Boys' lost *Smile* album. The concept is compromised, the context is wrong, and the artists who made it are not the Beach Boys. *Smile* is something else . . . something wonderful that was never finished, and something tragic that has yet to be released.

The *Smile* Music—A Tidal Wave of Broken Genius

"Surf's Up"

Perhaps the most advanced composition of the rock era. It is both melodically brilliant and lyrically abstract, and could have only been created by the spiritually perfect pairing of Brian Wilson and Van Dyke Parks. If this had been released in its time, early 1967, it would stand as the pinnacle of artistic statements in the pop/rock realm for that year, Beatles be damned. An amazing solo piano performance by Brian from December 1966 survives on film. The track was exhumed against Brian's wishes, augmented and overdubbed by the Beach Boys, and became the title track of their 1971 LP *Surf's Up*. By that time, the magic of one of music history's most ambitious steps forward was somewhat diffused.

"Cabin Essence"

A quirky fireside aura at its beginning, with banjo, harmonica, and gentle Carl Wilson voice, quickly ignites into some of the most haunting, manic, and evil-sounding music the Beach Boys ever made. The "who ran the iron horse?" section with demonic chanting, buzzing cellos, and rail-spike pounding, is truly ominous. The song's "crow cries uncover the cornfield" tag apparently caused major friction between Mike Love and Van Dyke Parks, making this recording the epicenter of *Smile* conflict. The Beach Boys dug it up and released it on their 1969 *20/20* LP.

"Our Prayer"

Smile-heads have argued for decades whether this incredible wordless a cappella performance by all six Beach Boys was going to open or close the *Smile* album. Regardless, it's one of the most beautiful moments in the entire Beach Boys canon. No other '60s rock band could have pulled this off. It is absolute proof of the vocal superiority the Beach Boys held over all of their competition. The group later overdubbed more voices onto it and released it on their 1969 LP *20/20*.

"Heroes and Villains"

Written in his infamous sandbox in 1966, "Heroes and Villains" is in many ways the centerpiece and main connective tissue that would potentially hold the *Smile* album together. It was recorded in over 20 separate recording sessions, and was more expensive than "Good Vibrations" to complete. The song is a rollercoaster ride of major textural and feel shifts. Some elements are whimsical and joyous, while others, like the "bicycle rider" chant and its creepy keyboard motif, project a nearly nightmarish aura. It is generously filled with fantastic Beach Boys vocal harmonies and genius musical twists and turns. Brian's evolving concepts for the song included edits that were as long as seven minutes or more. The released version timed out at less than four minutes, and though its brilliance is apparent, it has a disturbingly muddy sound quality, which undoubtedly hurt its commercial appeal.

"Child Is Father to the Man"

Among the most ambitious and beautiful sections of *Smile*. Unfortunately, it is also one of the pieces that went unfinished, and one whose place in a larger work confounded Brian. The track has a brooding and expansive aura, with a plaintive harmonica line not dissimilar to those heard on Ennio Morricone spaghetti-western soundtracks. The repetitive vocal chant is both hypnotic and unsettling. A tag that used the "Child Is Father to the Man" lyric, but with a different musical feel, appears on the released version of "Surf's Up."

"Do You Like Worms?"

Also known as "Do You Dig Worms?" this section of *Smile* lumbers darkly towards its "Plymouth Rock roll over" refrain, and then pivots into multiple versions of the bicycle-rider motif and back. It eventually transitions into a faux Hawaiian section. This track, as bootlegged, epitomizes the unfinished and schizophrenic nature of *Smile*. Just the fact that a Beach Boys album almost appeared in 1967 with a song called "Do You Like Worms?" is a mind-blower. On the 2004 Brian Wilson version, a previously unheard melody line was added to the song with its original Van Dyke Parks lyric, and the title was switched to the far less freaky "Roll Plymouth Rock."

"Wonderful"

A gorgeous and gentle harpsichord-adorned ballad sung by Brian and overdubbed with lovely horns. A rerecorded version sung by Carl appeared on the *Smiley Smile* LP and has its own unique appeal, although *Smile* purists will always prefer the original.

The Elements

Brian conceived a suite based on the elements of earth, air, fire, and water. In particular, the water and fire portions became major factors in the *Smile* legend. "Water," or "In Blue Hawaii," featured an eerie group vocal chant that somehow communicated a liquid aura. Other elements of the water section have a bouncy drip-drop-like feel. The Beach Boys used parts of this track and developed it further for their 1970 LP *Sunflower* under the title "Cool, Cool Water." Even more impactful was Brian's frightening interpreta-tion of the sound and fury of "Fire" or "Mrs. O'Leary's Cow." After a silly cartoonish slide-whistle bit that evokes hook-and-ladder trucks racing to their duty, the doors of hell are suddenly kicked open in a way that no pop artist has ever matched before or since. Brian's "Fire" track is so thoroughly demonic that it could be the scariest thing ever put on tape. A primitive, pounding beat whips a roaring section of moaning strings, underlined by wicked fuzz bass, crackling sounds, and topped with a chorus of tormented

"Mrs. O' Leary's Cow" was the "Fire" element within the *Smile* concept, and was the track that haunted Brian the most. With its wicked demonic sound unleashed, Brian believed it had actually started fires around L.A. Ironically, after he rerecorded it in 2004; it was the piece of music that gave Brian his first and only Grammy Award.

voices. The track somehow sounds like the very essence of Satan's flames. The result freaked Brian out entirely, especially when a sudden fire engulfed a building near the studio directly after he'd created this incredible track.

"Wind Chimes"

One of the first *Smile* songs committed to tape, "Wind Chimes" was potentially slated as the "Air" portion of the "elements" suite. It provides an obviously stoned point-of-view dedicated to the many wonders of suspended wooden tubes clanging in the breeze. The lyric admitting "though it's hard, I try not to look at my wind chimes" may be a window into the paranoia that was slowly enveloping Brian. A Carl lead vocal is featured on the original; and, as they did with "Wonderful," a rerecorded and rearranged version appeared on the *Smiley Smile* LP, with lead vocals shared by the group.

"Vega-Tables"

One of the last *Smile* songs to receive a flurry of Brian's attention prior to the final collapse of the project, it was possibly slated to be the "Earth" element. More than any of the project's songs, "Vega-Tables" projects the humor vibe that Brian so badly wanted to express. It features carrot-crunching, celery-munching, and juice-gurgling sounds. With *Smile* nearing its death throes, none other than Paul McCartney dropped in on a "Vega-Tables" session in April '67, escalating Brian's Beatles paranoia at a really bad time.

Odds and Ends

A project as vast and varied as *Smile* included everything from major compositions to tiny snippets, each having the potential to have been used in full, or split and spliced to fit Brian's ever-changing vision. Some of the remaining potentially key *Smile* sections include "I'm in Great Shape," likely pointing the way to Brian's sometimes on, but mostly off, health obsession; "Holidays," featuring a jaunty clarinet; "Barnyard," complete with bleating animal sounds and a wondrous vocal harmony figure; and "Old Master Painter," which includes a past-tense rendering of "You Are My Sunshine" languidly sung by Dennis. This is far from a complete rundown of every inch of *Smile*. The bounty of *Smile*-era compositions and recording sessions, and the bits and pieces within them and without them, has spilled over into the living, breathing body of the Beach Boys' music for many years.

But Wait! There's More ...

Beach Boys' Lost *Smile* Album to See Release in 2011
by Ed Christman
Billboard.com, March 11, 2011

It's an event that pop-music fans have been waiting for since the Summer of Love: Capitol Records is planning to release the Beach Boys' great lost album, Smile, *later this year.*

Two longtime Beach Boys associates—engineer Mark Linett and archivist Alan Boyd—are coproducing the release, which Capitol has titled The Smile Sessions.

The project will be released in three versions: a two-CD set, an iTunes LP digital album, and a limited-edition boxed set containing four CDs, two vinyl LPs, two vinyl singles, and a 60-page hardbound book written by Beach Boys historian Domenic Priore.

The Smile Sessions is being released with the support of the band, including Beach Boys mastermind Brian Wilson. Wilson wasn't immediately available for an interview, but he expressed his excitement about the [album] in a statement released through Capitol.

"I'm thrilled that the Beach Boys' original studio sessions for Smile will be released for the first time, after all these years," Wilson said. "I'm looking forward to this collection of the original recordings and having fans hear the beautiful angelic voices of the boys in a proper studio release."

The Smile Sessions doesn't yet have a specific release date, with Capitol saying only that it will arrive later this year. That will inevitably spark skepticism among long-suffering fans who've had their hopes dashed before. When Warner Bros. Records signed the Beach Boys to a record deal in 1970, part of the label's interest in the group was rooted in its hopes of releasing Smile. Linett, who has engineered Beach Boys reissues for more than two decades, recalls going through the Smile tapes as early as 1988. And in 1995, Capitol told Billboard that it was preparing to release a three-CD compilation tentatively titled The Smile Era for release in August of that year. But that set never saw the light of day.

"The major thing in the past, I don't think we had support from all the band, and now we do," says Bill Gagnon, GM/senior VP of catalog marketing at EMI Music North America. "All parties are supporting it coming out. Everybody is onboard now."

Also backing the project are the related rights-holders. Capitol owns The Smile Sessions master recordings, with publishing rights controlled by Universal Music Group's Rondor Music, the Beach Boys' own Brother Records, and, depending on which tracks are included on the final release, Wilson himself.

Since Smile was never completed, what exactly will be issued? Linett says the goal is to present "the whole piece as close to as it was envisioned, or as is envisioned, as possible . . . and obviously with input from Brian and from everybody else."

Linett is a better judge than most, having recorded and mixed the critically acclaimed 2004 version of Smile that Wilson recorded with his road band for Nonesuch.

Although a track listing hasn't been finalized, Linett says he expects that an approximation of the original Smile album will occupy one CD or three sides of vinyl, with session outtakes and studio chatter occupying the rest of each version of the release.

"When you say 'album,' it presupposes everything was recorded and finished, and that's not the case," he says. "We have gaps where we are missing some vocal parts. But all the music was recorded, which is heartening." All of the vocals were recorded by the Beach Boys, usually at the same time around the same mic, including the lead vocal, Linett says. The music was mostly played by the Wrecking Crew, the legendary group of Los Angeles session musicians that played on numerous Beach Boys hits,

although some Smile *tracks feature Carl Wilson on guitar and Dennis Wilson on drums, Linett says.*

Linett says Wilson's 2004 Smile *album has served as a blueprint for the current project, which will be mixed in mono because that's how Wilson (who's deaf in his right ear) intended it. But Linett adds that other selections from the 30 hours of* Smile *session recordings will more than likely be issued in stereo.*

"Some of these questions are hard to answer because not only haven't we assembled them yet, this has to be played for Brian and the other members of the group to see what kind of input they have," he says. "Just because Brian did it the way he did it in 2004 [doesn't mean] he won't say, 'Well, let's add "You're Welcome,"' which was the B-side on the 'Heroes and Villains' single."

"The main thing I am getting from everybody, after waiting 40 years to have it officially released, is, 'We want to make sure it is right,'" Linett says.

But is there any doubt surrounding the project this time around? "No," Gagnon says. "It's coming out."

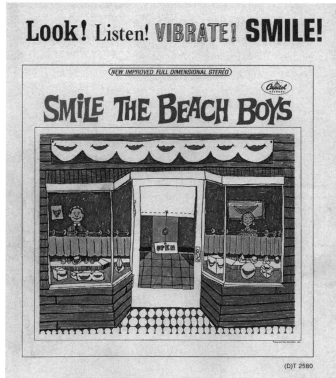

Capitol Records got a little ahead of themselves in late 1966 when they began publishing advertisements for the Beach Boys *Smile* album. They also printed hundreds of thousands of album cover slicks for *Smile*, an album that never materialized.

Official Press Release—3/14/2011

The Beach Boys' Legendary *SMiLE* Album Sessions to Be Released This Year by Capitol/EMI

Never-Before-Released Original 1966–'67 Album Sessions Compiled for Two-CD and Digital Packages and Deluxe, Limited-Edition Box Set

Hollywood, California—March 14, 2011—Between the summer of 1966 and early 1967, the Beach Boys recorded, in several sessions, a bounty of songs and drafts for an album, SMiLE, *that was intended to follow the band's 1966 masterpiece,* Pet Sounds. *The sessions were ultimately shelved, and the Beach Boys'* SMiLE *has never been released. With the full participation of original Beach Boys Al Jardine, Mike Love, and Brian Wilson, Capitol/EMI has collected and compiled the definitive collection,* The SMiLE Sessions, *for worldwide release this year in multiple physical and digital configurations.*

The SMiLE Sessions *presents an in-depth overview of the Beach Boys' recording sessions for the enigmatic album, which has achieved legendary, mythical status for music fans around the world.* The SMiLE Sessions *will be released in two-CD and digital-album packages, and a deluxe, limited-edition box set.*

Coproduced by Mark Linett and Alan Boyd, all of The SMiLE Sessions' *physical and digital configurations will include an assembled album of core tracks, while the box set delves much deeper into the sessions, adding early song drafts, alternate takes, instrumental and vocals-only mixes, and studio chatter.* The SMiLE Sessions *invites the listener into the studio to experience the album's creation, with producer, singer, and bassist Brian Wilson's vision leading the way as he guides his fellow Beach Boys, singer Mike Love, drummer Dennis Wilson, lead guitarist Carl Wilson, rhythm guitarist Al Jardine, and newest member Bruce Johnston (who'd replaced Brian Wilson in the touring group during 1965), through the legendary sessions.*

"I'm thrilled that the Beach Boys' original studio sessions for SMiLE *will be released for the first time, after all these years," says Brian Wilson. "I'm looking forward to this collection of the original recordings and having fans hear the beautiful angelic voices of the boys in a proper studio release."*

"One of my favorite songs from The SMiLE Sessions *is 'Wonderful,'" says Mike Love. "The song truly lives up to its title, as do many of the tracks on* SMiLE. *Cousin Brian was at his creative peak during those sessions. I'm unaware of anything that comes close in pop music."*

"I recently played some of my personal acetates from The SMiLE Sessions, *and they held up really well," says Al Jardine. "We would come home from touring and go straight into the studio to record. Brian couldn't wait to show us his latest ideas. We were recording* SMiLE *and* Pet Sounds *material simultaneously, so the tracks*

and vocals all have the same great quality. Most of the vocals were done at Columbia Studios in Hollywood , across the street from Western Studios, where most of the tracking was done. "

"For me, it's always been about the way Brian Wilson brilliantly composed and 'voiced' his amazing chord progressions and melodies, " says Bruce Johnston. "SMiLE really made me SMiLE!"

"Personally, I loved it, " the late Carl Wilson said in 1994 of the SMiLE sessions (from the Don Was–directed documentary Brian Wilson: I Just Wasn't Made For These Times*).*

"In my opinion it makes Pet Sounds *stink—that's how good it is, " the late Dennis Wilson told a journalist in 1966 of the planned SMiLE album.*

What Brian Wilson brought to the table, in his effort to maintain the Beach Boys' position among the top rock-and-roll bands of the day, was beyond what anyone could have expected. Beginning with "Good Vibrations, " then into SMiLE, Wilson had begun to construct songs in a modular form, crafting individual sections that would later be edited together to form a coherent whole. In several intense bursts of creative energy, Wilson , drawing on the talents of the finest studio musicians in Los Angeles and utilizing the best studio facilities available on any given day, laid down dozens and dozens of musical fragments, all designed to fit together in any number of possible combinations. No one had done this in pop music, and Wilson had just created "Good Vibrations, " the Beach Boys' bestselling record in a long string of hits, by using this method. His next endeavor would be an album-length version of this unique and luxurious songwriting parlance: SMiLE.

In 1965, Brian Wilson had met an up-and-coming session keyboard player and songwriter, Van Dyke Parks. Noticing Parks's conversational eloquence, Wilson felt that he could help to volley the Beach Boys' songwriting into the wave of broader-messaged and socially conscious rock and roll that would come to define the '60s. They were soon collaborating on keynote songs for SMiLE, including "Heroes and Villains, " the band's follow-up single to "Good Vibrations. " Wilson and Parks would also co-write "Surf's Up, " "Vegetables, " "Cabin Essence, " "Do You Like Worms?" "Wonderful, " "Wind Chimes, " and other bits and pieces of the SMiLE tapestry. Parks also introduced beat-pop artist Frank Holmes to create album-sleeve art and a booklet interpreting the album's James Joyce–mode lyrics.

The reason SMiLE did not see a release in early 1967 had more to do with back-room business that obscured the creative side of the program than anything else. In late 1966, the Beach Boys formed Brother Records, initially to produce outside artists. Soon, however, the Beach Boys would become embroiled in a court action with Capitol Records with the goal to become the top-selling artists on their self-owned, independent label. The group withheld "Heroes and Villains" and announced they would instead release "Vegetables"—recorded with the band's own money in April '67—on Brother

Records. By July 1967, Capitol Records and the Beach Boys had come to terms, with Capitol agreeing to distribute the band's Brother Records, and it was agreed that SMiLE was no longer to be the band's next album.

The SMiLE Sessions' global release date, complete track lists, and artwork will be unveiled soon.

The *Smile* Curse Or Labor Pains, Either Way It Hurts

As the 2011 *Smile* project is being prepared, predictable tales of tensions, power plays, conceptual disagreements, and general madness are leaking from the inside. All the while the fan base waits with baited breath, on the edge of their seats, hoping art wins out over commerce, and respect for the original vision wins out over ego. Will the team assembled to finally compile a *Smile Sessions* insist that the template of *Brian Wilson Presents Smile* is adhered to, or bravely push for something more 1967-ish? Brian, as usual, remains relatively detached. He's been walking down the path of least resistance for decades; don't expect him to change course just because *Smile* is happening again. No matter how it all comes down, we can be assured it won't sell a million units in January, but maybe the *Smile* they send out will return to them anyway.

12

I Just Wasn't Made For These Times

The Tragedy and Strategy of Brian Wilson

Shyness, sensitivity, parental abuse, obsessive compulsiveness, stage fright, sandboxes, fear of flying, fear of failure, fear of shower heads, fear of Phil Spector, drug abuse, paranoia, schizophrenia, reclusiveness, over-eating, overmedication, over-analysis, and being still crazy after all these years . . . Brian Wilson's personal problems are the stuff of legend. And while there is undoubtedly a tragic element to the life of Brian, he has at times used his problems as a shield, a crutch, and a convenient excuse for some seriously inappropriate behavior. And then there's the never-ending cycle of rehabilitation and redemption. Brian's back . . . again and again and again. People are strange, and Brian is one of the strangest. But has mental illness actually worked to Brian's advantage? Let's just say it's afforded him a generous amount of love and mercy.

To even get to the place where such things are possible and are debated is a sad thing. Brian's story veers into the abnormal at an early age. Anyone researching Brian will automatically find wildly differing perspectives on his stability and inner well-being. Some will insist that Brian was a happy kid, a popular athlete, and even a leader. Others will say he was painfully shy, a social outcast, and the child who never really fit in. The truth, of course, is somewhere in the middle. Brian wasn't one of the cool kids, but he wasn't a total nerd either. He wasn't a great athlete, but he was a good one. He didn't fit in everywhere, but in his neighborhood he was respected, and, yes, a leader. Brian's ace in the hole was his sense of humor. In a way, it still is.

There are many testimonials from people who believe that Brian's father Murry mentally and physically abused him at an early age. The most believable stories of this abuse come from Brian himself, and also came from his deceased brother Dennis. Whether or not Murry's harsh discipline was at the core of Brian's mental-health problems, he had other issues to deal with as well. Brian was predisposed to the potential for addictive and obsessive behaviors. There was definitely alcoholism in his extended and immediate family. Another trait that Brian had to manage was his extreme sensitivity. This ability to process sensory data more deeply than the average person is one of the reasons Brian's creativity is so outstanding, and it also is a reason everyday life is more of a challenge for him. It's hard for Brian to just deal with stuff. He'll be completely engaged in it, engulfed by it, and obsessed with it, or he will shut down, block it, and feign ignorance or indifference because he can't cope or doesn't want to try. With Brian, it's usually all or nothing.

The compulsive traits began to appear when Brian was a teenager. And they manifested themselves in a very fruitful way. Brian was highly sensitive toward sound: music, melody, and particularly harmony. Considering that he has nearly complete hearing loss in his right ear, Brian's ability to process and memorize complex musical arrangements is astounding, and is the foundation of his genius. He spent incalculable amounts of time examining the minutia of musical arrangements within the songs of his heroes, such as the Four Freshmen and Phil Spector. This went beyond a healthy fascination, and became something much closer to an unnatural obsession. Brian's savant-like ability to build fantastic rainbows of sound is a direct result of his combination of sensitivity and compulsion. He had the obsessive energy to explore and memorize the smallest details, and the creative antennae to receive and process his discoveries in an original way. Brian was built for constructing incredible musical mobiles.

But when the Beach Boys' early success led to the need to perform live and travel to distant cities, Brian tried to opt out. He was profoundly unhappy whenever the band had to leave Los Angeles and their homes to tour the States. As early as the spring of 1963, Brian recruited Al Jardine back into the Beach Boys so that he could stay home while Al, David, Carl, Dennis, and Mike slogged through a tour (by car) of the Midwest. Brian's stage fright and negative feelings toward travel became a bigger issue when David Marks left the Beach Boys in late 1963. The band was becoming more popular, and they were in demand in more diverse locations. Constant air travel was the only solution. But Brian hated to fly.

A Rock in a Landslide

Murry insisted that Brian put his fears aside and become a full-time touring Beach Boy. A tour of Australia and New Zealand was undertaken in early 1964, and a European promotional tour was booked for November. In between were multiple concerts in Washington, Nevada, Utah, Texas,

Hawaii, Arizona, New Mexico, Oklahoma, Missouri, Iowa, Kentucky, Indiana, Wisconsin, Illinois, Colorado, Ohio, Massachusetts, Connecticut, Florida, Idaho, Alabama, Georgia, Tennessee, Virginia, New Jersey, Rhode Island, California, and New York. Simultaneous to the concert performances, there were TV appearances to tape and promotional duties to fulfill. On top of all of that, Brian had to write, arrange, produce, and perform on the Beach Boys records, of which Capitol Records constantly wanted more. It was a huge job for one man, especially a sensitive man like Brian. But Brian stepped up, did his job, and the Beach Boys became even more popular . . . which

Brian Wilson's intense sensitivity is one reason his creativity is so genuine, and also one of the reasons why he is mentally unstable.

made the demand greater and made his job even harder. He met the challenge, at first, and everybody thrived. The money was rolling in. It worked out great for about a year . . . and then Brian cracked.

On December 5, 1964, during a flight to a concert in Houston, Texas, the limit was reached. Brian experienced what has been described as a severe nervous breakdown while in his seat on the plane. The other band members have described his state as inconsolable and irrational. He had to be restrained. The same day that Brian melted down, the Beach Boys gained their first number-one LP on the national charts. Brian played the show in Houston that night, but returned to L.A. the next day, and those close to him insist he was never quite the same again. He informed the band in no uncertain terms that he would not be performing with them anymore.

At first Glen Campbell filled in for Brian, and then permanent replacement Bruce Johnston became the sixth Beach Boy in spring 1965. Truthfully the group did suffer in their live presentation. Something about having had Brian standing center stage with his bass guitar gave the Beach Boys a balance which they never regained. The nonstop pressure of being a performing Beach Boy and their main creative source had short-circuited

Brian in a way that was semi-permanent. He'd take the stage on occasion for a big national TV appearance, or a local or very special gig. But as the years went by, Brian sightings in public, and especially in concert, became an increasingly rare thing.

Doin' In My Head

The next thing to tear at Brian's mental stability was the combination of continuing stress and increasing drug use. During the 1965–1967 period Brian began to use marijuana, LSD, and amphetamines, some more than others. His use of hallucinogenic chemicals may have been relatively limited compared to someone like John Lennon, who took acid nearly every day during parts of 1966 and 1967, but for Brian the danger of taking it even once was genuine because of the extreme sensitivity and apparent instability of his psyche. During the *Smile* period, Brian reportedly was given a large dose of very pure LSD. This particular episode had a lasting effect, and some claim that it was an extremely bad trip, and one that shattered him. He was also taking speed on a regular basis during that period, a routine that set the table for a massive emotional crash when *Smile* was abandoned. Brian's taste in drugs eventually shifted to cocaine, and even heroin, in the years ahead. The compulsive side of his being was on a constant pursuit of the "big rush," and Brian had no self-control with which to temper his cravings.

At first Brian's sometimes eccentric behavior was viewed as humorous. Having the band crawl around the studio floor snorting like pigs, or singing their vocals while lying at the bottom of an empty swimming pool, was weird and funny. But during the *Smile* sessions, people began to witness things that went beyond quirky. Collaborator Van Dyke Parks found Brian's behavior so troubling that he exited the project. This particularly manic period was then followed by a giant letdown. For the next year or so, Brian withdrew somewhat gradually, cancelling sessions and missing meetings. A studio was installed in his home so that he could record without going out. There was a darkly paranoid element that began to creep into his being. He spoke of how Phil Spector's "mind gangsters" were haunting him, and how David Anderle's portrait of him had stolen his soul. Brian expected that something new to fear was waiting around every corner.

Nineteen sixty-eight was the first year when Brian's issues became so severe that he was temporarily institutionalized. The details are sketchy, but family members will admit that something seriously troubling happened that year. It was a fork-in-the-road moment. Brian came home, but the old Brian never came back all the way. Although Brian continued to contribute, sometimes wonderfully, to the Beach Boys' recorded output, his days as the leader and dominant creative force in the band were over. Instead, he became something of an inconsistent but effective mentor to the others, giving tips on arrangements, filling in with an idea here, and adding a harmony line there.

Brian regularly showed glimpses of the genius that was still in him, but he also showed that he was more and more reluctant to let it come out. He completely lived up to his bizarre reputation when meeting with the Warner Bros. executives who were considering signing the Beach Boys to a new record contract. Everyone was nervous that he might ruin the band's chances if he had one his episodes of inappropriate behavior in front of the label bosses. But when Brian met them he was nicely groomed, freshly shaved, and neatly dressed . . . with his face painted green. The deal went through anyway.

One more crushing blow courtesy of his father came in 1969, when Brian learned that Murry had sold the entire Sea of Tunes catalog, the publishing rights to Brian's songs, for a lump sum of cash. Brian reportedly cried when he found out. The magic and joy that his songs represented, and the meticulous effort that had gone into their crafting, had been thoughtlessly commoditized by Brian's father. It was heartbreaking, to say the least. Brian withdrew even further; and as the 1970s got underway, he spent many days alone in his bed smoking, drinking, eating, and taking drugs. In 1973, Murry died of heart failure, and a freaked-out Brian did not attend the funeral.

Surfin' Sasquatch

It was a shocking thing to see the photos leaked in 1974 and 1975 of the once lanky and fresh-faced Brian. His weight had ballooned to over 250 pounds, his hair was long and dirty, and an unkempt beard semi-covered his bloated face. Brian was a reclusive addict too paranoid to take a shower or cut his fingernails. He usually dressed in a bathrobe and sweatpants, and his eyes projected a near-permanent weariness. His stare was glazed, red, and glassy, but still intense in a semi-vacant way. And Brian's music was still on top. An LP of his classics from a decade earlier titled *Endless Summer* became the number-one album in the U.S. in October 1974. The pressure on Brian to come back was building.

But Brian had no interest in coming back. He was hiding, and didn't want to be found. Whether it was the potential for increased revenue or genuine concern for Brian, or a combination of the two, his family and his band decided it was time for Brian to get out of bed. Brian's long-suffering wife Marilyn brought in a new 24-hour therapist to lead the reclamation project. The controversial psychologist's name was Dr. Eugene Landy. He was a former race-records distributor, promoter, drug counselor, and teacher known for using Gestalt Therapy as the foundation for his treatment philosophy. Within months of coming under Landy's full-bore treatment, Brian was off drugs, writing songs, losing weight, and looking happier. Nineteen seventy-six became the year of "Brian's Back." The press delighted in showing the blubbery Beach Boy exercising, getting clean, reentering the studio, and even taking the stage with the Beach Boys. But Landy's expensive, controlling, and demanding ways wore out their welcome with the extended Beach Boys family, and he was ultimately told his services were no longer needed.

Throughout 1976 and 1977, Brian maintained a reasonable level of normality without adhering to the Landy regimen. Brian still smoked, drank beer, and even consumed cocaine on occasion, and his once-magnificent voice was shot, but he was also writing and recording, and semi-consistently appearing at Beach Boys concerts. By 1978 he was slipping again, gaining back the weight, and showing signs of addiction. There became a tug-of-war over Brian within the Beach Boys' political framework. The Transcendental Meditation devotees and clean-livers, Mike, Al, and Mike's brothers Steve and Stan, pulled Brian one way; and the free-livers, the more creatively progressive and substance-fueled Dennis and Carl, pulled Brian the other way. On one hand, Brian was likely to have a healthier lifestyle if he remained loyal to the Love contingent, but Dennis and Carl understood Brian's creative side in a way that Mike never could, as they believed it was something far more precious than a commodity.

From 1978 to 1982, Brian bounced back and forth between battling factions, his mental health again declining and his weight eventually hitting an alarming 300 pounds. He disappeared for days on end, and was discovered wandering barefoot in a boulevard medium in San Diego. On another occasion, he was found face down in the Venice Beach sand having seizures from a cocaine overdose. He was hospitalized multiple times during this period. Those closest to him were certain he was going to die.

The Doctor Has Returned

Once again, Dr. Eugene Landy was brought in to see if he could turn Brian's life around. This time the band and Brian's family agreed to whatever Landy wanted. They basically turned Brian over to him. Landy got fast results. By 1983, Brian had slimmed down to 190 pounds; it was a huge transformation. Brian also participated more consistently in Beach Boys concerts, and his voice improved. But while everyone was running around trying to save Brian, brother Dennis slipped through the cracks. Dennis had become a severe alcoholic and drug addict; and, in December 1983, he drowned in Marina del Rey. Brian was completely haunted by the thought of his brother drowning in the Pacific Ocean, and he never really got over it. Just the mention of Dennis often causes Brian to shut down to this day.

Meanwhile, Dr. Landy continued his absolute focus on Brian. He and his team of assistants controlled "every aspect of (Brian's) physical, personal, social, and sexual environments." As the years rolled by, Landy isolated Brian from his friends, family, and band to the point where he was accused of having brainwashed him. When Brian appeared to promote his first solo LP in 1988, he looked like another person. He was robotic, drone-like, super skinny, and seemingly had received cosmetic plastic surgery on his face. Some said he looked and sounded great. Others were alarmed at the transformation, and claimed that Landy had basically molded Brian into something that was unnatural. But Landy shook off the criticism, reminding everyone that he was the one who had saved Brian when no one else could, and he just dug in further.

In 1976, when Brian emerged from years of reclusion, Beach Boys fans were shocked to see his physical condition. Wracked by mental health issues and ongoing substance abuse, Brian had also ruined his formerly gorgeous voice with cigarettes.   *Photo by Mark Sullivan*

Landy's name began to appear alongside Brian's on songwriting and production credits. Their production company was called "Brains & Genius." Landy had gone from being a therapist to a full-time manager and collaborator. Landy exercised complete control over Brian's considerable finances, too. While Landy lived in a Malibu Colony mansion, Brian lived in the guesthouse. Rumors swirled that Landy had overmedicated Brian and that he'd suffered a stroke and permanent motor-skill damage. Brian's speech seemed to be permanently slurred, he had noticeable facial tics, and his general presence was stunted and shaky.

By the late 1980s, at the urging of the Wilson family, the California Board of Medical Quality charged Landy with ethical and license-code violations, including the improper prescription of drugs and of having an improper relationship with his patient. These charges ultimately cost Landy his professional license, and his reputation. In 1992, Dr. Landy was barred by court order from further contacting or pursuing any personal or professional relationship with Brian. When asked about Landy more than a decade later, Brian lamented that he missed him. Eugene Landy died from lung cancer in 2006.

Meanwhile, Brian kept going. Following Dennis's tragic death in 1983, his other brother Carl passed away from cancer in 1998, the same year that his mother Audree died, making Brian the lone survivor of the Wilson family. It was an unlikely thing. Brian, the one that everybody fretted was going to go early, the one that was so fragile, so deeply troubled, the one that everyone worked so hard to save . . . he outlived them all.

I Feel Just Like an Island

With his new wife Melinda, and their growing gang of adopted children, Brian moved on to a new life as a solo artist with a wonderful new backing band. His new crew's job was to support, protect, and spur Brian on towards new achievements, and above all to mask his deficiencies. Usually reluctant, semi-engaged, partially present, and not completely there, Brian is damaged goods. But just *how* damaged is the question. That would depend on the day or moment or situation that he's in.

At times Brian can come off completely normal, even dynamic, funny, and personable. At times his leadership streak even reappears, and he takes charge of a conversation or a situation—and on rare occasions, a performance. But more often than not, Brian idles through life in semi-shut-down mode. He can seem borderline catatonic at times. Brian suffers from constant auditory hallucinations. He describes them as demons telling him they are going to kill him. He does what he can to block them out and to ignore them. Mike Love insists that Brian is a paranoid schizophrenic who fried his mind on acid. Others aren't quite so harsh. But even if Brian's behavior is perceived as that of a highly damaged individual, he always has a built-in excuse. And things are always getting better if you ask Brian's public-relations machine. Normality is right around the corner. He's had "serious issues" in the past, but he's "working hard" to overcome them, and "now" he's doing better. That's the mantra.

However, I think we'd be lucky to still have the 1976 version of Brian around. Watch the Lorne Michaels–produced *It's OK* TV special. In those interviews from his bed, or in the other interviews from that time period, it's obvious that Brian was still present. The difference between those days and now is huge. Admittedly he was overweight and very troubled, but today the Brian we have is much less present and much less Brian . . . I'd say he's operating at 60 percent on his good days, in comparison to 1976. Don't take my word. Look at a filmed interview from '76 and look at one from the last ten years. In '76, he was nervous, weird, and unhealthy, but he was there, he was present. Now he's completely on autopilot the majority of the time. Maybe he's healthier physically, but the guy that used to be Brian is diminished, partial, vacant. Anybody who thinks he's more "back" now than he was in 1976 is fooling themselves. And I would argue that the songs he wrote in '76/'77 are closer in spirit to the real Brian than most of his writings since. I guess that's the last time we weren't receiving Brian's offerings through a giant filter.

His solo career has been inconsistent, some of it quite good, some of it embarrassing. And how much of it is really Brian? Again, it depends on whom you ask, and how freely they are speaking when you do. His band and his collaborators in the studio do an awesome job of dialing in a Brian Wilson-esque sound. And they always defer to Brian should he come through with a kernel of creativity. I've been told by multiple sources as close to Brian as you can get that he really doesn't want to be there. Working in the studio and especially touring is not really his choice. His handlers, managers, and wife insist that he work. It's all a bit Landy-like when you look behind the curtain. Brian himself has claimed that going on stage is the worst part of touring for him. He doesn't mind the travel. Airplanes are scary, hotels can be stressful, but going on stage in front of people is the ultimate nightmare.

And then there are the good nights, when he's happy to perform, and he actually accepts the adulation from his adoring audience. And even if Brian would rather stay home, is that really what's best for him? What is the alternative to having yet another regime in place that controls Brian's agenda? If he is fully independent, does he revert to the guy facedown having seizures from an OD on Venice Beach? Is he back to 300 pounds and near death? Any way you slice it, Brian has beaten his life expectancy. His semi-helplessness and troubled core has given him wave after wave of people trying to help him. And at times they have become a source of problems instead of a solution to eliminate them.

Brian is a cork on the ocean, and a rock in a landslide. He's a leaf on a windy day. He's one of the greatest musical geniuses of all time, and one of the most troubled souls you'd ever want to meet. He's funny and he's tragic. He's bright and he's vacant. He's a giving tree that can never shake the expectation that it must give again.

These things he'll be until he dies.

Obituary—Eugene Landy—Psychotherapist to Brian Wilson

by Peter Ames Carlin
Saturday, 1 April 2006
The Independent

Eugene Ellsworth Landy, psychologist: born Pittsburgh, Pennsylvania 26 November 1934; four times married (one son); died Honolulu, Hawaii 22 March 2006.

The controversial psychotherapist Eugene Landy was best known for his relationship with the Beach Boys' troubled leader Brian Wilson. In a life that included stints as a music promoter, a radio producer, a pop-culture analyst, and a psychologist, Landy earned his greatest notoriety during the years he served as Wilson's 24-hour-a-day therapist.

At first, Landy earned credit for weaning the musician off the drugs, alcohol, and junk-food binges that had swollen his body and dampened his creativity. But by the late 1980s, after Landy eased into the role of his patient's co-writer, coproducer, and financial manager, the psychologist became the target of lawsuits and a government investigation.

In the early 1990s, Landy surrendered his psychologist's license and was barred from contacting Wilson. The episode proved so explosive that, even 15 years later, the central figures in the drama—Landy, Wilson, the minders hired to enforce the psychologist's rules, musicians, and collaborators—usually refused to speak about it on the record. "I can't say anything, because you just don't know what Landy's going to do," one former employee said to me last year while fending off an interview request for my Wilson biography, Catch a Wave: The Rise, Fall & Redemption of the Beach Boys' Brian Wilson.

Unpredictability had long been a Landy hallmark. Born in Pittsburgh in 1934, he was the son of a doctor, Jules, and a psychology professor, Frieda. Despite his family's academic background, Landy dropped out of school after sixth grade (he later claimed to be dyslexic) and worked in the fringes of show business. An early supporter of the jazz guitarist George Benson, Landy served briefly as the then-struggling musician's manager.

Landy served in the American Peace Corps and VISTA (Volunteers in Service to America) before returning to school in the early 1960s. He earned a bachelor's degree in psychology from the California State College, Los Angeles, in 1964, then a master's degree in psychology from the University of Oklahoma in 1967, capping his training with a PhD in 1968. Moving to Los Angeles, Landy set up a practice that specialized in treating drug abuse, particularly among young people. He soon parlayed his mastery of the hippie lexicon into a reference book, The Underground Dictionary, *published in 1971.*

Working with drug addicts helped Landy design a therapeutic system he called "milieu therapy," during which the doctor and his assistants would control every aspect of a patient's life. The programme proved especially popular among Hollywood's élite class of dissolutes—Landy later claimed patients ranging from the shock-rock star Alice Cooper to the actor Rod Steiger. And when Brian Wilson's first wife, Marilyn, sought help for her famous husband in late 1975, Landy was the first, and only, psychologist she called.

What Landy found, tucked into the shadows of Wilson's mansion, was an over-weight, unwashed 33-year-old musician whose once-flawless ear for creating dazzlingly innovative pop music had been dulled by years of depression, drugs, and alcohol. Given free rein to restore his patient's mental health, Landy threw water on Wilson to get him out of bed in the morning. He enforced rigid exercise and diet regimes, then led him to the piano to write new songs. Within weeks, Landy had Wilson back in the recording studio. Six months later, the trimmed-down Wilson made a dramatic return to the stage, just as the Beach Boys' new album, 15 Big Ones—*the first to be produced by Wilson in a decade—soared up the sales charts.*

You couldn't argue with the results. But Landy's skyrocketing bills infuriated the Beach Boys' managers, who fired him in November 1976. By the early 1980s Wilson was in even worse shape than he had been in 1975. Contacted by the Beach Boys' management, Landy agreed to take on his old patient with one condition: this time he would have complete control over Wilson's life, with no exceptions.

Once again, Wilson got free of drugs, lost weight, and got back to work. By 1985 he looked healthier and happier than he'd been in two decades. But friends and colleagues noticed troubling things, too. The bodyguards surrounding Wilson—nick-named "the surf Nazis" by his friends—had become a constant, sinister presence. Old friends and even family members said they had been barred from contacting him. And Landy had also added his name to his patient's creative and personal affairs.

A 1988 solo album, Brian Wilson, *earned rave reviews. But Wilson confessed to one reporter that he heard voices in his head. Friends and colleagues were dismayed by the amount of medication Wilson was given, and by the tremors and blackouts it seemed to cause.*

The California Board of Medical Quality Assurance filed an official case against Landy, accusing him of "grossly negligent conduct" in his treatment of Wilson and other patients. In 1989, Landy agreed to surrender his license, but his work with Wilson continued. The duo set up a corporation, Brains & Genius, and worked together on a new album, titled Sweet Insanity. *The album was never released. In 1991, a court ordered Landy to stay away from Wilson.*

The late Dr. Eugene Landy (left) with Brian in 1990. Dr. Landy's heavy-handed therapy style is credited with both saving Brian's life and with inflicting permanent damage to his brain.

"His one regret was that he didn't get out sooner," says Landy's wife, Alexandra Morgan. "If anything, he lost sight of what was best for Eugene in his desire to help Brian."

Landy moved to Honolulu in 1993, where he set up a new practice. His primary hobby in his final years was Argentinean tango. "The last chapter of his life was very quiet," his wife says. "He was starting over."

As had Brian Wilson. And though the musician often spoke angrily about the control the psychologist wielded over him, he also spoke warmly of him, as in a 1998 interview with the American radio interviewer Terry Gross. "I miss him," Wilson said.

"Meeting the Reclusive Brian Wilson"

by Gene Sculatti

Seventy-three and '74 were rough times for fans of the Beach Boys and robust California pop. But we tried, especially the handful of L.A. writers who coalesced around Phonograph Record magazine, where editors Greg Shaw and Marty Cerf made it their business to pour fuel on even the slightest spark of a record that in any way suggested a return to breezy harmony and fun themes. In May 1973, it was PRM's "Surf Music Revival" issue: vintage Beach Boys photo on the cover, coverage inside on the Wilsons, the Legendary Masked Surfers, and American Spring's new "Shyin' Away" single. Even though Brian was largely an unseen public presence then, he had agreed to be interviewed, with Marilyn and Diane Rovell, at the magazine's offices inside United Artists Records on Sunset.

The idea that we were going to be in the same room with Brian, much less ask him questions about his work, kept me, and probably Shaw and Ken Barnes too, in a kind of suspended animation in the weeks leading up to the (frequently rescheduled) appointment. I mean, all that music, all those records—I was the king BB freak in my hometown clique, endlessly beguiled by everything from the radio hits down to "This Car of Mine" and Our Favorite Recording Sessions; *inviting pals over as soon as I got "Little Deuce Coupe" and "All Summer Long"; studying those LP covers like a forensic cop for clues to what the guys who made that music were really like. Now I'm going to meet Brian Wilson . . . ?*

The actual event, with eight or nine of us huddled together in that small office (I remember sitting on the floor), would have to be judged anticlimactic, I guess. Brian was out of shape, distracted, and not especially forthcoming with answers to the questions we could barely coax out of our throats. We inquired about his recording of [the band] American Spring, whether or not there'd be an album, [and if] he and his band [were] working on a record. The whole thing lasted maybe half an hour, with Brian quite ready to leave way before then.

When he left, we PRM guys just sort of looked at each other in silence. We didn't know what to say. Part of it, I think, was the shock of seeing Brian in such a less-than-healthy condition. But most of it, for me anyway, was the utter stun of just seeing him, of having been just feet away from the guy responsible for so much incredible beauty. Spiritual is what it was.

13

Sail On Sailor

The Best Things Sometimes Come in Unpopular Packages

In December 1967, in the wake of the *Smile* and *Smiley Smile* debacles, with a teetering Brian Wilson gradually receding from the scene, the Beach Boys refocused, regrouped, got serious, and released a string of nine albums in less than six years that are some of the best of the rock era . . . and they didn't sell a fraction of their earlier LPs. Despite their lack of commercial reward, the Beach Boys tried really hard to do the right thing before they sold out.

At first Brian was still fairly engaged, although nowhere near the puppet master he had been from 1963 to mid-1967. He had a backlog of songs and ideas that could fill another album or two, but it would be up to the other Beach Boys to take up the slack in the years ahead. As the '60s wound down, the Beach Boys became something closer to a team of equals. By 1972 Brian would be among the least contributing members of the team. Carl Wilson evolved into the group's de facto record producer. Dennis Wilson became the band's most prolific songwriter. Bruce Johnston and Alan Jardine each contributed as composers, arrangers, and occasional producers. Mike Love continued to write lyrics and be an influential presence in the band. The Blondie Chaplin–and–Ricky Fataar period injected new energy into the Beach Boys sound. And Brian contributed too . . . just not as often as before, and less and less as the years went by.

The period that is often described as the Beach Boys "lean years" was not lean in terms of quality and quantity. Their late-1967 to 1973 body of work is a goldmine of underrated gems. It is the period when the Beach Boys regained their dignity and found traction with a new audience. It was a progressive and mature time for their music. In a way it was like a second career. This time they were the hard-working, soulful, racially diverse, socially aware band of scruffy musicians jamming away on rowdy college campuses and in marijuana-clouded concert halls. For several years they tried to ignore the iconic hits from their early days and just move forward with new material. But it was a losing battle.

The Beach Boys' former selves eventually engulfed and overtook their current selves. Their past became so popular again that it eventually made their present irrelevant. This was not a good thing for art's sake. It was financially rewarding . . . to mine the gold from days of old. But it also compromised the new respect the Beach Boys had slowly and carefully built between 1968 and 1973. Suddenly none of it mattered, because too many people realized all at once that the endless summer of 1964 was like a giant hit of sunshine crack. All they wanted was more of the same. One more hit of sunshine.

But hidden in the dusty record bins while nostalgia ruled was a string of bearded, beaded, denimed, and afroed classics. There may not be any hot rods or woodies to be found on or in them, but there are waves. Waves of harmony, and melody, and waves of classic grooves. There is plenty of Wilson magic in them too. None of these albums topped the charts. None of them even came close. But some of them are as just as good as the ones that did. If you think of the Beach Boys as an early- to mid-1960s band, think again. The Beach Boys might have been the best American pop/rock group in the world from 1963 to 1966; but then, when no one was looking, they got better.

Wild Honey

Released in December of 1967, the *Wild Honey* album was the Beach Boys' first act of starting over. The artistic triumph of *Pet Sounds*, the euphoria of "Good Vibrations," the crash and burn of *Smile*, and the pathetic thud of *Smiley Smile* were all in the past. *Wild Honey* signaled a fresh beginning, and a breath of fresh air it was. Even the cover was bright and clean in its simplicity, showing a colorful stained-glass window that adorned Brian Wilson's home. Gone were the heavy themes and lush productions of recent times, and equally gone were the embarrassingly stoned fumbles of their aftermath. Instead *Wild Honey* projected a crisp, soulful, compact collection of two-minute songs written by Brian and Mike, and produced by the entire band.

This wasn't a return to the clean-cut Beach Boys sound of 1964. It was something completely new. It was a back-to-the roots record that presented the Beach Boys in a pop-meets-rhythm-and-blues framework. The main voice was Carl Wilson, although everyone other than Dennis showed off their singing chops. The instruments were fairly minimal and mostly played by the Beach Boys themselves with the emphasis on modest guitar, cheesy keyboards, and primitive drums. *Wild Honey* is mainly a vocal album, and one with many great songs.

Among the best is the hot-soul title track with Carl's larynx-shredding vocal. "Aren't You Glad" is another lovely Wilson/Love collaboration that is understated in its sunshine-pop simplicity and probably too delicate for the freakadelic world of 1967. The Beach Boys also tackled Stevie Wonder's "I Was Made to Love Her" and lived to tell the tale with heads held high. "Country Air" is majestic and quirky, and I'm sure nobody understood it in its time. "A Thing or Two" bounces along until it finds a happening guitar groove that grounds the song just long enough to make it cool.

The album's absolute standout is the amazing "Darlin'." This is, without a doubt, one of Brian and Mike's classic songs, and that's saying something. "Darlin'" is pure blue-eyed-soul magic featuring one of Carl's best vocals ever. The tasteful brass arrangement and rich harmony vocals add a happy sheen to the production. How this single only made it to #19 is absolutely mystifying. The relatively mediocre chart performance of such an obvious

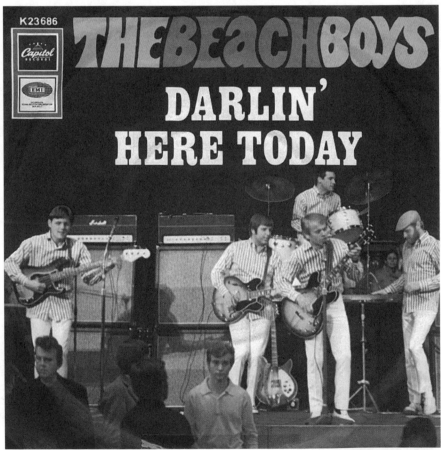

Written by Brian, sung by Carl, and produced by the Beach Boys, "Darlin'" is one of their most underrated singles, and should have been a giant hit. Unfortunately, it was released just as the group's popularity was seriously waning in the U.S.

classic was an early hint of the widespread indifference that the Beach Boys would face in the years ahead.

Brian showed he still had great lead-vocal abilities on both "I'd Love Just Once to See You" and "Here Comes the Night." His creepy "Let the Wind Blow" is the closest thing on this LP to a *Smile* vibe (other than the album's closing chant "Mama Says," which had been excised from "Vegetables"). The album refocuses on its pop/soul vibe with the chirpy rocker "How She Boogalooed It." Bruce, Al, and Carl created the song, and it represents one of the band's best bubblegum-meets-garage-rock moments. The organ solo is so fantastically cheesy that it seems ready made for a retro-dance sequence in a modern-day Target television commercial or an episode of *Glee*. Carl's lead vocal sounds so much like Al that people are still arguing about it 44 years later.

Wild Honey reached a modest #24 on the U.S. album charts and a somewhat fairer #7 in the U.K. Despite the lukewarm sales in the States, the LP is an almost perfect statement of anti-psychedelia released smack dab in the era of Jimi Hendrix and Cream. *Wild Honey* is pioneering in its back-to-the-roots sentiment. Soon the Beatles, Stones, and others would be taking a similar path to a simpler and cleaner sound. But the Beach Boys and *Wild Honey* got there first. Too bad hardly anyone noticed.

Friends

The June 1968 release of *Friends* signaled the true beginning of the Beach Boys as a group of six relatively equal creative partners. They were no longer solely Brian's band, and the songwriting credits on this LP reflected it. *Friends* was actually a bit of a coming-out party for Dennis, as he took four co-songwriting credits; he was also lead vocalist on two of those songs. This LP had a decidedly Wilson Brothers slant (with a strong assist from Al Jardine), as Mike Love focused on his Transcendental Meditation activities including a much-celebrated trip to India alongside the Beatles.

In fact, all of the Beach Boys had recently been initiated in the TM process, and *Friends* reflects the peaceful and quietly centered aura that surrounded them during this time. The title track written by Brian, Carl, Dennis, and Al has a lilting quality to the vocals and a helium-like feel to the track. It is somewhat unusual for a rock song to be written in 3/4 time, which is a waltz. It is even more unusual to have that song be a single release, which "Friends" was. Needless to say, it wasn't exactly a strong commercial choice, topping out at #47 on the U.S. charts. But the song undoubtedly has a timeless appeal, and it has worn well through the years.

"Wake the World," co-written by Brian and Al, is one minute and twenty-eight seconds of sweet melodic beauty. It's incredible to think that such a well-developed composition and arrangement could be shorter than any song on the *Surfin' U.S.A.* LP. "Be Here in the Morning" is another fabulous musical arrangement that is beautifully sung by Al, Brian, and Carl. It apparently has a brief vocal contribution from none other than Murry Wilson in the harmonic mix as well. "Anna Lee, the Healer" is an intimate tune from Mike and Brian about a spiritual acquaintance that includes a reference to "Rishikesh," where the Maharishi Mahesh Yogi's ashram was located, and where Mike and the Beatles had just been. It features another example of the unit's magical harmonies.

Among the true highlights of *Friends* is Dennis Wilson's great "Little Bird." Dennis's lead vocal has an immediate and compelling presence, and the song's catchy groove and progressive production elements make "Little Bird" one of the LP's most appealing tracks. Co-written with lyricist Steve Kalinich, and reportedly with an uncredited assist from Brian, "Little Bird" proved that Dennis not only had the ability to create outstanding material, but material that had its own unique style that nudged the Beach Boys into new territory. Dennis and Kalinich also contributed the stark poem/prayer "Be Still." Dennis's lead vocal is completely unadorned and quite raw, giving the song a genuine quality that again stands out on the album.

Brian's breezy and plainly honest song "Busy Doin' Nothin'" describes in detail the semiretired and disengaged state of his then-current life. It is both funny and disturbing, which is a perfect reflection of Brian himself. What makes "Busy Doin' Nothin'" stand out is Brian's great vocal and the charming samba-style arrangement adorned with acoustic guitar and gorgeous woodwinds. The last 30 seconds of the track is stunning in its musical inventiveness and sheer beauty. The thought of Brian gradually wasting away at home with all of this brilliance still at his fingertips is a very sad thing.

The quirky gentleness of *Friends* in the context of political protests, race riots, and the war-torn social landscape of 1968 makes it about as square a peg as one can imagine. The vaguely psychedelic cover, with the Beach Boys surrounded by clouds of obscure smiling faces, does nothing to lessen the ambiguous feeling projected by the album's content. But despite its total lack of edge and its soft focus, *Friends* is a beautiful and highly creative album. It proved to be an utter commercial disaster for the Beach Boys, limping to its peak chart position of #126 in August 1968 while the Doors and Cream battled for the number-one spot. The Beach Boys once-massive popularity was a thing of the past, and the path forward had to be negotiated with Brian only partially involved.

20/20

The February 1969 release of *20/20* signified the Beach Boys twentieth official album release, which would also be their last on the Capitol Records label. The band had seen the highest of highs with Capitol since their 1962 debut, and lately the lowest of lows. But there had been at least one recent ray of hope. As the failure of *Friends* became obvious the previous summer, Mike Love had convinced Brian to help him write something closer to the old Beach Boys' style, with a nod towards summer and surfing. "Do It Again" would be the first of many times Mike returned to that particular well. It turned out to be a decent #20 hit in the U.S. and a surprising number one in England. It also was included as the lead track on the *20/20* album.

"Do It Again" is nostalgia with a modern twist. Brian's production hints at a nearly techno vibe with its highly compressed electronic beat. The opening sounds a bit like something that would be played at a surfing robots' dance. Nonetheless, Mike infuses the song with typical Beach Boys imagery, and Brian lays on some harmonies for good measure. Carl adds a very compact guitar solo, and then the song kind of peters out from there. But all in all, it is a fun look back at an innocent time, but with a little fried mind seasoning thrown in.

Another great single added to the *20/20* package is "I Can Hear Music," a showcase for Carl's lead vocals. Carl built the lovely track himself with brother Dennis pounding the drums, and the group adding perfect harmony support. "I Can Hear Music" hit #24 on the U.S. singles chart and was a Top Ten in the U.K. It is the first Beach Boys hit to feature virtually no contribution from Brian, and the last Top Forty the band would have for seven years.

"Bluebirds Over the Mountain" is yet another single release from the period. It was mainly Bruce Johnston's baby, and like "I Can Hear Music" it is a cover of an oldie but goodie. Bruce's production is interesting, with great harmonies, a heavy drum feel, and a wild Ed Carter guitar solo. The song was heavily promoted internationally, more so than any competing Beach Boys single, but it didn't perform so well, hitting only #61 in the U.S. and #33 in the U.K. The fact that the Beach Boys were relying on non-original material for single releases is a direct result of Brian's increasing absence from the scene.

Dennis Wilson was again a major contributor to the *20/20* album. His track "Be With Me" is a beautifully orchestrated production with smoky brass and an innovative string arrangement by Van McCoy. There is a sinister quality to the song's fade, making Dennis the first Beach Boy other than

Brian to reach for a darker-than-expected Beach Boys sound. "All I Want To Do" is a full-out rocker written by Dennis, and sung as roughly as possible by Mike—who isn't exactly Little Richard. Why Dennis didn't sing this himself is a mystery, as he was much better at rasping out a hard-rock number than Mike.

Bruce is given the full spotlight on his lush instrumental "The Nearest Faraway Place." This is undoubtedly an ear-pleasing track, and shows that Bruce was gifted at both arranging and writing a gorgeous melody. There is a sentimental quality that often pops up in Bruce's work, and in this case it works to magnificent effect.

Side Two begins with Brian's production of the standard folksong "Cotton Fields," with Al nicely handling the lead vocal. Al himself would rerecord the song in the near future, changing the arrangement slightly and the production style completely, and arguably doing a better job of it than Brian. "I Went to Sleep" follows, and again reveals a barely there Brian could still pull out wondrous gems from his hidden bag of tricks. "Time to Get Alone" is another example of Brian's magical touch. The track was originally intended for the group Redwood (who evolved into Three Dog Night), an act that Brian had coveted for the Brother Records label. The Beach Boys' version is energetically sung by Carl, Brian, and Al, and would have made a great choice for a single release. Carl recorded his own production of the song, which paled in comparison to Brian's original, and went unreleased.

By far the most notorious song on *20/20* is Dennis's production "Never Learn Not to Love," which in its early form was titled "Cease to Exist" and authored by none other than murder-cult guru Charles Manson. Dennis polished Manson's rough gem, added some Beach Boys harmonies, tweaked the lyric and title, and took the songwriting credit. Apparently Manson wasn't pleased. While the world was still thinking of the Beach Boys as those stripe-shirted choirboys in white pants singing about surfer girls, they were recording and releasing Charles Manson's music. Were the Stones really the bad boys of rock? Sympathy for the devil? The Beach Boys gave him shelter and money.

Ironically, the *20/20* lineup follows the former Manson tune with one of the group's most spiritually beautiful pieces of music, titled "Our Prayer." The gorgeous a cappella track was a leftover from the *Smile* project, but sweetened for this release. The Beach Boys pulled it out at the perfect time to offset the residual bad vibes from the previous track. The album ends with "Cabin Essence," another exhumed *Smile* track, and a brilliant one for sure (see this book's *Smile* section for more details).

20/20 continued the trend of chart losers for the Beach Boys, reaching a disappointing #68 on the U.S. album chart. It was appropriate that Brian was not even pictured on the LP's cover, as he hadn't appeared in concert with the band in years, and his contributions in the studio were down to a trickle. Brian is shown inside the album's gatefold hiding behind an eye chart and looking fairly detached. Despite the somewhat schizophrenic and checkered nature of the *20/20* LP, it exhibits a very high level of quality, and was deserving of far more praise and attention than it received in its time. This LP catches the Beach Boys on the way out Capitol's door, talent intact, looking for new horizons.

Live in London

Recorded at Finsbury Park Astoria in North London in December 1968, *Live in London* was released in the U.K. on the EMI label in May 1970. Submitted to Capitol/EMI to fulfill the Beach Boys lingering contract requirements upon leaving the label, it was not released in the U.S. until late 1976. The record was another stiff in the sales department, completely failing to chart in the U.K. in 1970. But again, weak chart performance belied the excellent quality of the release.

The Beach Boys, without Brian, had evolved into a first-rate live act. They added a brass section and several other auxiliary musicians to enhance the core of Carl and Al on guitar, Bruce on keyboards and bass, and Dennis on drums. Ed Carter filled in on guitar, bass, or percussion, depending on what was needed; Daryl Dragon was a reliable asset behind the keyboards; and Mike Kowalski provided extra percussion. The result was a truly professional presentation of the Beach Boys sound, complete with incredible harmonies and crisp arrangements.

Most of the *Live in London* set is highly enjoyable and performed nearly perfectly. Several of the songs in this set even surpass their studio versions. In particular, "Wake the World" and "Aren't You Glad" are magnificent performances. The group's vocals are stunning. The band, including Dennis's drumming, is tight, tasteful, and energetic. And the entire vibe in the room is uplifting and even exciting. At a time when the Beach Boys' fortunes were nose-diving in the U.S., it's obvious they were still adored in Britain, and the group does nothing to disappoint the faithful who attended this concert.

For years it was speculated that this album must have been radically sweetened in postproduction because it sounded so clean and well balanced. But the fact is, other than a bit of equalizing and mixing, this is the sound of the '68 Beach Boys live, with nothing added. Too bad more people could not have enjoyed this record in its time as it is a modest classic, but it was not to be. Count it as yet another lost gem from the Beach Boys "lean" years.

Sunflower

As the 1960s passed, one of its most successful show-business stories, the Beach Boys, were staggering but still standing. With a new decade here, and just signed to their new record label Reprise Records (owned and operated by Warner Bros.), the Beach Boys were full of hope. They already had an impressive amount of recorded material in the can, and new sessions continued at Brian's home studio, as well as occasional recording dates at several other Los Angeles studios. All new Beach Boys releases would be appearing on their own custom Brother/Reprise label, signaling a semi-revival of their abandoned Brother Records label, which had been briefly in place during the *Smile* and *Smiley Smile* era three years earlier.

After a couple of false starts at getting a track selection approved by their new label bosses, the Beach Boys released *Sunflower* at the end of August 1970. It turned out to be one of their best efforts ever. The album's lead single, "Add Some Music To Your Day," was written by Brian and Mike with a minor assist from Brian's friend Joe Knott. The song is a virtual kaleidoscope of Beach Boys voices; all six members provide essential vocal elements to the song. Warner Bros. was thrilled by the initial response from wholesalers to the single, calling it the fastest-selling single in their history, but then reality set in. The single didn't receive any radio play, and it didn't move at all from retail bins. "Add Some Music To Your Day" eventually turned into a virtual boomerang of massive returns that Warner Bros. had to eat. Not exactly the start the Beach Boys were hoping for.

Despite the bad news regarding the single, *Sunflower* was certainly something to be proud of. Once again, Dennis Wilson's creative presence grew stronger on *Sunflower* as he took songwriting credits on four tracks and lead vocals on three, including the album's opener "Slip On Through." This song showed off the soulful side of Dennis's arsenal with its great chorus groove. Another killer track was Brian's gorgeous "This Whole World" with its awesome stack of "aum bop did-it" harmonies. One of *Sunflower*'s true delights is the fact that Brian was so involved in its creation, and "This Whole World" is clear evidence that Brian still had genius to spare.

Dennis tossed off a good-time rocker with his raucous "Got to Know the Woman," while Bruce with a little help from Brian contributed the whimsical "Deirdre." Side One ends with yet another strong Dennis Wilson track titled "It's About Time." Both Carl and Al were involved in the composition of this epic jam, as was lyricist Bob Burchman. Once again, "It's About Time" sees Dennis pushing the Beach Boys into progressive territory, and Carl's vocal chops are more than ready for the challenge. "It's About Time" became the Beach Boys' concert closer during this period, and its high-energy thrust often brought audiences to their feet.

1970's *Sunflower* LP may have been the finest group effort of the Beach Boys' entire career. It was a rare case when all of the band members, including Brian, were contributing in a major way. *Sunflower* was critically heralded but sold poorly in its day.

Side Two opens with Bruce's schmaltzy "Tears in the Morning," which shows off his deft arranging skills. Next Brian and Mike deliver a gleaming track with "All I Wanna Do," which features one of the best vocal performances of Mike's career. There is a shimmering sonic depth to "All I Wanna Do" that makes it unique compared to just about anything else from the period. One reason is that recording engineer Stephen Desper was a resourceful and forward-thinking technician who used newly acquired 16-track capabilities to record *Sunflower*. The resulting sound is the fullest the Beach Boys had presented to this point in their evolution.

Another *Sunflower* highlight is the classic Dennis Wilson ballad "Forever." Written and sung by Dennis with a lyrical contribution from his friend

Gregg Jakobson, "Forever" is perhaps Dennis's most beloved song. Brian has called it one of the most harmonically perfect Beach Boys songs, and he should know since he helped Dennis arrange the vocals. Brian also adds his wondrous falsetto to the song's fade. With "Forever," Dennis rose to the top tier of romantic balladeers. It stands as an evergreen classic, and one of the Beach Boys' most heartwarming songs. Carl adds another gorgeous flourish to *Sunflower* with his vocal showcase titled "Our Sweet Love." There is a quiet effervescence to this track that only Carl's voice could pull off. The song was composed by Brian, Carl, and Al, and it stands as another reason why *Sunflower* is one of the Beach Boys' best collections of brilliance.

"At My Window," with a lead vocal by Bruce and co-written by Brian and Al, nicely continues the sweet melodic and harmonious sound that is found throughout the entire album. *Sunflower* comes to a beautiful close with the incredible "Cool, Cool Water," which is five minutes of Beach Boys vocal magic. Written mainly by Brian with lyrics by Mike, "Cool, Cool Water" has elements left over from the *Smile* project as well as newly recorded sections that seamlessly come together in a liquid bouquet of harmony. *Sunflower* found the Beach Boys at the absolute top of their game singing-wise, making it one of the greatest rock-vocal records ever. But it didn't sell.

Early concert promoter Fred Vail, who was back promoting the Beach Boys at this point, insists that the group was completely devastated by the lack of reaction to *Sunflower* in the U.S., where it charted at a horrific #151. It was a critical favorite in the U.K. and made the Top Thirty there, but that did little to ease the disappointment felt from the American rejection, where no radio stations would play it. Vail recalls a program director from a major station telling him how great the Beach Boys were. The man enthusiastically went on about how big a fan he was and how wonderful their music was. But then he refused to play "Add Some Music To Your Day" on his radio station. His reason had nothing to do with talent, but with perception. Nobody would play or buy the record because the Beach Boys were not perceived as hip. They were yesterday's news, and they were over, at least as far as U.S. fans were concerned.

The Beach Boys were drawing crowds as small as 200 people to their concert appearances. The curtain would go up and the concert hall would be one-fifth full, or less. Just a couple of years earlier the Beach Boys had played to packed houses of thousands of screaming fans. It was a testament to their persistence that they were even bothering with such depressingly unattended concerts. But they hung together and kept moving forward, and slowly they began to turn it around. *Sunflower* is a perfect example of why. The Beach Boys were incredibly talented. It wasn't just Brian who had the gift. This was a family of brilliant artists, and when they pulled together, and when those harmonies blended, there was nothing else in the world like the Beach Boys.

Surf's Up

Following the painful realization that their beautiful *Sunflower* album had become a monumental commercial failure, the Beach Boys looked for new leadership. They hired a clever writer and disc jockey named Jack Rieley as their new manager. Rieley immediately set out to change the seemingly entrenched perceptions about the Beach Boys that permeated the rock world. He insisted that the group write more socially aware lyrics to their songs, and he pitched in as a lyricist, offering ecologically conscious and politically progressive themes. Rieley also demanded that the band appear on stage in tandem with the Grateful Dead at the Fillmore East concert hall to enhance their credibility with the emerging "FM underground" audience, which by 1971 was anything but underground.

The band had already stuck their toe into alternative water by playing the Big Sur Folk Festival the previous year, as well as a series of celebrated shows at the Whisky a Go Go club on Sunset Boulevard in L.A. Now with Rieley pointing the way, in August 1971 the Beach Boys put forth an LP titled *Surf's Up* that was specifically intended to appeal to a new generation of potential fans. Immediately noticeable was the striking album cover based on the legendary sculpture "The End of the Trail," originally created in 1894 by James Earl Fraser. This image played along nicely with the group's Brother Records logo, which showed a Native American on horseback with arms spread. With these two images, the Beach Boys projected a deep spiritual connection to the land and its roots.

Surf's Up possessed a good number of highlights, but overall was not as strong a collection of songs as its unsuccessful predecessor, *Sunflower*. However, the perception of *Surf's Up* somehow being more hip or progressive than earlier Beach Boys albums made inroads, as it was given more attention by radio and especially by the rock press. Among the best tracks on the LP is "Long Promised Road," which is one of Carl's strongest compositions. Carl wasn't as prolific a songwriter as either of his brothers, but when he came through with a good one, the quality matched Brian and Dennis's better work. "Long Promised Road," with a lyrical contribution from Jack Rieley, is a great example of Carl's soft-rocking, soulful style.

Another fantastic track is Bruce Johnston's iconic "Disney Girls (1957)." Surrounded by songs that are trying so hard to be hip, Bruce goes in the opposite direction and creates a sweet nostalgia classic. The word picture he paints is outstanding. The musical and vocal arrangements are even better. Brian Wilson himself was so touched by the song that he hailed it as a "masterpiece." Infused with gorgeous Beach Boys harmonies, "Disney Girls" is probably Bruce's finest moment.

Carl Wilson makes a second strong musical statement on *Surf's Up* with his ethereal track titled "Feel Flows." Again Carl collaborated with Jack Rieley, whose lyrics may be nonsensical but fit Carl's airy jazz-rock song perfectly. The trippy phasing and synthesizer elements in "Feel Flows," which are tailor-made for a stoner's headphones, undoubtedly delighted more than a few hippies who stumbled upon the *Surf's Up* LP. Like Dennis had on *Sunflower*, Carl takes the Beach Boys' music into a realm that would surprise anyone who thought of them as lightweight. "Feel Flows" is as modern and progressive as the majority of "heavy" music in the mainstream rock world of 1971.

Al contributes an appealing folk tune seasoned with psychedelic overtones with his and Gary Winfrey's "Lookin' at Tomorrow (A Welfare Song)." Following that is one of the most controversial songs the Beach Boys ever put to wax: "A Day in the Life of a Tree." Co-written by Brian and Jack Rieley, the track is driven by a mournful pump organ, which perfectly complements the piercing lyrics and raw lead vocal courtesy of Rieley (with an assist from Van Dyke Parks and Al Jardine). The song is thought of as either a truly moving cry from a suffering tree beset by "pollution and slow death," or a silly put-on with dodgy vocals. No doubt, however, that "A Day in the Life of a Tree" is a fabulously original creation, and one that has brought many listeners to tears.

Next, Brian Wilson delivers one of his last truly classic songs with the heartbreakingly beautiful "'Til I Die." Brian yet again finds a way to trump nearly everything around him with his originality and his melodic gift. "'Til I Die" proves that Brian could not only write beautiful music, but that he had the ability to communicate honestly and artfully with his lyrics as well. The track is decorated with a haunting vibraphone and organ bed, which frames the strong harmony vocal arrangement perfectly. Many fans feel that Brian never reached this level of beauty in his work again.

The legendary title track "Surf's Up" follows "'Til I Die" and closes the album. One of Brian's most written-about and coveted pieces of music, "Surf's Up" was born in the sandbox during the *Smile* era. It is undoubtedly a masterpiece, and although it went unfinished in its original 1966/1967 form, the Beach Boys fused some past elements with some newly recorded elements to create this gorgeous 1971 version. It was all done against Brian's wishes, although he reportedly contributed a vocal line to the ending section.

The *Surf's Up* LP is an excellent record, but sadly it could have been considerably better with a couple of additions and deletions. Dennis Wilson recorded at least two tracks that were slated for the LP: the moving Carl-sung ballad "Fourth of July," and his greatest lost classic, titled "Wouldn't It Be Nice (To Live Again)," which featured the most impressive lead vocal of Dennis's career. According to Jack Rieley, others in the band voiced jealousy of the songs on which Dennis sang lead, and were constantly maneuvering to exclude them. Dennis himself insisted that "Wouldn't It Be Nice (To Live Again)" follow "'Til I Die" as the album's closer, which Carl did not agree with. Regardless of the underlying reasons, the fact that no Dennis Wilson songs made the final *Surf's Up* lineup, but instead were replaced by the relatively

When Dennis tore his hand apart in the summer of 1971 Ricky Fataar became the Beach Boys' full-time drummer, a position he held until Dennis returned to the drums in late 1974. Ricky is still considered the most skillful drummer the Beach Boys band ever had.

weak Jardine number "Take a Load Off Your Feet" and Mike's "Student Demonstration Time," made the LP less than it could have been.

Nonetheless, *Surf's Up* performed well commercially compared to recent Beach Boys releases. It reached #29 on the U.S. album charts and #15 in the U.K. It also broke the Beach Boys into the FM radio market in some areas of the U.S., and found its way into the dorm rooms and apartments of many college students and young adults. The Beach Boys even found themselves on the cover of the October 28, 1971 issue of *Rolling Stone* magazine, which printed an extensive two-part article on their resurgence. Jack Rieley's strategy had worked to a modest degree, as the Beach Boys successfully repositioned themselves as a band with something current to say.

Carl and the Passions—"So Tough"

At a time when it seemed crucial to capitalize on the positive momentum generated by the *Surf's Up* LP, Warner Bros. and the Beach Boys instead threw up a dust cloud. *Carl and the Passions—"So Tough"* is conceptually the most confusing of all Beach Boys albums. The title is a tongue-in-cheek and extremely inside reference to the name of a pre–Beach Boys entity that lasted all of about a week in early 1961. The group committed marketing hari-kari by not mentioning the words "the Beach Boys" anywhere on the front cover of the album. Warner doubled down on the madness by slapping a reissue of the *Pet Sounds* LP onto the backside of the package. Customers looking for the new Beach Boys album would have to find it even though the artist listed on the cover was not the Beach Boys. If they successfully managed to negotiate that mind-maze and actually had the album in hand, then they would have to process whether this was something new, which it was, or something old, which it was.

On top of its suicidal packaging strategy, the May 1972 release of *Carl and the Passions—"So Tough"* had even more curveballs to throw. For the first time since 1965, the Beach Boys' lineup of official members had changed. Joining the party were guitarist Blondie Chaplin and drummer Ricky Fataar, both South Africans and former members of Brother Records recording artists the Flame. Gone from the Beach Boys was Bruce Johnston, who wasn't thrilled with the group's new musical direction and was even less thrilled with Jack Rieley's managerial concepts. Bruce added background vocals to a single *Carl and the Passions—"So Tough"* track and then bid the group adieu. Brian Wilson participated minimally, his photo having to be flown in to the group shot inside the gatefold. Dennis was still here, but operated independently, like a solo artist.

With all of this chaos in play, it's no surprise that *Carl and the Passions— "So Tough"* lacks continuity. However, it does have its charms. Certainly the lead track, "You Need a Mess of Help to Stand Alone," is a worthy rocker written by Brian and sung in a gritty style by Carl. "Here She Comes" displays the new edge that Blondie and Ricky brought to the turntable, sounding about as nontraditional "Beach Boys" as possible. Brian and Jack Rieley contribute a slinky boogie titled "Marcella," written about a hand-job queen that Brian frequented. "Hold On Dear Brother" is another Fataar/Chaplin number, and as with all of their material, it is very soulfully delivered.

An all-time favorite with many fans is the spiritually uplifting "All This Is That," written by Al, Carl, and Mike. Melodically ear-catching and uplifting, "All This Is That" contains Carl Wilson vocals that can only be described as otherworldly. There is a spine-tingling element to the swooping lines

Dennis sharing a microphone with Blondie Chaplin in 1972. Blondie gave the Beach Boys more soul vocally, and a harder edge as a guitarist.

delivered by the youngest Wilson brother with plenty of vocal support from Al and Mike. The other Beach Boys are clearly channeling Brian Wilson territory with much of this song, although its deep TM-related themes surely have Mike and Al's fingerprints on them. Still, the star of "All This Is That" is undoubtedly Carl Wilson, making it one of his finest vocal tracks of the 1970s.

The balance of *Carl and the Passions—"So Tough"* belongs to Dennis Wilson. It might have been wise to have his pair of emotionally epic tracks close the album instead of having them be separated by the lovely but light "All This Is That." Dennis's songs have a singularly weighty quality to them because of his penchant for projecting raw emotion with his voice, and his growing facility for creating moving orchestral arrangements. "Make It Good" is a virtual dreamscape of sound and feeling. It can't even be categorized as a "song." It is deeper, more cinematic, less contained than any song could be. I can imagine the other Beach Boys were unsure of just what "Make It Good" was. It is undoubtedly groundbreaking, and worthy of consideration when listing the Beach Boys' most original and progressive tracks.

Dennis closes the album with his wondrous ballad "Cuddle Up." Offering assistance was Daryl Dragon, who facilitated Dennis's musical expressions by translating his raw ideas into beautifully realized orchestrations; it was a fruitful collaboration that only lasted about two years. With "Cuddle Up," they left behind major evidence that a completed 1972 Dennis Wilson solo album would have been something special. It is again more than just a song, but something closer to a love-play, complete with a leading man, and celestial angels providing the heavenly vocal chorus behind him. "Cuddle Up" simply contains some of the most moving moments in any Beach Boys song, or any other song. With this as evidence, Dennis Wilson should be credited as the second musical genius to emerge from the Wilson family.

Despite the fabulous musical offerings that it contained, *Carl and the Passions—"So Tough"* was a disappointing seller, reaching only #50 on the U.S. album charts and a modest #25 in the U.K. No doubt the confusing packaging that housed it was a significant part of the problem. The toehold on minor album-sales success that the Beach Boys had seemed to have gained with their *Surf's Up* release had all but disappeared with *Carl and the Passions—"So Tough"*. Still, the band was gaining strength as a live act, and they clearly had piles of talent in their ranks. The '70s held promise, and the Beach Boys were primed to take advantage of their improving reputation.

Holland

In the summer of 1972, at manager Jack Rieley's urging, the Beach Boys and their families moved to the Netherlands, of all places, to live and to record their next album. Thus the title of their next LP would be *Holland*. The logistical difficulty, including the need to ship the materials to and build a fully functioning recording studio at their chosen destination of Baambrugge, in the Dutch province of Utrecht, made this their most expensive project to date.

After months of recording, the Beach Boys submitted their new album to Warner Bros. in October 1972. Their label promptly rejected the offering, saying that it lacked any trace of a potential single release. Back in L.A., and due to a suggestion from Van Dyke Parks, the band unearthed a vintage, unfinished Brian Wilson composition titled "Sail On Sailor." After some last-minute tweaking of the lyrics by Jack Rieley, a session was booked to record the song. First Dennis, then Carl, made brief attempts at singing the lead vocal over the rocking track featuring Ricky on drums, Carl on guitar, and Blondie on bass. Finally Blondie took a couple passes at the lead vocal, and his version is the one that stuck.

Warner Bros. was pleased, with "Sail On Sailor" slated as the lead track and single for the *Holland* album, and it was released in January 1973. The sound and feel of "Sail On Sailor" immediately advanced the Beach Boys into the now. The genius of the track is that it still sounds like Beach Boys music with its unmistakable harmony stacks that no other rock band could have sung so beautifully. But "Sail On Sailor" also has a distinctive groove and an incredibly soulful lead vocal from Blondie. This combination of Brian's seed of a song, and the group's classic voices—with new blood taking it into a more edgy realm—made "Sail On Sailor" an instant classic.

Continuing the edge is Dennis's swampy near-dirge titled "Steamboat." This song seems like it could be a message to Brian—"Don't worry, Mr. Fulton, we'll get your steamboat rolling"—with Brian as the inventor Mr. Fulton, and the resurgent Beach Boys as his steamboat slowly gaining momentum without him. There is an imaginative element to "Steamboat," with its bell-ringing, steam-pressure-valve-release, piston-driving, and paddlewheel-turning sounds that live within the music. A fantastically wild slide-guitar solo adds a liquid-metallic exclamation to an already diverse textural palette. "Steamboat" is proof that Dennis was the Beach Boy who never forgot the new territory discovered during Brian's *Smile* period, as its attitude is very similar.

A trilogy titled "California Saga" was created by Mike Love and Al Jardine, and continued the high level of creativity that permeates *Holland*. The opening section, titled "Big Sur," is one of Mike Love's finest songs. Casting himself as a folksinger, Love pulls off this country waltz incredibly well, with no trace of pretentiousness. Mike intimately evokes the majestic and simple qualities of living harmoniously with nature in the Big Sur forests. The second element of the trilogy is a spoken-word rendering by Mike and Al based on a poem by Robinson Jeffers titled "The Beaks of Eagles," which reflects on the evolving landscape and changing times through the perspective of the eagle. It also features three lovely musical interludes from Al lamenting the inevitable rape of the land by man's greed, and then concludes with an ultimately hopeful point-of-view, which leads to the final section of the trilogy, simply titled "California."

With a perfectly placed opening vocal line sung by Brian, "California" is one of the quintessential Beach Boys moments of the decade. Al Jardine wonderfully fuses a banjo-driven shuffle with Moog bass, and somehow re-creates the classic Beach Boys sound in a completely modern way. With crystalline harmonies and an appropriately "California Girls" style lead vocal from Mike, this time he name-checks numerous sites on the beautiful Central Coast of California and its historic Central Valley. Anyone who heard this song was aware that it referenced the mid-'60s Beach Boys style, but still there is nothing nostalgic about it. This would have been a great direction for the band to follow in the future. It offers a quality, forward-leaning musical and lyrical experience, with a mature attitude, but with a reverence toward the roots of their classic sound. The balance between now and then is perfectly reached with "California," and it's a trick the Beach Boys never pulled off as well in the years ahead.

Side Two of *Holland* opens with Carl Wilson's great track titled "The Trader." His three-year-old son Jonah is heard kicking off the song with the simple greeting "Hi," and from there one of Carl's true musical masterpieces unfolds. The lyrics written by Jack Rieley relate a tale of imperialism and its negative effect on indigenous peoples and their cultures. The song is presented in two sections; the first is up-tempo and features an epic production with stellar harmonies. The closing section is soft and intimate with harmonies creating a ghostly backdrop. Carl's lead vocals throughout the song are typically perfect, as his gift for sounding supple and unforced, but emotionally engaged, makes "The Trader" both a heartbreaking and musically pleasing experience.

"Leaving This Town" is a song that is probably the strongest example of original material by Ricky and Blondie to appear on a Beach Boys record. Blondie's vocal gift is perfectly suited for this melancholy reflection on life's

constant changes and challenges, and the forks in the road that constantly appear. An extended synthesizer solo takes the song into an area that sounds more Emerson, Lake & Palmer than Beach Boys. But as Blondie's vocal returns, the stark beauty and feeling of "Leaving This Town" are again underlined.

The relationship between Dennis Wilson and Mike Love was never a smooth one. Even in the band's early days, there were major points of contention between them.

Al Jardine added his folk-influenced songwriting and arranging style to the Beach Boys late-'60s and early-'70s output, which gave them one of their many unique textures.

But there were also periods of camaraderie. As the years passed, the vast differences between them intensified and magnified, eventually leaving their relationship in ugly tatters. If nothing else, the combination of the two left behind a truly beautiful offering with the ballad "Only With You." With music by Dennis and a lyrical collaboration between Mike and Dennis, "Only With You" is the lone purely romantic song on *Holland*. Carl sings it with a gentleness that perfectly communicates the song's heartfelt message, while Dennis once again displays his masterful ability to create a piano-driven love song that has a lasting presence.

The presence of Brian Wilson is certainly felt on *Holland*, even though his active participation was minimal. He contributed just one fully formed new song, the strangely cosmic "Funky Pretty." The tune projects a clumsily catchy Moog-driven groove with a quirky lyrical slant written by Brian, Mike, and Jack Rieley. In a typically savant-like Brian way, the song, originally titled "Spark in the Dark," is ingenious, displaying oddly hesitant piano transitions, multimember lead vocals, gobbledygook word rounds, and a killer group-sung tag. No one really knew exactly what Brian was going for, but "Funky Pretty" sounds like he almost got there.

Truthfully, Brian virtually quit the *Holland* project partway through. He'd put forth a concept titled "Mount Vernon and Fairway (A Fairy Tale)" which referenced the location of Mike's boyhood residence. His hope was that this would be the centerpiece of the new album. He set about recording a typically inventive but equally strange musical fairytale inhabited by a bizarre pied piper and a magical radio. The rest of the group, especially Carl, was not as enthusiastic about the direction Brian was headed with his childlike theme. When he was met with skepticism, Brian simply stopped recording and walked away, leaving the fairytale only partially complete.

It was decided that by including "Mount Vernon and Fairway (A Fairy Tale)" as a bonus seven-inch EP attached to the *Holland* album that it would increase Brian's presence on the release, and still leave the rest of the album intact as a coherent musical statement. Jack Rieley and Carl set about patching together Brian's bits and pieces as best they could, with Rieley adding the connecting narration. In its released form, "Mount Vernon and Fairway (A Fairy Tale)" is an odd but welcome slice of Brian Wilson music and humor. Brian himself provided the voice of the Pied Piper, while Carl contributed some of the singing. The brief musical themes woven throughout the fairy tale are tantalizingly great and show that Brian was still able to come up with truly unique ideas.

Holland received excellent reviews in the rock press and proved to be one of the Beach Boys' most enduring favorites with its fans. It is without a doubt among the most listenable Beach Boys albums from beginning to end. It reached a respectable #36 on the U.S. album charts and an even better #20 in the U.K., while both "Sail On Sailor" and "California" received significant airplay on FM radio in selected markets across the U.S. The Beach Boys also saw their domestic concerts grow consistently in audience size. At the end of 1973, *Rolling Stone* magazine named *Holland* as one of its choices for record of the year. With their 19th studio album, the Beach Boys once again created a classic, but unfortunately it would be their last group album of new material to earn universal acclaim.

The Beach Boys In Concert

As the Beach Boys' fortunes slowly improved, their live performances began to take on an "event" status wherever they went. The sets now combined a tasteful smattering of '60s Beach Boys classics alongside the newer material they were currently promoting. It was inevitable that the group would give in and move into a more oldies-friendly direction. In every city, they were constantly besieged with requests shouted throughout their concerts for "California Girls" or "I Get Around" or "Surfin' U.S.A." There was no way to avoid it. The social landscape was suddenly developing a voracious appetite for 1950s and early-1960s nostalgia, and the Beach Boys were living legends associated with those times. *The Beach Boys In Concert* album released in November 1973 finds the band at a crossroads, both trying to remain a current entity, and also relenting into giving their fans what they wanted.

The Beach Boys In Concert is also the last of their albums to feature Blondie Chaplin and Ricky Fataar. Their impact on the quality of the Beach Boys' live performances is still thought of by many hardcore fans as a high point for the band. No doubt they added versatility and dynamism. And for the second LP in a row, it's Blondie singing "Sail On Sailor" that leads off the album. Although the single of "Sail On Sailor" only peaked at #79 upon its 1973 release, and again entered the charts in 1975 and rose to #49, it will always be considered among the core of classic Beach Boys songs. It is perhaps the only perennial Beach Boys favorite to still thrive in the classic-rock and album-rock FM radio formats of the present. It was also featured in films and on television, giving Blondie Chaplin a voice that remains significant in Beach Boys history.

Another key to the success of *The Beach Boys In Concert* LP is the fact that it was a double album. There was once something substantial and valued when a group put forth a two-LP set, and other than the strange coupling of *Carl and the Passions—"So Tough"* and *Pet Sounds*, this was the Beach Boys first proper double album. It contained 20 songs recorded during the winter of 1972 and the summer of 1973. Six tracks were great live performances of songs from recent albums, while the rest covered material spanning the 1963–1967 period. Unfortunately Dennis Wilson seems to have been short-changed on the choice of tracks included on *The Beach Boys In Concert,* as none of his original material made the cut, and he isn't the featured vocalist on any the album's songs. Oddly, he is the only band member pictured on the front cover, shown with a microphone protruding from his groin towards the audience's faces.

In several cases, the versions of songs included on *The Beach Boys In Concert* somehow improved upon their original studio versions. "Let the Wind Blow" is arguably better with the guitar-heavy arrangement afforded it here, and Carl's vocal is truly magnificent thereon. "Marcella" rocks harder than the studio cut and has better energy. "Funky Pretty" loses the stunted quality of the studio version, and becomes a slithery groover in this wild concert performance. Also included is Blondie's and Ricky's "We Got Love," which had been removed from the *Holland* album to make room for "Sail On Sailor."

All in all, *The Beach Boys In Concert* album has to be counted as a solid success for the Beach Boys. It was their bestselling LP since 1968, as it reached a peak of #25 on the U.S. album charts in early 1974, and was awarded RIAA Gold Record status. It also marked the end of an era in which the group shook off widespread indifference and gamely fought their way back towards the top by proving they were still creatively viable. From here a series of events would vault them even higher, as the demand for tickets to their concerts exploded, causing *Rolling Stone* magazine to vote the Beach Boys its "Band of the Year" for 1974. But the attention that the mid-'70s nostalgia boom brought them eventually turned into a double-edged sword, and had a debilitating effect on their future creative choices. Nineteen sixty-seven to 1973 was an incredibly productive period, and should be counted as the Beach Boys "other" golden era. And as they sailed on to their next phase, they knew they'd once again proved themselves worthy of the label "legends."

14

A Day in the Life of a Tree

The Beach Boys May Have Created Global Warming . . . or Saved the Planet!

Since 1962, the Beach Boys have made a lot of money singing about gas-guzzling, air-polluting, planet-killing, hot-rod cars. They'll forever be associated with real fine 409s, fuel-injected Sting Rays, and little deuce coupes. But somewhere along the way they hung an environmental U-turn and wrote some of the greatest pro-ecology songs in rock history. The Beach Boys' conflicted relationship with environmental issues mirrors their equally Jekyll and Hyde–like wrangles with social morality and politics.

Things were simpler in 1962. If you wanted to be cool, you had to have a fast car. Gas was dirt cheap. The air, even in L.A., was still relatively clean. The base price of a brand new 1962 Corvette was $4,038. A 409 Chevy coupe, a big-block Dodge, or a 390 Ford were far cheaper. The "hot rod" had already been a Southern California staple for decades by the time the Beach Boys came along. The term was coined in the late 1930s around a social clique that raced their modified cars on dry lakebeds east of Los Angeles. The key was simple: you needed a lightweight vehicle with lots of horsepower that went faster than the other guy's. Gearheads began tearing apart old cars, stripping them down to the bare essentials, and then cramming in the biggest engine they could find. If it all held together while you pushed for the top end, you were in luck.

By the 1960s, drag-racing had become a definite craze in Southern California, and all over the U.S. The local dragstrip became an eardrum-blasting, toxic-fume-inhaling, eyeball-burning extravaganza that was ongoing and heavily attended. Street racing was illegal, but it was just as prevalent, if not more so, than legal drag racing. "I shoulda kept my mouth shut when I started to brag about my car." That's how these things get started. A guy

The Beach Boys

DENNIS   DAVE   CARL   BRIAN   MIKE   Capitol RECORDS

The Beach Boys gathered around Dennis Wilson's 1963 Corvette Stingray for an early publicity shot. Due to their great car songs, the Beach Boys became synonymous with hot-rodding; and, just as it had been with surfing, it was Dennis who was the serious gearhead of the group.

rolls up to the burger stand in his precious ride. Another guy already parked there sees him and makes an offhand remark that his car is so ugly it's gotta be slow. Game on. The kids make a beeline for a country road, or out-of-the-way boulevard, and the race is on.

Spirit of America

The Beach Boys had an incredible knack for writing the soundtrack to those unfolding car-related scenes occurring around the U.S. They somehow managed to record car songs that sounded like hot rods look. They projected a sound that was shiny, fast, metallic, and loud . . . but loud *and* pretty, just like a cool car. I don't know how they did it, but they sure made it seem like an easy job. Brian and the boys just turned the key, pumped some gas to the carbs, and floored it. The band got traction, went in a straight line, and beat every other "car band" by several lengths. There were other groups that created a few timeless classics about having fun in fast cars. And there were many more that tried but got shut down. But there is no doubt that the Beach Boys ruled the pavement when it came to classic car songs. Among the runners-up were the Rip Chords, Ronny and the Daytonas, Bruce & Terry, Gary Usher, Dick Dale, the T-Bones, and the appropriately named Challengers. There was only one act that came within exhaust-sniffing distance of the Beach Boys when it came to classic car songs, and that was Jan and Dean. With classics like "Dead Man's Curve" and "Drag City," Jan and Dean knew how to flex their musical horsepower. One reason why was that Brian was co-writing their songs and singing with them.

But Brian wasn't really a car guy. He dug cool cars but he never seriously raced them, or worked on them, and he didn't really know that much about them. He got help from collaborators like Gary Usher, who was a real hot-rodder, and Roger Christian, who also knew his way around a custom machine. Mike Love gave the Beach Boys an immediately identifiable fast-car-sounding voice the second he uttered those classic words, "She's real fine . . . my 409." There was a quality to Mike's delivery on that song that sounded credible. If you ran into a guy with a scarily fast car in those days, he usually talked like Mike Love, all nasal and California sounding. I don't know what came first, the chicken or the Love, but it was not unusual to hear a Mike Love–esque voice coming out of a guy sitting behind the wheel of a cool ride.

Check My Custom Machine

The one Beach Boy who completely immersed himself in the hot-rodding culture was Dennis Wilson. That awesome dark blue, fuel-injected, 1963 split-window Corvette Stingray on the cover of the Beach Boys' *Shut Down Volume 2* album belonged to Dennis. It's the first thing he bought when the Beach Boys made a little bread. He also bought a Jaguar XKE, and eventually an AC Cobra, which is just about the fastest street-legal car ever made. Dennis raced his Cobra all around Southern California, and won stacks of trophies, even setting a track record or two. The inventor of the Cobra, Carroll Shelby, saw to it that Dennis received one of the first 427-cubic-inch Cobra motors to install in his formerly 289-cubic-inch small-block-powered Cobra. Either way it was a monster, but with the big block it would literally jump off the pavement when Dennis punched the accelerator. He ran it with a specially mixed fuel, hitting top speeds of 160 MPH and more.

In 1965, Dennis purchased a Ferrari coupe that had been formerly owned by the late, great soul singer Sam Cooke. Dennis's driving partner on sprints up the Pacific Coast Highway was actor Steve McQueen, who also had a Ferrari, a Jaguar, and a Cobra. I guess Steve and Dennis had similar tastes in cars, and women, and drugs, but let's stick with cars for now. The bottom line is that Dennis was the real car guy in the Beach Boys, just as he had been the real surfer. Brian wrote about it, and Dennis did it. That was the pattern.

In 1971, Dennis was cast as the "Mechanic" in the classic road film *Two-Lane Blacktop* alongside James Taylor as the "Driver." Dennis brought a legitimate knowledge of drag cars to his role of keeping the pair's '55 Chevy and its ground-shaking 454 cubic-inch motor in racing shape. He'd gone from being in a band that sang about fast cars, to a guy who raced them, to an actor who portrayed a guy that fixed them. Dennis was creating art that was commenting on life, living life that was imitated by art, and then imitating living said life through art. It must have been surreal for Dennis.

But it's not like the other Beach Boys didn't relieve themselves of a bit of their wealth while pursuing the joy of owning great cars too. Carl had an Aston Martin DB4 and a Bentley; Brian had a Porsche and a Rolls-Royce; Mike had a Porsche, a classic MG, and a Rolls-Royce; Bruce had a Jaguar and a Bentley; and Al had a vintage T-Bird and a HemiCuda. For the Beach Boys, "Our Car Club" wasn't just a song, it was a way of life. But as the 1970s rolled on, a nationwide gas shortage became a reality. Long lines formed at fueling stations, gas prices skyrocketed, and the Beach Boys went green.

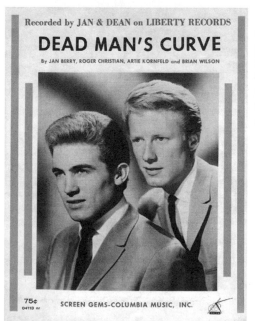

Jan and Dean may have been the only pop act that seriously competed with the Beach Boys for consistent chart success when singing about fast cars. One of the reasons they did so well is that Brian Wilson was helping them as a co-writer and singer on some of their best records.

Let the Grass Grow

Manager Jack Rieley pointed the Beach Boys in an environmentally friendly direction. Suddenly they wrote about saving the ecology instead of burning rubber. Their 1971 song "A Day in the Life of a Tree" is one of the most devastatingly sad pro-environment songs ever released by a major act. And there were others. "Don't Go Near the Water" warned of pollution ruining our oceans. Mike and Al's trilogy "California Saga" is another very moving environmentally conscious piece of art. Dennis Wilson's 1977 solo track "Pacific Ocean Blues" laments the gruesome slaughter of whales and other sea life, while his "River Song" condemns the overpopulation and polluted air of L.A. There are many more pro-environment compositions from Al, a folkie at heart; he has championed a number of environmental causes with his music and his wallet. Bruce has been an advocate for the beach-protecting philosophy of the Surfrider Foundation. Mike too has done his share through his TM and earth-conscious philosophies.

In 1983, the Beach Boys went head to head against one of the most controversial environment-related figures in America. Reagan administration

By the early '70s, the Beach Boys were singing about environmental causes instead of drag racing. They may be one of the only acts in history to have written several of the greatest pro-ecology songs as well as some of the all-time hot-rod anthems.

Secretary of the Interior James Watt declared that the Beach Boys had been attracting "the wrong element" to their annual Independence Day concerts on the Washington, D.C. National Mall, which in the previous years had drawn up to 500,000 people. He barred them from playing, and instead asked Wayne Newton to perform in their place. The backlash from the public was so severe that President Reagan, who declared himself and the First Lady "fans" of the Beach Boys, publically admonished Watt. An apology was offered to the band, who were invited to perform at the White House; and by the next year they were back playing in the Washington, D.C. National Mall on July 4.

In the court of public opinion, the Beach Boys' vast popularity had virtually crushed the man who has been called the most blatantly anti-environmental political appointee in American history. Watt's tenure as Secretary of the Interior was marked by controversy, stemming primarily from his alleged hostility to environmentalism and his advocacy for the commercial development of federally protected lands and forests. He is rumored to have said that Jesus will return when the last tree falls. According to the environmental advocacy group Center for Biological Diversity, Watt held the

After their early-'70s stint as environmentalists, the Beach Boys returned to the familiar territory of promoting gas-guzzling cars and pure speed in the '80s and '90s. This *NASCAR Salute* CD included the guitar of David Marks, who had rejoined the Beach Boys in 1997.

record for protecting the fewest species under the Endangered Species Act in United States history. (Two decades later his record was broken when George W. Bush's second appointee to the position, Dirk Kempthorne, protected exactly zero species.)

Still Cruisin' and Usin' Those Fossil Fuels

So the Beach Boys had championed the environment in song, and they'd taken on tree-killer James Watt and won! Hail the Beach Boys, the planet's best friends. Well, not exactly. Actually the Beach Boys, or at least the Mike Love faction of the Beach Boys, has shown a consistently pro-corporate and pro-Republican slant in their politics. They befriended Ronald Reagan, performed at his second inaugural ball in 1985, and actually campaigned for George H. W. Bush. In 1989, they were back in their hot rods promoting their "Still Cruisin'" single in a procession of gas-guzzling Corvettes.

Yes, it's a massively conflicted three-way dance between the Beach Boys, the environment, and their fossil-fuel-draining and corporate-fawning proclivities. Dennis was either driving a Ferrari or hitchhiking. He was either wearing expensive Italian leather boots or he was barefoot. He lived in a mansion or he was homeless. Mike advocates inner enlightenment *and* pursuit of personal wealth. Bruce is a Surfrider *and* a country-clubber. They love the planet and they love their money and their stuff. They are Americans after all. Tach it up, Tach it up . . . but don't go near the water.

15

No-Go Showboat

The Beach Boys' Image Problems

Mike Love's nasal voice, those embarrassing lyrics, their girlish high voices, associations with trends that aren't hip, striped shirts, white tennis shoes, "Barbara Ann," Mike Love's outfits, Mike Love's between-song patter, Dennis's friendship with Charles Manson, Brian's failing voice, too many cigarettes, too many drugs, too many beards, too many fat guys, too much alcohol, too much rehab, too much TM, going country club, tennis shorts, Tommy Bahama–wear, Hawaiian shirts, cheerleaders, "Kokomo," ponytails on old men, John Stamos, and *Baywatch*. There seems to always be something that someone hates about the Beach Boys. But some of the things that some people hate are *exactly* what other people love about them. It has been a five-decade circus of confusing aesthetic choices from a band of diverse individuals and crazy people. The following are just some of the issues that have made the Beach Boys less popular and/or have caused endless disagreements among the fans about them.

Striped Shirts

The end of the Beach Boys' striped-shirt phase didn't come until late 1967, over two years too late. The Beatles were still wearing matching suits when they performed on their last tour in August 1966, but their choice of stage-wear was tasteful, Mod, solid-color suits. The Rolling Stones ditched matching stage outfits back in 1963. But the Beach Boys continued to wear those candy-striped referee shirts that might have looked cool in 1964, but looked completely ridiculous in the context of 1967. They switched to matching ice-cream-white suits in late 1967, which weren't much better. They finally went to non-matching gear sometime in 1969.

It's not as if the Beach Boys were alone in their insistence on wearing stage uniforms. There were many groups performing in matching outfits in 1967. The Dave Clark Five, Paul Revere and the Raiders, the Monkees, the Four Seasons, the Moody Blues, the First Edition, Vanilla Fudge, the Brooklyn Bridge, the Five Americans, and many other hit rock/pop acts were still performing in matching outfits in the late '60s. But the Beach Boys stood out because those striped shirts had become so iconic. To see them still wearing candy stripes so many years later would have been equal to seeing the Beatles wearing collarless jackets in 1967. That would have been ridiculous; and in the case of the Beach Boys, it was.

Voices

For Beach Boys fans it's hard to imagine, but it is true that many people can't stand the band because of their voices. How could it be true? The Beach Boys have the greatest vocal abilities of any rock band in history. Apparently some don't see that as a positive. Particularly, Mike Love's ultra-nasal voice gets under people's skin. The Beach Boys themselves made it worse by dialing up Mike's nearly caricature-ish nasality in later years, and sometimes in inappropriate places. To hear Mike, with that voice, singing John Lennon's "Imagine" during early-'80s concerts was nails-on-chalkboard material, for sure.

And then there are those who don't like Brian's super-high falsetto. It's just too much for some ears. Here is a perfect example of something

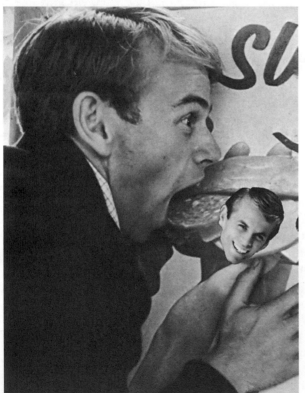

that most Beach Boys fans consider brilliant, and most non-fans think sounds wimpy or whiny. One thing that seems to find universal agreement is the fact that Carl Wilson was a great singer. But some will say that it's unfortunate Carl was in a band with that guy who sang through his nose, or the other guy who sang like a girl.

Due to a myriad of image problems, some deserved and some circumstantial, the Beach Boys had to eat it periodically as their popularity waxed and waned.

Trends

The Beach Boys caught a lot of flak, especially in the late 1960s and early 1970s, for being associated with teen trends like surfing and hot rods. They couldn't win. The surfers hated them because they were poseurs. The hippies hated them because they were jocks. And then the energy crisis happened after the Beach Boys had been promoting car clubs, dragstrips, and fuel injection for years. Eventually those associations turned back into a positive, but there was a period where the Beach Boys' classic themes seemed about as uncool as you can get.

"Barbara Ann"

The single "Barbara Ann" was a big hit for the Beach Boys in early 1966, but it kind of put them into an oldies bag that was hard to shake. Even though the incredible *Pet Sounds* closely followed "Barbara Ann," to some it didn't penetrate. "Ba, Ba, Ba, Ba, Bar-bara Ann" not only penetrates, it amounts to near brainwashing. To this day the song continues to be a double-edged sword. Some cannot get enough of it. To many low-information consumers, it's the Beach Boys most recognizable song. People continue to scream for it during encores. It's the Tourette anthem of rock and roll. But to others, just the mere fact that the Beach Boys sang this mind-numbing song is reason enough to dislike them.

Mike Love

He's the frontman, and the coolest guy ever according to some Beach Boys fans. To a seemingly larger majority, he's repulsive. The one thing his detractors usually point to is the genetically unfortunate fact that Mike is relatively bald, and was so at a young age. There's no room for baldness in rock and roll. Geez, tough crowd. But aside from that fairly shallow point, Mike does have some additional issues that have made him a target.

Mr. Love's teasing demeanor can come off uncomfortably cocky to some, and his between-song patter and purposely dumb jokes are an irritant to many. And then there are those outfits. From Mr. Natural in a white robe, to country Jesus, to hippie pimp, to gold lamé and turbans, to Bob Hope–like golf wear, to Tommy Bahama, casual country club, and a tsunami of Hawaiian shirts, Mike Love's clothes really piss some people off. For others it's a constant source of humor. And to reiterate, to many Beach Boys fans, he's just cool, so get over it.

At times the Beach Boys fortunes were flatter than a blown tire, and it seemed the rain would never stop falling on them. This bootleg disc includes material from their disastrously drugged 1978 Australian tour, on which even the normally reliable Carl Wilson was too stoned to maintain his balance.

Not Turned On and Tuned In

In 1967, as the "Summer of Love" unfolded, the Beach Boys were still singing "Barbara Ann" in their striped shirts and white tennis shoes. The acid generation was listening to Jefferson Airplane, Cream, and the Doors. The Beatles managed to deftly negotiate the changes and still led the pack. But the Beach Boys stumbled and fell behind. John Lennon and Paul McCartney seemed to have had the perfect vision to articulate the massive shifts happening in the culture. "Tomorrow Never Knows," "Strawberry Fields Forever," "A Day in the Life," "I Am the Walrus"—all of them felt like John and Paul knew something had happened, or something was happening, or something was going to happen that was both mind-blowing and brilliant.

Brian, on the other hand, seemed like he was scared. He was sticking his toe in the frightening place, but the dark parts of "Heroes and Villains" and *Smiley Smile* sounded like a potentially terrified vision trying to whistle its way

Carl Wilson, pictured here with Wolfman Jack, became disillusioned with the Beach Boys highly dysfunctional state in the late '70s and early '80s. After a bout with substance abuse, he cleaned up his act and temporarily left the band in 1981 to record and promote a solo LP.

through the graveyard. And due to Brian's sensitivity and his hesitation in releasing a potentially game-changing *Smile* album, people missed the fact that he had been *the* pioneer in finding the creative envelope and probing its limits. Instead the Beach Boys were perceived as lightweight fluff, while the Beatles were given the credit for leading the artistic progression of the acid generation with their *Sergeant Pepper's Lonely Hearts Club Band* LP. This was an image problem that the Beach Boys had a particularly difficult task in reversing.

Charles Manson

In 1969, when the Manson family committed one of the most brutal and sensationalized series of murders in U.S. history, being known as their good friend and host wasn't exactly a positive association. But Dennis Wilson managed to drop that bomb on the Beach Boys after he'd allowed Charlie and his devoted girls to live at his home through much of 1968. Of course

Dennis had no idea they'd become infamous murderers, and to his credit when he started feeling bad vibes from the family he cut his ties to them. That was a half-year or more before the horrific Tate/LaBianca slayings, but there was a lingering problem. Dennis had polished up and recorded one of Charlie's songs and taken the credit for it. Oh, and the Beach Boys had put it on one of their albums. They'd never be able to live down their Manson connection, which to this day follows them like a bad dream.

Brian's Back, But His Voice Isn't

In 1976, Beach Boys fans were thrilled to see Brian come back to an active status with the group. The joy disappeared when they saw his 270-pound body and heard his cigarette- and cocaine-ravaged voice. In the late '70s, it was torturous to hear Brian attempt to croak out "In My Room" or "Surfer Girl" in concert. Al Jardine insists that Brian sabotaged his voice purposely because he was embarrassed that he sounded like a girl and he wanted a rough voice like Dennis. If that's the case, he got his wish and more. Brian's vocals remained unreliable and raspy until the mid-'80s, when he quit smoking and got healthy. But in truth, they were never the same.

Brian came back to "theoretically" lead the Beach Boys back to the top in the late '70s, but his poor physical condition and shaky mental state made his contributions less than stellar.

Too Loaded to Stand Up

The 1978 Australia and New Zealand Tour featured multiple shows with a very unsteady Carl, who was reportedly doing heroin with his brothers. The drug also affected his usually golden voice, and while singing "God Only Knows" he sounded like Elmer Fudd on Valium. Carl's fundamental ability to normally stay balanced on his feet had left him, and at several concerts he actually stumbled around the stage in front of a horrified audience. At one show, he actually fell to the floor.

Mike Love and Dennis Wilson had the most volatile relationship within the Beach Boys family. What began as a competitive and often testy friendship devolved into onstage fistfights and a mutual hatred for everything the other represented. Despite the animosity, they still managed to collaborate on several great songs.

The drugs had a different effect on Brian, who was bouncing around the stage, dancing bizarrely, and marching in place while playing his bass. Dennis seemed much healthier and physically together than either of his brothers during this tour, which probably only means he had a higher tolerance for the hard substances they were all sharing. Carl apologized to the fans for his behavior, but the Beach Boys received some very bad image karma from this tour.

Drinking and Fighting

I was at the Beach Boys Universal Amphitheatre show in 1979, sitting among the Wilson/Martin/Hinsche families, when a drunken Dennis made a comment about Quaaludes to the audience that didn't go down well with Mike. There were several verbal exchanges between the two, and a little later Dennis dramatically pushed his drums off the riser and onto Mike. He then jumped over them and chased Mike across the stage as everyone tried to separate them. I'll always remember that Audrey said, "Oh dear," as she watched the calamity break out on stage in front of 15,000 fans. There was a sudden break—let's call it an unscheduled intermission—while the road crew was called upon to clean up the mess. Dennis was the first of the Beach Boys to return to the stage, and he walked directly to a microphone and said, "I love Mike Love."

Perhaps an even more physical confrontation had already happened behind the scenes. Carol Ann Harris, Lindsey Buckingham's ex-wife, published her memoirs recently. In them she describes being backstage at a Beach Boys 1979 Universal Amphitheatre concert. She witnessed Mike yelling at Dennis for missing the preshow soundcheck. Dennis's response was to knock Mike out with one well-placed punch.

There were so many public confrontations between Dennis and Mike that it's hard to sort one from the other. The animosity between them infused an air of ugliness into the Beach Boys experience. This was a severe image problem that hit its peak in 1979, at which time Dennis was temporarily forced out of the band with the instruction to sober up. His sobriety reportedly never lasted more than two consecutive days.

Pony Tails and Tennis Shorts

A good many fans think of the Beach Boys' 1980s and 1990s appearances on TV's *Full House, Home Improvement,* and *Baywatch* as some kind of peak. They think of the "Kokomo" period as golden days for the Beach Boys. Dennis was dead, but they still had Carl in the band's

The Beach Boys of 1977 sometimes seemed like middle-aged men vainly trying to reclaim their teenage mojo. When Brian was given some creative slack, he came up with the decidedly odd *The Beach Boys Love You* LP. It turned out to be a warped classic that didn't sell and confused critics, but stands as another example of Brian's wacky brilliance.

lineup, and Brian too on occasion. Some former fans just cringed when they saw what the Beach Boys had become during that era. Many were astonished and horrified to see David Marks re-appear with them during their *Baywatch* appearance 32 years after his departure from the band. The reality that the Beach Boys were his band too didn't matter, because balding old men in Hawaiian shirts with pony tails was a painful thing to process. The rapidly aging boys along with their baseball caps, short-shorts, cheerleaders, cheesy presentation, and questionable aesthetic sense had a radioactive-like effect on the group's legacy.

The Beach Boys had died their creative death. To some they lost any hope of being relevant in about 1980. It seemed they had shed any last traces of coolness by the 1990s, and everything that came afterwards was embarrassing. In reality they'd already stopped progressing artistically back in 1973, other than Dennis's *Pacific Ocean Blue*, which was undoubtedly a creative step forward. The *Keepin' the Summer Alive* album, with its cover literally showing the Beach Boys locked in a beach bubble, was the last straw for many longtime Beach Boys fans. Conversely, there was a large chunk of fans that actually remained loyal, and some new ones that came onboard during the "shorts" years of the '80s and '90s. It all comes down to perspective: one fan's image problem is another fan's pleasure.

16

What's Wrong?

Artistic Missteps by the Beach Boys

They shelved their greatest album, they blew off the Monterey Pop Festival, they toured with the Maharishi *after* the Beatles had rejected him, and they put an incapacitated Brian Wilson back in charge when everything was on the line. Yes, the Beach Boys have made a few mistakes. The following is a brief evaluation of how the Beach Boys blew it, and how they regularly got together and blew it again.

More Guitar, Please

While rock and roll became more and more guitar-based, the Beach Boys went keyboard. Although they had established themselves early on as one of the first electric guitar–centric groups, by 1966, when rock-guitar gods were rising, the Beach Boys dialed it down. If Dave Marks, who developed into an incredible guitarist, hadn't left the Beach Boys in late 1963, it would have certainly improved their guitar-based identity. Although the Beach Boys had a very distinct guitar identity by 1966, their excellent surf/hot-rod guitar sound had run its course. Subsequently the Beach Boys' guitar sound became a smaller part of the big production on their records, and only a mild support system in concert.

While everything around them was becoming *more* guitar-centric, the Beach Boys became less of a guitar band, and this is part of why they became viewed as so uncool so quickly. The Beach Boys had almost everything. They had great songs, great production, great vocals, and great instrumentation, but the one thing they didn't have was a tangible guitar identity like the Beatles, Stones, Who, et cetera. You might say, "But that's what made them special" . . . but it wasn't. A great guitarist would have only helped. Someone the caliber of David Marks could have taken "Barbara Ann" in concert and turned it into "Crossroads" for a few bars, and that would have made a big difference along the way.

Certainly great LPs like *Wild Honey* would have been better with some tasteful guitar textures woven into some of the tracks. It would have made them sound more mature, more FM radio friendly. The Beach Boys early-'70s updated live sound, with Blondie augmenting Carl, could have already been underway in 1966 if Marks had stayed. There would have been less ground to make up with the typical rock audience. Brian Wilson would have taken advantage of the fact that he had another weapon to fire in his arsenal, and maybe Dave's ax would have been a really good one at a crucial time, like on *Smile* . . . but we'll never know. Just remember this: in June 1967, when the Beach Boys bailed out of playing the Monterey Pop Festival, David Marks was 18 years old and playing fantastic lead guitar with his psychedelic band the Moon.

A Smile Turned Upside Down

In May 1967, when publicist Derek Taylor let it be known that Brian Wilson was scrapping his epic *Smile* album, he barely disguised his complete disgust. Taylor wasn't alone. Brian and the Beach Boys had labored over this project for more than half a year, expectations were through the roof, Capitol Records was in companywide cerebrovascular panic over the building cost, everything was riding on its delivery. To shelve the project was one of the all-time flakes in music-business history. As rock music grew into a serious art form, the nationwide approval rating of the Beach Boys went into freefall.

Capitol had become so fed up waiting for *Smile* that they virtually pulled the financial plug on Brian. His reaction was to shrink into a passive mode. The Beach Boys were forced to throw a studio together in Brian's home and slap together an album there on the cheap. The resulting release *Smiley Smile* proved to be the worst seller in Beach Boys' history to that point. It would be eight years before the Beach Boys fully recovered from this disaster. The non-release of *Smile* turned out to be one of the worst artistic missteps in music history.

Monterey Pop Party Poopers

The Beach Boys were scheduled as the closing act for Saturday night, June 17, 1967, at the Monterey Pop Festival. Brian Wilson was on the festival's Board of Governors, and helped choose the talent. The Beach Boys' state-of-the-art sound system, and their talented engineer Stephen Desper, were donated to ensure that all of the festival's acts sounded their best. Monterey was destined to be a one-of-a-kind event, with diverse artists from several continents coming together to launch the Summer of Love. In retrospect, the festival turned out to be even greater than anyone had imagined, with wondrous performances by a long list of luminaries including Jefferson

Airplane, the Who, Ravi Shankar, Otis Redding, the Grateful Dead, Simon & Garfunkel, the Byrds, and so many more. More significantly it signaled the coming-out party for future rock icons Janis Joplin and Jimi Hendrix, who absolutely slayed the audience and jump-started their national popularity.

It could have been the moment that the Beach Boys rose to meet the expectations of thousands of turned-on minds with their blissful harmonies and "Good Vibrations." This could have been their chance to command the respect they deserved as one of rock's most progressive entities. But instead, they cancelled at the last minute. To many it seemed that the wealthy, mainstream, clean-cut Beach Boys were afraid to be judged by a skeptical hippie generation. It ingrained a perception of the Beach Boys as being part of the square establishment. They not only didn't play, but they chickened out.

The exact reason that they pulled out has been speculated upon for years. One rumor was that the greedy Beach Boys didn't want to play for free. Another theory is that Mike Love was leery of Monterey's Coca-Cola corporate sponsorship and cancelled to protest unhealthy beverages in principal. A third possibility is the fact that Carl Wilson was facing jail time for refusing to be sworn in after receiving a U.S. Army draft notice, claiming conscientious-objector status, and was too distracted to perform. Brian claimed *he* was responsible for canceling the Beach Boys appearance simply because they were under pressure to complete their next single "Heroes and Villains." Simultaneously Dennis's wife Carole was preparing to file for divorce, leaving Dennis too despondent to attend the festival. Regardless of the reason, or reasons, when you add it all up, missing Monterey Pop equaled one of the worst decisions the band ever made.

The Maharishi Mess

In 1968, the Beach Boys embraced the teachings of Maharishi Mahesh Yogi and were motivated to help him promote Transcendental Meditation to the world. Dennis had met Maharishi at the Beach Boys' December 1967 UNICEF benefit concert in Paris, France, and introduced him to the other boys. It was Mike Love who traveled to Rishikesh, India along with the Beatles in February 1968 to gain enlightenment in the presence of the Maharishi. An enamored Mike and the Beach Boys scheduled a joint 30-city tour with the beloved Maharishi. The concept was that the Beach Boys would perform, and then the Maharishi would lecture sitting cross-legged on a flower-covered platform. Unfortunately, after a short period of following him, the Beatles (other than George) ultimately rejected the Maharishi as a fraud. Deserved or not, this anti-endorsement damaged the Maharishi's credibility in the eyes of music fans, and the timing couldn't have been worse

The Beach Boys out for a cruise on Dennis's sailboat, the *Harmony*, in 1976. By this time there were two clear factions in the band: the clean-living TM practitioners—Mike and Al; and the partying free-livers—Dennis and Carl. A nonplussed Brian was often pulled at from both sides, but tended to gravitate toward his brothers when given free rein.

for the Beach Boys. As the Maharishi's star crashed, the joint tour bombed. In the end, due to anemic ticket sales, the Beach Boys/Maharishi tour was cancelled after seven poorly attended dates. The Beach Boys reportedly lost hundreds of thousands of dollars on this particular misstep.

The Downer About *Surf's Up*

By 1971 Jack Rieley had certainly improved the general perceptions of the Beach Boys. He'd gotten them some good press, and he'd raised their profile. But Rieley didn't exactly turn them around creatively. *20/20* and *Sunflower* were better LPs than *Surf's Up* and *Carl and the Passions—"So Tough"*, although much less popular. If taking inferior product and getting more attention for it makes you a genius, then Jack Rieley was one. But he presided over the dismantling of, or dumbing down of, what could have been the *greatest* Beach Boys LP: *Surf's Up*. Instead it turned into a political compromise that satiated members with less artistic vision while great songs disappeared from it. Bruce Johnston called *Surf's Up* a "hyped-up lie," and in a way he was right. The cover is impressive, and some of it is genius, but the whole thing could have surpassed *Sunflower* as a statement of art. Instead it fell significantly short of even matching it. *Carl and the Passions—"So Tough"* falls short of even that. Rieley was their manager; and if he gets credit for the good, then folks should be reminded that he was by no means a savior in every way. This misstep has a lower profile one than most of the others, but it is nonetheless significant.

15 Bad Ones

The Beach Boys had a nearly pristine history of high-quality releases until their *15 Big Ones* album. In the context of 1976, it was a huge artistic disappointment. Everything about it seemed cheesy and small. The worst part (besides the awful cover and the overall lack of originality and bite) is the fact that rock's greatest vocal group didn't sing well on it. It is glaringly shoddy in the vocal department.

Yes, it has its charms, like every other bad Beach Boys thing. The song "It's OK" is great, and offers just the right amount of nostalgia. But more nostalgia was piled on like too many toppings on a teetering banana split. Why the need for self-parody? Much of *15 Big Ones* sounds like a *Happy Days* type of soundtrack performed by middle-aged men with cigarette coughs. They were the fucking Beach Boys, and not Sha Na Na. In reality, *15 Big Ones* was the beginning of endless attempts to cash in on the Beach Boys' past with something from the present that wasn't as good.

Putting a shell-shocked Brian Wilson back in charge in the studio was a huge mistake. He'd been in bed while the industry and its recording process had changed. The whole world was waiting for the artistic progression of *Holland* to continue. What magical sound would the Beach Boys come up with next? Instead of magic, they got Potsie Weber meets Flash Cadillac. There *were* a few hints of magic. "Had to Phone Ya" showed Brian still had good track ideas, but he had no focus, no strength, he did not want to be there, and he phoned more than that song in. There was no polish, no soul, and no life in *15 Big Ones*. And still it was a hit. The Beach Boys were in such demand in 1976 that even a badly made banana split was wolfed down by American record buyers. But it had a detrimental effect. It was an artistic misstep that had a cost.

In 1976, Dennis and Carl knew their way around Brother Studio better than Brian did. They were adept at coaxing interestingly textured tracks, with choirs, strings, giant fat bass sounds, synth washes, tape manipulation, dreamy harmonies, and epic drums. They could handle production and arrangements just plain better than the other Beach Boys, including Brian. Dennis's productions from 1975 and 1976 sounded current, but artful and twisted in a Wilson-specific way. An LP with Dennis-produced tracks like "Rainbows," "River Song," and "Holy Man" would have kept the Beach Boys in the creative game. But instead they opted for Brian's tired oldies approach and several half-baked originals thrown in to fill out the album. The great tragedy of *15 Big Ones* is that in the lead up to it, the record industry and music fans of the world had their ear cocked toward the Beach Boys in a way they never would again. *15 Big Ones* is a big reason why.

L.A. Light, Disco Dud

The commercial failure of the Beach Boys 1979 LP *L.A. (Light Album)* was a *huge* disappointment for the band, their record label, and anyone else connected to it. This was the group's CBS Records debut after being given a contract worth $8,000,000, and being signed in a media-celebrated ceremony. The band experienced major trouble trying to deliver the LP on time, as Brian Wilson proved unable to produce an acceptable track lineup. Label head Walter Yetnikoff heard Brian's initial work and uttered the famous line, "I think I've just been fucked." Brian's solution was to send an S.O.S. out to former member Bruce Johnston. Bruce was put in charge in an attempt to implement damage control, and to hopefully bring in an acceptable product. The results were decidedly mixed.

L.A. *(Light Album)* admittedly had about four or five great tracks. Brian and Carl's "Good Timin'" was a smooth-harmony vehicle; Carl's "Angel Come Home" was a touching torch song with a rocking chorus sung by Dennis. Al's "Lady Lynda" had some very pretty moments, although it seemed somewhat self-conscious. Dennis's "Baby Blue" was a magnificent and moody ballad featuring a great vocal duet between Carl and Dennis. "Love Surrounds Me" was a dark and funky Dennis track, which, like "Baby Blue," had been poached from his doomed *Bambu* solo project. But despite the strength of this material, Bruce and the Beach Boys decided to put all their chips on an ultra-sterile disco dance version of "Here Comes the Night" complete with a blow-dried, spandex-clad, mirror-balled production.

The "Here Comes the Night" single was given a bigger promotional push than any Beach Boys record in their long history. A massive campaign was undertaken to ensure that both the single and the LP received maximum exposure. To this day, you can find L.A. *(Light Album)* promo materials by the armload on eBay. There were picture discs, colored-vinyl twelve-inch singles, posters, T-shirts, visors, postcards, and anything else CBS thought might help them break the new Beach Boys record. Radio was bombarded with offerings of swag, as was the print media. There was a high-profile TV appearance booked on *Midnight Special*. There were radio interviews by the dozen, and a Radio City Music Hall series of featured concerts. There were even joint record-store signings by all six Beach Boys, including Brian! An air of anticipation was building. Then people heard the disco-inflected "Here Comes the Night," and the whole thing went THUD!

Despite the fact that *L.A. (Light Album)* was pushed by the CBS/Caribou label like one of those Billy Mays (R.I.P.) OxiClean TV commercials . . . it flopped. CBS had done all they could. They'd practically made house calls and shoved the record under people's front door, but people rejected it, yawned at it, and more than a few verbally eviscerated it for the inclusion of a twelve-minute disco mistake (cue eleven people saying, "but I loved that track").

CBS and the Beach Boys ate dirt when the disco single not only failed to make the Top Forty, but the album failed to make the Top Ninety-Nine! The misguided disco effort smacked of bandwagon jumping, and essentially killed any chance of a successful launch on their new label. "Good Timin'" was rushed out as a follow-up, and did decently considering the Beach Boys' popularity had cliff-dived just prior to its release, but it was too late. *L.A. (Light Album)* showed just how fast you could fritter away a label's hope, a fan base's patience, and the media's interest. It was an epic disaster . . . oh . . . and the last fairly good Beach Boys LP.

17

The Thing That Wouldn't Die

A Brief History of Beach Boys Comebacks

T he Beach Boys have been at a seeming career dead end too many
times to count. And yet, history has shown there is always one more
hit, one more resurgence, one more rise to the top in them. From
"Do It Again" to *Endless Summer*, from "Brian's Back" to America's Band,
from "Kokomo" to *Sounds of Summer*, they just won't go away. The following
is an examination of the Beach Boys' uncanny ability to reanimate.

"Surfin' U.S.A."

You're saying to yourself, how could something recorded so early in the
Beach Boys career be considered a comeback? However, after the relative
failure of the "Ten Little Indians" single in November 1962, the Beach Boys
were flirting with one-hit-wonder status. "Surfin' Safari" had been a #14 hit,
and the Beach Boys' next single was expected to fair even better. But "Ten
Little Indians" fizzled with a very poor #49 placing on the singles chart, the
lowest for any Beach Boys single until 1968. In January 1963, Brian reacted
by cutting his next single at Western Recorders instead of at the Capitol
Tower Studios, and his instinct was right. "Surfin' U.S.A." hit #3, and not
only put the Beach Boys career back on track, but vaulted them into the
realm of national stars.

"Good Vibrations"

In a way, the Beach Boys had nothing to come back from in late 1966,
when "Good Vibrations" hit number one on the charts. But in a sense it
was a comeback moment for them. They had tasted the top of the charts
in 1964 and 1965 with "I Get Around" and "Help Me, Rhonda," and in the
subsequent months they came close with "California Girls, "Barbara Ann,"

The Beach Boys became one of the top concert attractions in the U.S. again in the mid-1970s. After years of scraping by playing smaller venues, by 1975 they were filling stadiums, and regularly performing to 50,000 fans or more per show.

and "Sloop John B." But "Good Vibrations" was such a universal success, both critically and commercially, that it transcended perceptions and actually momentarily gave the Beach Boys a level of prominence that they hadn't enjoyed since late 1964. It not only was a hit, but it renewed and redefined the Beach Boys and became their ultimate anthem. It also marked a temporary farewell to superstar status as they embarked on an eight-year struggle through the pop wilderness.

"Do It Again"

Following a series of bombs on the charts, in the summer of 1968 Mike Love convinced Brian to collaborate with him on a new single that evoked the Beach Boys' old signature style. It would reference the thematic touchstones of summer, surfing, fun, and girls in a way the group hadn't in several years. Brian made it work by adding a cutting-edge production element of distorted drums that added a hint of freakiness to the nostalgia party. "Do It Again" turned out to be the first of many Beach Boys returns to the sand-and-sun well, but it was also one of the most successful. The "Do It Again" single hit a respectable #20 in the U.S., and surprised everyone by rising all the way to number one in the U.K. It was a short-lived comeback, but a notable one for sure.

Surf's Up

Between 1967 and 1970, the Beach Boys had recorded four great albums in a row, but the consumer response to them was horrible and getting worse.

1970's *Sunflower* was one of their best efforts ever, yet it only managed a chart placing of #151. This was so bad that it seemed the Beach Boys had little chance of recovering. But a new wave of energy hit them when manager Jack Rieley stepped in and pushed them in what he thought would be perceived as a "heavier" direction. He was right. When the *Surf's Up* album was released in August 1971, the modern rock press, especially *Rolling Stone* magazine, for the first time began to treat the Beach Boys with respect. Simultaneously the band improved its credibility with the college and young-adult audiences by performing in hip venues like the Fillmore Auditorium and Winterland. Suddenly a noticeable improvement occurred in record sales as *Surf's Up* peaked at a very decent #29 on the album charts, the highest placing for a Beach Boys LP in four years.

Endless Summer

This was the comeback that changed everything. The Beach Boys had done their share to improve the landscape on which their fortunes were to be determined. After bottoming out in 1970, they had incrementally worked their way back up the rock-and-roll ladder. They had paid their dues to remake themselves while growing into an in-demand concert attraction. The Beach Boys and Reprise Records had recently taken advantage of that swelling popularity with a new live double album *The Beach Boys In Concert*, which hit #25 on the album chart in early 1974. But what happened next made that success look very small.

A nostalgia wave had begun to build in America that met its perfect synergistic companion with the summer 1973 film *American Graffiti*. The film followed the ups and downs of a group of high-school seniors on the final night of their school year in 1962. Directed by George Lucas, there was a beautifully bittersweet quality to the story that was nicely enhanced by the classic late-'50s and early-'60s rock music that was its soundtrack. The movie became a huge success; and, by sheer luck, added great momentum to the Beach Boys' building fortunes.

In the film, two Beach Boys songs were placed in pivotal moments that became unforgettable to anyone who saw the movie. "Surfin' Safari" is featured in a hilarious and revealing exchange between actors Paul Le Mat, an aging hot-rodder who can't stand that "surfin' shit," and Mackenzie Phillips, a preteen pixie who thinks the Beach Boys are "bitchin'." It communicated a perfect example of how and why the Beach Boys were both hated and loved in 1962, in 1973, and why they still are today. The second song featured in the film was "All Summer Long," and its choice as the closing music that followed a chilling onscreen epilogue was profound. A silent montage of words and images revealed the reality four key characters faced in the years ahead, and the jarring moment was only magnified by the beautiful innocence that the sound of the Beach Boys represented.

With all of this attention swirling about them, Mike Love caught wind that Capitol Records was planning to release a compilation of 1962–1965 Beach Boys classics in the summer of 1974. Mike suggested the title *Endless Summer*, which was basically the same as a classic 1966 surfing documentary minus the word "the." But that title, the timing of the release, and the 20 songs that were chosen to fill the double album proved to be commercial gold. Released in June 1974, *Endless Summer* was a massive success. It returned the Beach Boys to a level of prominence they had not seen since the golden days of "Good Vibrations."

By October 1974 the *Endless Summer* album had risen to number one on the U.S. album chart, displacing Bad Company's self-titled debut. Over the next several years it would spend an astonishing 155 weeks on the *Billboard* chart, while selling 3,000,000 copies. The album crossed over in every direction and would be seen in the record collections of wildly varied consumers sitting as comfortably alongside Led Zeppelin as Barry Manilow.

In short order, the Beach Boys went from being a popular act that filled large halls and auditoriums in 1973 to a headliner that packed 50,000-plus fans into the biggest stadiums all over the world in 1975. They were voted *Rolling Stone* magazine's "Band of the Year" for 1974, and by summer 1975 they outdrew Mick Jagger and the Rolling Stones while touring in the same markets with their co-headliner Chicago. Suddenly the Beach Boys were back at the very upper echelon of rock artists, just as they had been a decade earlier. They were once again wealthy, and they were household names. And ironically, all of it happened at a time when they had not released an album of new material in years.

Brian's Back

This was the most artificially hyped of the many Beach Boys comebacks. In early 1976, with the residual momentum of the *Endless Summer* success still in play, the Beach Boys upped the ante by announcing Brian Wilson would be producing their next album. Brian had been virtually unseen in more than two years, and hadn't performed with the Beach Boys since 1970, and not regularly since 1964. More importantly, he had not been the Beach Boys' primary record producer since 1967, and had contributed little to their post-1970 output.

Reportedly, Brian was not interested in spending enough time at Brother Studio to truly engage in the project. At first, it was suggested that he record

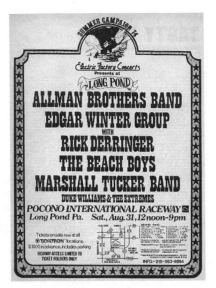

The 1973/1974 Beach Boys often found themselves on concert bills opening for the current crop of FM radio rock favorites, but it never fazed them. Their set included so many beloved '60s-era classics that they could play for two hours and still have encore material to spare. Audiences became so enamored with the Beach Boys performances that by early 1975 no act wanted to follow them. They remained a top-billed attraction from this point forward.

some oldies to "warm up," and then record an album of originals once he had reacclimated to the recording process. A compromise or fallback was put in play when the two ideas were combined to make up the tracks on the July 1976 release of *15 Big Ones*. The album was seen as something of a sellout, and was not a favorite of Brian's brothers Carl and Dennis, who criticized it in the press. But *15 Big Ones* was a comeback in that it was the first album of newly recorded material by the Beach Boys to make the *Billboard* Top Ten since *Pet Sounds* a decade earlier. Even more significant was the Brian-produced single "Rock and Roll Music" which rose to #5, making it the Beach Boys' most successful single release since "Good Vibrations."

America's Band

In the post–"Brian's Back" years, the Beach Boys were beset by internal tensions and substance problems. After the glow of *Endless Summer* had worn off, the band's live concerts had become somewhat shoddily performed, although still well attended. Sales of their new releases had again tanked, earning relatively poor chart performances and worse critical reviews. But all it took were a few negative words from one national political figure, and like magic, the Beach Boys were back in the spotlight and being hailed as "America's Band."

In 1983, Reagan Administration Secretary of the Interior James Watt took it upon himself to inform the press that the Beach Boys had been attracting "the wrong element" to their annual Washington, D.C. Fourth of July concerts. His solution was to ban rock groups from the National Mall Independence Day celebration and invite Las Vegas crooner Wayne Newton as their replacement. The public's reaction to this proclamation was devastating for Watt, and a giant boost for the Beach Boys. Overnight, HONK IF YOU LOVE THE BEACH BOYS signs began appearing in the hands of random protestors in major cities around the U.S. And it seemed like everyone was honking. Even President Reagan blew his horn in support of his fellow Californians and proclaimed that he and Nancy were fans. Reagan publically admonished Watt, who apologized to the Beach Boys; and just like that, another comeback had materialized out of thin air. By 1984, the Beach Boys were back performing in front of 500,000 happy fans at the Washington, D.C. Fourth of July celebration.

"Kokomo"

In 1988, Mike Love and Terry Melcher got together and spruced up an older song originally written by John Phillips (of the Mamas and Papas) and his collaborator Scott McKenzie. The song was called "Kokomo," and told of the tropical delights on a fictitious Caribbean island. It was conceived as a typical trop-rock production, but with classic Beach Boys harmonies added to the obligatory steel-drum–and-conga-driven groove. The Beach Boys had been experiencing little success on the charts in recent years, and were currently without a record contract. Brian Wilson, on the other hand, had recently completed a solo album, which was seeing its much-anticipated release on Sire Records. Just when it seemed likely that 1988 would be Brian's year, Mike Love's "Kokomo" rose from nowhere and eclipsed everything.

"Kokomo" had the good fortune of being placed in a new Tom Cruise film titled *Cocktail.* To take advantage of such, a one-off July 1988 single release was thrown together on Elektra Records, which strangely featured a non–Beach Boys B-side in Little Richard's "Tutti Frutti." More good fortune struck when the "Kokomo" video showing the Beach Boys performing in the sand at a Florida resort was added to MTV's regular rotation. The video, which also featured guest percussionist and full-time heartthrob John Stamos, became one of music television's most requested clips. Simultaneously, adult contemporary radio completely fell in love with "Kokomo," giving it exposure in every dentist office, hotel lobby, supermarket, and tiki bar in America.

While Brian Wilson's 1988 solo LP was getting good reviews but not selling great, "Kokomo" went viral. By November it had overtaken Phil Collins and was sitting in the number-one position on the *Billboard* national singles chart. "Kokomo" was the Beach Boys' first number-one single in the U.S. since "Good Vibrations" 22 years earlier. This represented the longest gap between number ones by any artist in *Billboard* chart history. What it all meant was that somehow, even though they should have been dead and gone ten times over, the Beach Boys had risen to the top of the music business once again. "Kokomo" became the group's biggest hit ever, logging 15 weeks in the U.S. Top Forty, where it went platinum. It also became their biggest hit ever in Australia, reaching number one there, and staying at the top of the charts for two months. Add to that Top Ten chart rankings in Germany, France, Denmark, Sweden, and New Zealand and the picture is clear: "Kokomo" was a worldwide phenomenon.

It must have all been extremely disconcerting for Brian. He'd had no part in the recording of "Kokomo," saying he had not been given adequate notice to make the session. Terry Melcher's production of "Kokomo" does reference Brian's harmonic feel, with Carl singing the hook in a classic Wilson high voice. But the single was undoubtedly Mike's triumph, and he had no problem letting everyone know Brian wasn't involved. To have it occur just as Brian was sticking his toe into the solo waters, and for it to be such a massive international hit, was undoubtedly a shocker for him and his management.

"Kokomo" became so overexposed so quickly that there was an inevitable backlash. Especially since the middle-aged Beach Boys, grinning and swaying in their resort wear, were seen on MTV every day until the song hit brainwash levels of saturation. It also popped up in endless TV shows, including John Stamos's *Full House*, and was even covered by Kermit the Frog and the Muppets, and referenced on *Friends* and *The Simpsons*. It became one of the most celebrated *and* hated songs in popular culture, mirroring the up-and-down fortunes of the Beach Boys. "Kokomo" was not only nominated for a Grammy Award and a Golden Globe Award, but it was voted one of *Blender* magazine's "50 Worst Songs Ever." Despite the controversy, "Kokomo" represents one of the most amazing and unexpected comebacks by any recording artist in history.

Sounds of Summer

In June 2003 Capitol Records released the most extensive Beach Boys single-disc CD compilation to date. It was titled *Sounds of Summer* and included 30 classic hits from their long career. The Beach Boys have likely had more compilations and greatest-hits packages released worldwide than any other recording act, but something about this one struck a chord with consumers. Its release timed nicely with the proliferation of CD sales at mainstream retail chains like Wal-Mart, Target, Best Buy, and Borders. *Sounds of Summer* was one of those ubiquitous items positioned perfectly alongside checkout lines that became something of an impulse buy for shoppers. With its generic sunset cover art behind a golden Beach Boys logo, *Sounds of Summer* became the *Endless Summer* of a new millennium. Despite the Beach Boys not having had a Top Twenty album on the pop charts since 1976, *Sounds of Summer* hit #16 and spent 104 weeks on the *Billboard* album charts. Its sales hit 2,000,000 in 2006. Once again, the Beach Boys had risen to a head-shaking level of commercial success several eras removed from their heyday. When considering their long-term pattern of cyclical comebacks, it seems likely they will never completely fade away.

18

Rhonda, Wendy, Caroline . . . and Those California Girls

Who Were They?

B rian Wilson and the Beach Boys are responsible for some of the most familiar love songs in pop history. They also have a history of failed marriages and inter-band partner swapping. Their connection to those "girls on the beach" and the resulting relationships with them are fascinating in that much of what happened played out in song. It's a blurry line that separates the fantasy from the reality when it comes to Beach Boys' relationship songs.

Did Caroline Really Mean Marilyn?

The ultimate examples of Beach Boys love songs are in the grooves of the magnificently romantic *Pet Sounds* album. It was written with the ups and downs of Brian's first marriage to Marilyn Rovell in mind, but also mainly articulated by his lyricist Tony Asher, who brought his own relationship sagas into the thematic mix. Asher has recounted that while writing the *Pet Sounds* classic "Caroline, No" he was singing a line about an old girlfriend of his with the lyric "Oh Carole, I know," which Brian misheard as "oh Caroline, no." Brian liked it better the second way, and it stuck. But whom was the song actually written about?

Asher claims he'd run into an old flame of his in New York and she'd cut her long hair and changed her appearance, which inspired the song. But Marilyn heard the lyric and believed it was written about her, as she too had recently cut her long hair to a shorter length, and of course Caroline and Marilyn are very similar-sounding names. And then there is Brian's high-school classmate, Carol Mountain, over whom he obsessed for many years. There has long been speculation among Brian's friends that "Caroline,

Brian and his first wife Marilyn Rovell, pictured in 1964. Marilyn was the inspiration for some of Brian's greatest songs. She managed to cope with the severe up-and-down personality of Brian for over 15 years, and refuses to say a bad word about him to this day.

No" was actually written about her. Brian even showed up at her door unannounced in 1966, making for a very uncomfortable reunion. "Caroline, No" is a perfect example of how various legends regarding the source of a classic song can grow and mutate over the years.

Rhonda, You Look So Fine

Sometimes a girl you barely know can become the subject of a classic for the ages. The "Rhonda" celebrated in Brian and Mike's "Help Me, Rhonda" lyric was apparently a one-night stand. No one was jumping up and down to take credit for being the inspiration as both Brian and Mike were married when the song was written. However, the tune did inspire an awful lot of mom and dad's to name their little girls Rhonda, which is slightly creepy considering the subject matter. Interestingly Brian recorded the song twice, and on first take he spelled his subject Ronda, only adding the "h" on his second try. Maybe the mystery girl gave Brian or Mike a call and said something like, "and you didn't even have the courtesy to spell my name right, you cheating bastard!" Just a thought.

Wendy Left Me Alone

Legend has it that Dennis was "dating" a devastatingly hot young girl named Wendy Vines, and her dad Arvy Vines was the manager of the apartment building where Dennis lived. When Mr. Vines caught his teenage daughter sneaking out of Dennis's pad at four AM, there was holy hell to pay. But Dennis, being Dennis, somehow charmed Mr. Vines into a more reasonable state of mind and took him fishing. The two subsequently became regular fishing buddies. The result of this new friendship was Wendy completely losing interest in Dennis and going off with some greasy biker.

At some point, Dennis related the story to Brian and/or Mike, and they took the raw material and sculpted a classic song titled "Wendy." It's one of the many examples of when a Dennis story, anecdote, or idea turned into a Brian and Mike song, much the same way Ringo's quips inspired so many Lennon and McCartney songs. Brian and Marilyn must have really liked the song, or at least the title, as they named their second daughter Wendy in October 1969.

California Girls and More

The Beach Boys catalog is filled with wonderful songs about girls . . . girls on the beach, girls driving T-Birds, girls in colorful clothes, surfer girls, wild honeys, car-crazy cuties, and farmer's daughters. Even though the Beach Boys are thought of as a surfing-, cars-, and summer-themed band, their favorite subject matter was girls by a leg, a long leg. With so many females on their minds, and so much effort made writing about them, they must have become experts on relationships and love. However, the results don't look so good if you examine the Beach Boys' personal lives. The five Beach Boys who were inducted into the Rock and Roll Hall of Fame have had a total of 16 marriages! Mike and Dennis can claim ten of those.

And then there are those rumored examples of the Beach Boys sharing partners and various members of their extended family. Dennis was named in Mike's divorce from his wife Suzanne as an example of her philandering. Dennis's first wife Carol also dated Mike. Brian has

The Beach Boys spent much of their career singing about the many girls who were in and out of their lives. Mike and Dennis were particularly prolific in the romantic-relationships department with ten marriages, countless flings, and numerous illegitimate children to their joint credit.

admitted that his relationship with his wife Marilyn's sister Diane became something more than innocent. He wrote a beautiful song of regret titled "My Diane" that supposedly expressed his grief over losing her. Multiple sources have claimed that all three Wilson brothers were guilty of having dalliances with one or more of the other's wives. Dennis took the "family on family" trend to the nth degree when he married and had a child with Mike's alleged illegitimate daughter Shawn Love. That meant Mike was not only Dennis's first cousin, but also his father-in-law, and his son's grandfather. I get around, indeed.

But to live and love is a part of life, a more entangled part of life for some than others. For the Beach Boys, love was the emotional fuel that ran their creative engine. And girls were the obsession that went far beyond big waves, powerful engines, and fun, fun, fun. Sometimes, as in the case of "Marcella," "Anna Lee, the Healer," and "Susie Cincinnati," it had nothing to do with love, but a simple fascination with unique people who just happened to be female. But more often than not, the Beach Boys laid their souls bare in

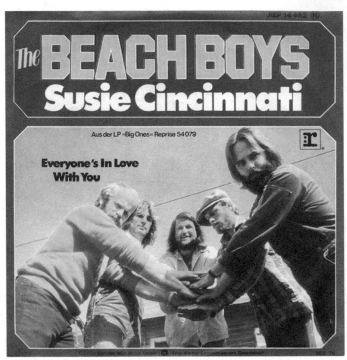

Al Jardine immortalized a chain-smoking cab driver named Susie with this lively single released in 1976. The Beach Boys often found the inspiration for their songs from the everyday women they encountered, and sometimes in a completely platonic way.

song for the women in their lives, who sometimes just happened to also be the women in their bandmates' and brothers' lives, too.

Girl, Don't Tell Me You'll Write

The first time I heard the Beach Boys' 1965 song "Girl Don't Tell Me," or the first time it really penetrated into my being, it nearly made me cry. I was 16 years old and crying was a truly uncool thing to do. But when I heard the song I knew exactly what Brian was trying to communicate with it, and it deeply moved me. Just as the song relates, I'd met a girl in the summer while vacationing on a lake in the California mountains. We enjoyed an intense week of sweet teen passion. Her name was Susan, and I can still feel her warm skin, and soft blonde hair. I was 15 and she was 16. I can remember the thrill of telling my friends back home about this awesome girl I'd met. And I remember the excruciating sadness when she didn't respond to the two letters I wrote her. I was crushed.

The next summer, I went back to the same place with my folks . . . and guess what? Susan was there again, too. Just like in the Beach Boys song, her hair was longer, those shorts fit her fine, and she obviously felt no guilt about not writing me back. I was hurt, but I still told her to jump on the back of my Honda and ride into the woods with me. I made out with her again, and we laughed and ran around together just as we had the year before, but it seemed so hollow in comparison. Deep down, I knew that to Susan I was just temporary fun, and that once I was gone she wouldn't think about me, and wouldn't write me. That was the last time I saw her.

When I heard "Girl Don't Tell Me," it was like the Beach Boys had reached right into my life, into my heart, and into the most personal place where *no one* went. They said, "Yeah, it's sad, Jon, but it's a beautiful sadness." It's that kind of bittersweet sadness you learn to cherish as time goes by. Once life sands away all the rough edges and all the truly new and fresh experiences are in your past, the memories of warm, sparkling summer nights with girls like Susan stand out. And every time I hear the Beach Boys sing "Girl Don't Tell Me," she comes back to me. Thanks to that song I cherish the beautiful sadness I still feel inside, three decades later. When I reflect on things like this I'm sure it may seem silly to some, but I know it's true that Brian Wilson and the Beach Boys gave me so much. Like the chance to revisit how Susan broke my heart, and how time takes that pain and turns it into something kind of sweet.

19

Make It Good

Great Musical Moments by Each Beach Boy

There are an endless number of great moments by each individual Beach Boy that stood out on their records. Here's a selection of some of the best things each guy brought to the table—on songs that will live forever.

Brian Wilson

"We'll Run Away" (lead vocal)

Brian's lead vocal on this beautiful ballad is one of his very best. During the bridge, he sings in his natural lower register with a fantastic vibrato that is hugely appealing.

"Hushabye" (lead vocal)

Brian's voice shines among the great vocal performances by all of the Beach Boys on this amazing cover song. At the 1:45 mark, Brian takes it all to another level with his "pillows lying on your bed . . ." section. It truly is one of his best vocal moments.

"Don't Worry Baby" (lead vocal)

Singing one of pop's most memorable melodies over blissful harmonies sung by he and his brothers, Brian delivered an absolutely timeless classic with this one. There have been many, many cover versions, but Brian sang it better than anyone ever will.

"When I Grow Up (To Be a Man)" (keyboards)

Brian doesn't get a lot of props for his keyboard work; but on this song, his electric-harpsichord flourishes are a major part of the arrangement's charm. This tune is a great example of the self-contained musicianship that the Beach Boys rarely get credit for. "When I Grow Up (To Be a Man)" is all Beach Boys, and it's all great.

"Kiss Me, Baby" (production/arrangement/lead vocal)

The incredible arrangement and production alone on this song should be enough evidence that Brian was the greatest studio artist in pop history. He uses the whole group perfectly, giving crucial vocal roles to each Beach Boy, but saves the most difficult and beautiful parts for himself. A masterpiece.

"Don't Talk (Put Your Head On My Shoulder)" (lead vocal)

A mind-bogglingly gorgeous solo vocal performance by Brian. One of the most perfectly bittersweet songs ever, sung by the only vocalist on Earth who could have done it justice.

"Surf's Up" (lead vocal)

A near-operatic vocal from Brian on perhaps the most compositionally sophisticated pop song ever written. His solo piano performance on the *Leonard Bernstein: Inside Pop—The Rock Revolution* documentary filmed in December 1966 is as deeply spiritual as anything that exists in 20th-century art.

Carl Wilson

"I Get Around" (lead guitar)

Carl's guitar performance on this song nicely defines his dynamic yet economical early style. The solo is uniquely Carl: he darts around choosing quickly plucked double and single notes, some slightly muffled, some stingingly clear. His genius is how he playfully toys with the rhythmic feel, pours out a nice flurry of runs, and makes it all sound as if he's doing it with a laid-back California casualness.

"God Only Knows" (lead vocal)

It's hard to make any list of great rock vocal performances and leave this one out. Carl has a gentle but deeply moving quality that is in peak form on this classic song. Put this in the dictionary to define "perfect."

"Good Vibrations" (lead vocal)

Just having the credit of being the lead vocalist on one of rock's greatest songs is an amazing honor. But Carl is so much more than just a credit. His sublime vocal performance on "Good Vibrations" is a living, breathing gift to all of us. It's a classic sound, a recording for the ages, and Carl's lovely voice is a major part of its enduring charm.

"I Can Hear Music" (lead vocal, production)

Carl created a great-sounding record with this Ronettes cover. His vocal is pure and soulful, and his production is unique in that it sounds like Beach Boys music, but doesn't ape Brian's style too closely.

"Let the Wind Blow"—live 1973 version (lead vocal)

"Otherworldly" is the only way to describe Carl's stunning lead vocal performance on the version of "Let the Wind Blow" included on *The Beach Boys In Concert* album from 1973. It ranks among the best of his career.

"Baby Blue" (lead vocal)

Carl sang lead on a number of Dennis's compositions, and this sweet ballad is among the best of the "Carl sings Dennis" songs. The gentle care with which his voice settles into this beautiful melody is a spiritual gift to anyone who hears it.

Dennis Wilson

"The Girls on the Beach" (lead vocal, middle section)

It's only two lines of an otherwise gorgeous song led by Brian, but when Dennis briefly takes over during the middle eight bars, he absolutely owns it. He manages to communicate a longing, fleeting, sexy vibe, and all with just ten words.

Dennis Wilson might have been underrated as a musician because his wild lifestyle seemed to override everything else. But like Brian, it was the combination of Dennis's sensitivity and intensity that made him unique as a performer and as an artist. His passionate drumming, tender songwriting, and heartfelt vocals contributed mightily to the Beach Boys' body of work.

"When I Grow Up (To Be a Man)" (drums)

For anyone who claims that Dennis was not a good studio drummer, this song is emphatic evidence to the contrary. His playing is both artful and lively, giving the track exactly what it needs, plus a little extra in the passion department.

"Do You Wanna Dance?" (lead vocal)

Dennis was the first Beach Boy other than Mike or Brian to sing the lead vocal on a hit single. His rocking approach gives this song a slightly tougher edge than any Beach Boys release prior to it.

"Be With Me" (production)

This haunting track features truly epic production. That such a dramatic and sweeping sound didn't come from the golden ear of Brian, but from his black sheep brother Dennis, is still hard for some fans to get their minds around.

"Forever" (lead vocal)

There is a genuinely heartfelt quality to Dennis's voice that comes through perfectly on this ballad from the *Sunflower* album. Perhaps he was not as gifted a singer as Carl or Brian; but like his brothers, Dennis had an ability to project earnest and touching emotions into in his vocals that few others can claim. Murry often insisted that his sons sing "from the heart." Dennis might have been the best of the three at hitting that mark.

"Barbara" (lead vocal)

A 1971 Dennis Wilson demo that didn't see the light of day until 1998's *Endless Harmony* documentary, it features one of Dennis's most beautiful vocal performances. His voice was at its purest during this period, but unfortunately much of what he recorded from this era remains unreleased.

"Angel Come Home" (lead vocal)

I'm not sure if Carl wrote this song with Dennis in mind to sing it, but it seems tailor-made for him. Dennis beautifully brings out both a tender and wistful element as well as his rough and rocking side. He wasn't in the best of shape by this time in his career, but the broken-down quality of his voice only adds to this great performance.

Mike Love

"Surfin' U.S.A." (lead vocal)

An iconic song that defines an era, and one big reason why is Mike's definitive lead vocal. He gave the Beach Boys a major part of their early identity with his distinct vocals, and on this song he successfully sold the Beach Boys message to a million kids.

"Fun, Fun, Fun" (lead vocal and lyrics)

Once again, Mike is the singing narrator of an era-defining story in song. His ability to maintain a strong level of musicality and rhythm while reeling off vivid word pictures is reminiscent of Chuck Berry at his best. As in many cases, Mike's lyrics on this classic are extremely underrated because they are so accessible. The underlying inventiveness of how Mike's words are casually rolled out and perfectly placed to enhance the feel of the music is something that is often overlooked, but is crucial to the appeal of a song like "Fun, Fun, Fun."

"The Warmth of the Sun" (lyrics)

Brian's magnificent melody and lead vocal are perfectly enhanced by the tender lyrics written by Mike. Proving conclusively that his ability to write went beyond teen trends and novelties, this song is one of Mike's most artful moments.

"California Girls" (lead vocal)

Another of Mike's signature moments, his lead vocals and lyrics on this song are as significant and recognizable in popular culture as "Stairway to Heaven" or "Hey Jude." Mike may not get the respect that McCartney or Plant do, but his message penetrated the masses just as thoroughly.

"Sloop John B" (lead vocal)

As Brian's fabulous arrangement unfolds one piece at a time, momentum builds, Brian sings, harmonies join him, and the whole thing finally hits its stride just as Mike Love takes over the lead vocal. The reason is that Mike's voice has become such a signature element in the Beach Boys sound that when you hear it, you *know* all the cylinders are firing.

"All I Wanna Do" (lead vocal)

Even among the biggest Mike Love detractors, this *Sunflower* track seems to be a unanimous favorite. There is a softer quality to Mike's voice on this one that he rarely duplicated. It stands as one of his best lead vocals.

"California Saga: Big Sur" (lead vocal)

Mike takes a country-folk approach on this song, and surprisingly makes it work. Versatility is not a word that one often uses to describe Mike's vocals, but this track from the *Holland* album actually *does* show that Mike could be a broad-ranged performer when choosing to stretch out a bit.

Al Jardine

"Catch a Wave" (bass)

Few fans are aware that Al played bass on more Beach Boys classics than he did guitar. This song's deep groove is enhanced by Al's simple but effective bass performance.

"Help Me, Rhonda" (lead vocal)

Al is a great singer in a band of great singers, and sometimes his contributions are overlooked. But no one can overlook this classic pop moment, when Al was truly given a chance to shine. His dynamic lead vocal on the number-one hit single version of "Help Me, Rhonda" seems an even greater achievement with the knowledge that a drunken Murry Wilson was in the studio hassling him while he was recording it.

"Cotton Fields" (lead vocal, production)

Al took this traditional, classic folk tune and made it his own. After Brian had tried a version with Al on lead vocal, Jardine took another crack at it, dialing up both the country and the Beach Boys' harmony elements. His instinct proved excellent, as it became a significant international hit.

"Lookin' at Tomorrow (A Welfare Song)" (lead vocal)

An appealing showcase for Al's distinctive voice. He'd apparently written this song with his friend Gary Winfrey many years before its eventual release on the *Surf's Up* album. Al's vocal quality is well suited for the folk-flavored vibe that this tune offers.

"Lady Lynda" (lead vocal)

Al brings his signature vocal quality to this performance that certainly stands out on the group's *L.A. (Light Album)*. There is a clarity and presence to Al's voice that becomes more recognizable as some of the other Beach Boys vocal abilities begin to deteriorate. Since Al never abused his vocal cords with cigarettes, alcohol, or drugs, his voice remains in excellent condition to this day.

David Marks

"Surfin' U.S.A." (rhythm guitar)

The great rhythm-guitar performance adds an essential texture to Brian's production of this classic track. Beach Boys fans have often underappreciated David's guitar contributions to the early years. There was a unique rocking element that his playing gave the band. When he was gone, it was gone.

"Let's Go Trippin'" (rhythm guitar)

On this Dick Dale cover from the *Surfin' U.S.A.* album, David lends excellent support to Carl's lead, with much more than a straight rhythm performance. Dave's ringing chords and surf licks help the two guitars create an interlocking and weaving sound that makes it hard to tell where one starts and the other ends. That's called jamming.

"In My Room" (rhythm guitar)

Dave's smooth chording on this song is fairly subtle in the mix at first, as Carl's arpeggios stand out. But as the song builds, David's guitar becomes the more prominent sound. To basically be the primary instrumental bed supporting one of rock's greatest vocal blends proves a notable moment for David.

"Your Summer Dream" (rhythm guitar)

David takes the main guitar role on this song with his dreamy chording. He chose his old Silvertone acoustic to create the unique sound, giving the song its perfect vintage texture.

Bruce Johnston

"Girl Don't Tell Me" (celesta)

Bruce's delicate keyboard performance on this song is both tasteful and essential. His ringing celesta gives the production a big piece of its magic.

Although there's nothing fancy in his playing, the result of his effort is notable because it's a standout part of a classic track.

"The Nearest Faraway Place" (keyboards, production)

This song is a sublime trip into the land of melody with Bruce and his keyboards. To write it off as "easy listening" ignores the craftsmanship involved in a song of this quality. It's beautiful and impressive in every way.

"At My Window" (lead vocal)

A perfectly whimsical vocal delivery from Bruce gives this *Sunflower* song just the right vibe. There is a near Syd Barrett–like quality audible as this track veers from childlike to slightly warped and back, and Bruce's sweet voice is a big reason why it all works so well.

"Disney Girls (1957)" (production/arrangement/lead vocal)

Bruce has done some great work in his long career in music, but topping this classic song will be impossible. Not only is it a fantastic composition, it is also a masterpiece of production and arrangement. Add to that the excellent lead-vocal performance by Bruce, and you have his finest moment as a Beach Boy.

Blondie Chaplin

"Wild Honey"—live 1972 version (lead vocal)

To include this is kind of cheating the premise, as the Beach Boys never "officially" released this song with Blondie on lead. But it was included in their *Good Vibrations From London* TV special, and Blondie's vocal on it is an incredible thing to behold. "Soulful" doesn't even begin to describe the primal fury with which he belts out the classic Brian Wilson composition. If you haven't heard it, find it.

"Sail On Sailor" (lead vocal)

It's impossible to mention Blondie Chaplin without giving him props for one of rock's iconic lead-vocal performances. If he had done nothing else in his career, this vocal would be enough to give him a major claim to rock and roll glory. It's a classic; he nailed it, sail on, Blondie.

Ricky Fataar

"Funky Pretty"—live 1973 version (drums)

Ricky put down some great drum tracks for the Beach Boys during his two-and-a-half years with the band. This track from *The Beach Boys In Concert* stands out because Brian, not Ricky, played the skins on the *Holland* studio version of "Funky Pretty" in an exceedingly minimal form. To hear Ricky stretch the feel of the song out a bit with some excellent drumming is a revelation.

"River Song" (drums)

This is another choice that is out of the usual boundaries because it was released on Dennis Wilson's solo album, and not by the Beach Boys. But Ricky's drum performance on Dennis's epic "River Song" may be the single best drum track on any Beach Boys–related song through their entire 50 years. It's that good.

20

We're Singin' That Same Song

A Guide to Which Beach Boy Sang Which Song

The following is a guide to which member of the Beach Boys sang lead on each specific song. It is a difficult thing to sort out because nearly every Beach Boys song features multiple vocalists, particularly on the background harmonies. This list concentrates specifically on LEAD vocals, or significant solo vocal lines. The use of "and" and "with" separates a primary lead vocalist from a co-lead vocalist with a smaller role in the song. Hopefully this list will help illustrate the incredible vocal depth the group possessed, and how all of the Beach Boys had major roles as lead vocalists.

Surfin' Safari—1962

"Surfin' Safari"—Mike
"County Fair"—Mike
"Ten Little Indians"—Mike
"Chug-A-Lug"—Mike
"Little Girl (You're My Miss America)"—Dennis
"409"—Mike
"Surfin"—Mike
"Heads You Win, Tails I Lose"—Mike
"Summertime Blues"—Carl and David, with Mike
"Cuckoo Clock"—Brian
"The Shift"—Mike

Surfin' U.S.A.—1963

"Surfin' U.S.A."—Mike
"Farmer's Daughter"—Brian

"Lonely Sea"—Brian, with Mike and Dennis
"Shut Down"—Mike
"Noble Surfer"—Mike
"Lana"—Brian
"Finders Keepers"—Mike, with Brian

Surfer Girl—1963

"Surfer Girl"—Brian
"Catch a Wave"—Mike, with Brian
"The Surfer Moon"—Brian
"South Bay Surfer"—Mike and Brian
"In My Room"—Brian, with Carl and Dennis
"Little Deuce Coupe"—Mike
"Hawaii"—Mike and Brian
"Surfers Rule"—Dennis, with Brian
"Our Car Club"—Mike and Brian
"Your Summer Dream"—Brian

Little Deuce Coupe—1963

"Little Deuce Coupe"—Mike
"The Ballad of Ole' Betsy"—Brian
"Be True To Your School"—Mike
"Car Crazy Cutie"—Brian
"Cherry, Cherry Coupe"—Mike
"409"—Mike
"Shut Down"—Mike
"Spirit of America"—Brian
"Our Car Club"—Mike and Brian
"No-Go Showboat"—Brian and Mike
"A Young Man Is Gone"—Brian, Carl, Mike, and Al
"Custom Machine"—Mike

Shut Down Volume Two—1964

"Fun, Fun, Fun"—Mike
"Don't Worry Baby"—Brian
"In the Parkin' Lot"—Mike
"The Warmth of the Sun"—Brian
"This Car of Mine"—Dennis

"Why Do Fools Fall In Love"—Brian
"Pom, Pom Play Girl"—Carl, with Mike
"Keep an Eye on Summer"—Brian, with Mike
"Louie, Louie"—Carl and Mike

All Summer Long—1964

"I Get Around"—Mike and Brian
"All Summer Long"—Mike
"Hushabye"—Brian and Mike
"Little Honda"—Mike and Dennis
"We'll Run Away"—Brian
"Wendy"—Brian and Mike
"Do You Remember?"—Mike and Brian
"Girls on the Beach"—Brian and Dennis
"Drive-In"—Mike
"Don't Back Down"—Mike and Brian

Beach Boys Concert—1964

"Fun, Fun, Fun"—Mike
"The Little Old Lady From Pasadena"—Mike
"Little Deuce Coupe"—Mike
"Long Tall Texan"—Mike
"In My Room"—Brian
"Monster Mash"—Mike
"Papa-Oom-Mow-Mow"—Brian and Mike
"The Wanderer"—Dennis
"Hawaii"—Mike and Brian
"Graduation Day"—Brian, Mike, Carl, Al, and Dennis
"I Get Around"—Mike and Brian
"Johnny B. Goode"—Mike and Brian

The Beach Boys' Christmas Album—1964

"Little Saint Nick"—Mike, with Brian
"The Man With All the Toys"—Mike and Brian
"Santa's Beard"—Mike
"Merry Christmas, Baby"—Mike
"Christmas Day"—Al
"Frosty the Snowman"—Brian

"We Three Kings of Orient Are"—Mike and Brian
"Blue Christmas"—Brian
"Santa Claus Is Coming to Town"—Brian and Mike
"I'll Be Home for Christmas"—Brian
"White Christmas"—Brian
"Auld Lang Syne"—Brian, Dennis, Carl, Mike, and Al (spoken message by Dennis)

The Beach Boys Today!—1965

"Do You Wanna Dance?" —Dennis
"Good to My Baby"—Brian and Mike
"Don't Hurt My Little Sister"—Mike and Brian
"When I Grow Up (To Be a Man)"—Mike and Brian
"Help Me, Ronda"—Al
"Dance, Dance, Dance"—Mike and Brian
"Please Let Me Wonder"—Brian and Mike
"I'm So Young"—Brian
"Kiss Me, Baby"—Mike and Brian
"She Knows Me Too Well"—Brian
"In the Back of My Mind"—Dennis

Carl Wilson was never volatile like his brother Dennis, and never eccentric like his brother Brian. Carl instead possessed a calmness and self-control that made him a superior stage leader and a reliable producer in the studio. He was also an excellent guitarist whose style inspired other musicians and helped define the Beach Boys' early sound. But any list of Carl's attributes begins and ends with his amazing voice. It was simply one of the best in rock history.

Summer Days (And Summer Nights!!)—1965

"The Girl from New York City"—Mike
"Amusement Parks U.S.A."—Mike, with Brian
"Then I Kissed Her"—Al
"Salt Lake City"—Mike, with Brian
"Girl Don't Tell Me"—Carl
"Help Me, Rhonda"—Al
"California Girls"—Mike and Brian
"Let Him Run Wild"—Brian
"You're So Good to Me"—Brian
"I'm Bugged at My Ol' Man"—Brian
"And Your Dream Comes True"—Brian, Carl, Mike, and Al

Beach Boys' Party!—1965

"Hully Gully"—Mike
"I Should Have Known Better"—Carl and Al
"Tell Me Why"—Carl and Al
"Papa-Oom-Mow-Mow"—Brian and Mike
"Mountain of Love"—Mike
"You've Got to Hide Your Love Away"—Dennis
"Devoted to You"—Mike and Brian
"Alley Oop"—Mike
"There's No Other (Like My Baby)"—Brian
"I Get Around"/"Little Deuce Coupe"—Mike
"The Times They Are a-Changin'"—Al
"Barbara Ann"—Brian and Dean Torrence, with Mike

Pet Sounds—1966

"Wouldn't It Be Nice"—Brian and Mike
"You Still Believe in Me"—Brian
"That's Not Me"—Mike with Brian
"Don't Talk (Put Your Head On My Shoulder)"—Brian
"I'm Waiting for the Day"—Brian
"Sloop John B"—Brian and Mike
"God Only Knows"—Carl, with Brian and Bruce
"I Know There's an Answer"—Mike, Al, and Brian
"Here Today"—Mike
"I Just Wasn't Made For These Times"—Brian
"Caroline, No"—Brian

Smiley Smile—1967

"Heroes and Villains"—Brian, with Al and Mike
"Vegetables"—Brian, Al, and Mike
"She's Goin' Bald"—Mike, Brian, Al, and Dennis
"Little Pad"—Mike, Carl, and Brian
"Good Vibrations"—Carl, Mike, and Brian
"With Me Tonight"—Carl
"Wind Chimes"—Mike, Brian, Carl, and Dennis
"Gettin' Hungry"—Mike and Brian
"Wonderful"—Carl, with Mike
"Whistle In"—Carl and Mike

Wild Honey—1967

"Wild Honey"—Carl
"Aren't You Glad"—Mike, Brian, and Carl
"I Was Made to Love Her"—Carl
"Country Air"—Carl, Brian, and Al
"A Thing or Two"—Mike, Carl, Brian, and Bruce
"Darlin'"—Carl
"I'd Love Just Once to See You"—Brian
"Here Comes the Night"—Brian
"Let the Wind Blow"—Mike, Brian, and Carl
"How She Boogalooed It"—Carl
"Mama Says"—Mike, Brian, Carl, and Al

Friends—1968

"Meant For You"—Mike
"Friends"—Carl, with Brian
"Wake the World"—Brian, Mike, and Carl
"Be Here in the Morning"—Al, Carl, and Brian
"When a Man Needs a Woman"—Brian
"Passing By"—Brian, Carl, and Al
"Anna Lee, the Healer"—Mike, Al, Brian, and Carl
"Little Bird"—Dennis, with Carl and Brian
"Be Still"—Dennis
"Busy Doin' Nothin'"—Brian
"Transcendental Meditation"—Brian

20/20—1969

"Do It Again"—Mike, with Carl
"I Can Hear Music"—Carl
"Bluebirds Over the Mountain"—Mike, Carl, and Bruce
"Be With Me"—Dennis
"All I Want to Do"—Mike
"Cotton Fields"—Al
"I Went to Sleep"—Brian and Carl
"Time to Get Alone"—Carl, Brian, and Al
"Never Learn Not to Love"—Dennis
"Our Prayer"—Brian, Dennis, Carl, Mike, Al, and Bruce
"Cabin Essence"—Carl, with Mike and Dennis

Live in London—1969

"Darlin'"—Carl
"Wouldn't It Be Nice"—Al and Mike
"Sloop John B"—Carl and Mike
"California Girls"—Mike, with Al and Bruce
"Do It Again"—Mike, Carl, and Al
"Wake the World"—Carl, Mike, and Al
"Aren't You Glad"—Mike, Carl, and Al
"Bluebirds Over the Mountain"—Mike, Carl, Al, and Bruce
"Their Hearts Were Full of Spring"—Mike, Carl, Al, and Bruce
"Good Vibrations"—Carl and Mike
"God Only Knows"—Carl
"Barbara Ann"—Al, with Mike and Carl

Sunflower—1970

"Slip On Through"—Dennis
"This Whole World"—Carl
"Add Some Music To Your Day"—Mike, Bruce, Brian, Carl, and Al, with
    Dennis
"Got to Know the Woman"—Dennis
"Deirdre"—Bruce
"It's About Time"—Carl and Mike
"Tears in the Morning"—Bruce
"Forever"—Dennis, with Brian
"All I Wanna Do"—Mike, with Brian
"Our Sweet Love"—Carl
"At My Window"—Bruce
"Cool, Cool Water"—Mike and Brian, with Carl

Surf's Up—1971

"Don't Go Near the Water"—Mike and Al
"Long Promised Road"—Carl
"Take a Load Off Your Feet"—Brian and Al
"Disney Girls (1957)"—Bruce
"Student Demonstration Time"—Mike
"Feel Flows"—Carl
"Lookin' at Tomorrow (A Welfare Song)"—Al
"A Day in the Life of a Tree"—Jack Rieley, with Van Dyke Parks and Al

Mike Love possesses one of the most distinctive voices in pop music. As the group's primary lead singer, he helped the Beach Boys become instantly identifiable on the radio. Despite being a sometimes controversial and divisive figure, Mike's great singing and classic lyrics are a big reason why the Beach Boys attained their iconic stature.

"'Til I Die"—Brian, Carl, and Mike
"Surf's Up"—Carl, Brian, and Al

Carl and the Passions—"So Tough"—1972

"You Need a Mess of Help to Stand Alone"—Carl
"Here She Comes"—Ricky and Blondie
"He Come Down"—Mike, Blondie, Al, and Carl
"Marcella"—Carl and Mike
"Hold On Dear Brother"—Blondie
"Make It Good"—Dennis
"All This Is That"—Carl, Al, and Mike
"Cuddle Up"—Dennis

Holland—1972

"Sail On Sailor"—Blondie
"Steamboat"—Carl, with Dennis
"Big Sur"—Mike
"The Beaks of Eagles"—Mike and Al
"California"—Mike, with Brian, Al, and Carl
"The Trader"—Carl
"Leaving This Town"—Blondie
"Only With You"—Carl
"Funky Pretty"—Carl, Al, Blondie, Ricky, and Mike
"Mount Vernon and Fairway (A Fairy Tale)"—Carl, Brian, Mike, and
    Blondie, with Jack Rieley

In Concert—1973

"Sail On Sailor"—Blondie
"Sloop John B"—Carl and Mike
"The Trader"—Carl
"You Still Believe in Me"—Al
"California Girls"—Mike, Al, and Carl
"Darlin'"—Carl
"Marcella"—Carl and Mike
"Caroline, No"—Carl
"Leaving This Town"—Blondie
"Heroes and Villains"—Al and Carl
"Funky Pretty"—Carl, Al, Blondie, Ricky, and Mike

"Let the Wind Blow"—Carl
"Help Me, Rhonda"—Al
"Surfer Girl"—Al, Carl, Mike, Dennis, and Billy Hinsche
"Wouldn't It Be Nice"—Al and Mike
"We Got Love"—Ricky and Blondie
"Don't Worry Baby"—Al and Carl
"Surfin' U.S.A."—Mike
"Good Vibrations"—Carl and Mike
"Fun, Fun, Fun"—Mike

15 Big Ones—1976

"Rock and Roll Music"—Mike
"It's OK"—Mike, with Dennis
"Had to Phone Ya"—Mike, Al, Carl, Dennis, and Brian
"Chapel of Love"—Brian
"Everyone's in Love With You"—Mike
"Talk to Me"/"Tallahassee Lassie"—Carl
"That Same Song"—Brian
"TM Song"—Al
"Palisades Park"—Carl
"Susie Cincinnati"—Al
"A Casual Look"—Mike and Al
"Blueberry Hill"—Mike
"Back Home"—Brian
"In the Still of the Night"—Dennis
"Just Once in My Life"—Carl and Brian

The Beach Boys Love You—1977

"Let Us Go On This Way"—Carl and Mike
"Roller Skating Child"—Mike, Al, and Carl
"Mona"—Dennis, with Brian
"Johnny Carson"—Mike and Carl
"Good Time"—Brian
"Honkin' Down the Highway"—Al
"Ding Dang"—Mike, with Carl
"Solar System"—Brian
"The Night Was So Young"—Carl
"I'll Bet He's Nice"—Dennis, Brian, and Carl
"Let's Put Our Hearts Together"—Brian and Marilyn Wilson

"I Wanna Pick You Up"—Dennis and Brian
"Airplane"—Mike, Brian, and Carl
"Love Is a Woman"—Brian, Mike, and Al

M.I.U. Album—1978

"She's Got Rhythm"—Brian and Mike
"Come Go With Me"—Al
"Hey Little Tomboy"—Mike, Brian, and Carl
"Kona Coast"—Mike, Al, and Brian
"Peggy Sue"—Al
"Sweet Sunday Kind of Love"—Carl
"Wontcha Come Out Tonight?"—Brian and Mike
"Belles of Paris"—Mike
"Pitter Patter"—Mike and Al
"My Diane"—Dennis, with Brian
"Match Point of Our Love"—Brian
"Winds of Change"—Al and Mike

L.A. (Light Album)—1979

"Good Timin'"—Carl
"Lady Lynda"—Al
"Full Sail"—Carl
"Angel Come Home"—Dennis
"Love Surrounds Me"—Dennis
"Sumahama"—Mike
"Here Comes the Night"—Carl and Al
"Baby Blue"—Carl and Dennis
"Goin' South"—Carl
"Shortenin' Bread"—Carl and Dennis

Keepin' the Summer Alive—1980

"Keepin' the Summer Alive"—Carl
"Oh Darlin'"—Carl and Mike
"Some of Your Love"—Mike and Carl
"Livin' With a Heartache"—Carl
"School Day (Ring! Ring! Goes the Bell)"—Al
"Goin' On"—Mike and Carl, with Brian
"Sunshine"—Mike, Brian, and Carl
"When Girls Get Together"—Mike, Brian, and Carl

"Santa Ana Winds"—Al and Mike
"Endless Harmony"—Bruce and Carl

The Beach Boys—1985

"Getcha Back"—Mike, with Brian
"It's Gettin' Late"—Carl
"Crack At Your Love"—Al and Brian
"Maybe I Don't Know"—Carl
"She Believes In Love Again"—Bruce and Carl
"California Calling"—Mike and Al
"Passing Friend"—Carl
"I'm So Lonely"—Brian and Carl
"Where I Belong"—Carl and Al
"I Do Love You"—Carl and Al
"It's Just a Matter of Time"—Brian and Mike

Still Cruisin'—1989

"Still Cruisin'"—Mike and Carl, with Al and Bruce
"Somewhere Near Japan"—Mike, Carl, and Al, with Bruce
"Island Girl"—Carl, Al, and Mike
"In My Car"—Brian, Carl, and Al
"Kokomo"—Mike and Carl
"Wipe Out"—Damon Wimbley, Darren Robinson, Mark Morales, and Brian
"Make It Big"—Carl, Mike, and Al, with Brian

Summer in Paradise—1992

"Hot Fun in the Summertime"—Mike and Carl, with Adrian Baker
"Surfin"—Mike and Carl
"Summer of Love"—Mike
"Island Fever"—Mike, with Carl and Al
"Still Surfin'"—Mike, with Adrian Baker
"Slow Summer Dancin' (One Summer Night)"—Bruce and Al
"Strange Things Happen"—Mike and Al, with Carl
"Remember (Walkin' in the Sand)"—Carl and Al, with Mike
"Lahaina Aloha"—Mike and Carl
"Under the Boardwalk"—Mike and Carl
"Summer in Paradise"—Mike
"Forever"—John Stamos, with Mike and Carl

21

White Punks Play Tonight

A Select List of Important Beach Boys Concerts

(co-written with Ian Rusten)

T he concert dates highlighted below are a sampling of some of the more notable shows in the band's long history. Considering there have been close to 5,000 shows performed under the Beach Boys banner between 1961 and 2011, it would be impossible to name the best, or even the most important, handful of performances. The concerts listed here are all very significant for one reason or another. To have attended any one of them is to have witnessed an important moment in the Beach Boys' history.

Long Beach Municipal Auditorium, Long Beach, California, Dec 31, 1961

With a single on the local charts, the Beach Boys made their first professional concert appearance (other than a brief unpaid walk-on during an earlier Dick Dale concert) at the "Ritchie Valens Memorial Dance and Show" on the last night of 1961. While the still-green group probably made little impact on the crowd, most of whom were there to see headliners Ike and Tina Turner, the Beach Boys themselves never forgot this concert for which they were each paid $60 in cash.

Big Reggie's Danceland, Excelsior, Minnesota, May 3, 1963

With the single "Surfin' U.S.A." heading up the charts, the Beach Boys hit the road for their first real tour outside California in April and May 1963. It was hardly a glamorous affair. The band traveled together in one small car and had no roadies to help them lug their instruments and amps back and forth from gig to gig. Nevertheless, the still-teenage Beach Boys had a blast, and Mike Love has frequently referred to this concert on the shores of Lake Minnetonka as the moment when he knew the group had really made it. Not only did the show sell out, but cars full of fans eager to catch a glimpse of the California phenomenon created a four-mile-long traffic jam along the highway!

Fox Theater, Brooklyn, New York, August 30, 1963

The Beach Boys complete a grueling six-week tour with this Murray the K–promoted concert, their first in New York. This was a wonderfully varied bill, with Stevie Wonder, Smokey Robinson and the Miracles, the Drifters, the Beach Boys, Jay and the Americans, and Gene Pitney all sharing the same stage. This show also has historical significance because David Marks and Murry Wilson got into a confrontation while traveling to this concert,

The Beach Boys pictured performing at the T.A.M.I. Show concert in October 1964. This was the apex of their classic striped-shirt era, with Brian front and center during his most dynamic period as a live performer. Within a few months Brian retired from regular live performances, avoiding the stage for over a decade.

which led to David's departure in the months ahead. "Surfer Girl" was the Beach Boys' hit single at the time of this show.

Memorial Auditorium, Sacramento, California, December 21, 1963

This was the first of three concerts recorded for, and used in part on, the group's massively successful *Beach Boys Concert* LP released in late 1964. Those who witnessed the early Sacramento concerts insist that they were

The Sacramento Municipal Auditorium is significant in the history of the Beach Boys as it was the site of some of their most frenzied fan reaction during the band's first years of fame. Capitol Records took advantage of this popularity hot spot by recording several Beach Boys shows there and releasing the exciting *Beach Boys Concert* album, which went to number one in 1964.

the site of the most frenzied fan reaction that the Beach Boys had received to date. It was at this show that the iconic introduction of the band was rendered by concert promoter Fred Vail. Less than two months prior to this date, Al Jardine officially replaced David Marks as the fifth Beach Boy.

Teenage Music International Show, Santa Monica, California, October 28–29, 1964

The Beach Boys were at the height of their popularity when they took part in this phenomenal musical event. Director Steve Binder filmed exciting performances by a once-in-a-lifetime concert lineup that included the Beach Boys, the Rolling Stones, Jan and Dean, James Brown, Marvin Gaye, the Supremes, Chuck Berry, and others. Since Brian Wilson was soon to quit touring with the band, this film is our best document of what the original lineup was like onstage. Based on this evidence, they kicked ass! The resulting footage was shown in movie theaters across the world, and is now available on DVD.

Hammersmith Odeon, London, U.K., November 14, 1966

With both the *Pet Sounds* LP and the "Good Vibrations" single near the top of the U.K. charts, the Beach Boys were greeted in London as superstars, even momentarily eclipsing the popularity of the Beatles. These Hammersmith Odeon shows were the epicenter of a Beach Boys groundswell that saw many of Britain's top celebrities standing in line to see the California singing group. This may have been the very peak of the Beach Boys' worldwide popularity.

Finsbury Park Astoria, London, U.K., December 8, 1968

The Beach Boys went through a rough period in the U.S. in the late '60s, with declining record sales and fewer fans turning up for gigs. But across the pond, the Beach Boys' British fans remained loyal as the group flew over seven times between 1966 and 1972 for concert tours and TV appearances. The two shows that the Beach Boys performed this night were taped and released in the U.K. in 1970 on an LP called *Live in London*. Fans in the U.S. had to wait until 1976 to hear this exciting concert album, which showcases the touring group's amazing ability to re-create their beautiful vocal harmonies onstage.

Beverly Hilton Hotel, Beverly Hills, California, April 18, 1969

All of the Beach Boys, except Mike Love, attended Hawthorne High School, and the group graciously agreed to play at their alma mater's senior-prom dance for a fraction of the pay that they usually received for gigs. The group got into the spirit of the occasion, providing an opening act for no extra cost and even donning formal tuxedos. Attending fans say the band seemed to have a blast. It was quite a night for the students as well. Few, if any other high-school graduating classes, can boast that one of the top bands in the world played their senior dance!

Seattle Opera House, Seattle, Washington, February 28, 1970

When Mike Love suddenly came down with an illness, the increasingly reclusive Brian Wilson volunteered to take his place for a short but memorable Pacific Northwest tour. A low-quality tape of this concert survives and shows what the band might have sounded like if Brian had continued to tour with them regularly. With his high falsetto still in good shape, he adds a spark to the harmonies that was often lacking at concerts without him. The performance of their new single "Add Some Music To Your Day" is a highlight, with Brian singing both his own and Mike's parts.

Whisky a Go Go, Hollywood, California, November 4–7, 1970

The group took on a four-day residence at the legendary Sunset Strip location, playing a total of eight shows. Considering the Whisky has a capacity of less than 400, and even though the Beach Boys' popularity was at its low ebb, lines formed around the block, making it a standing-room-only situation. Brian even participated in the initial three performances, and then removed himself for the balance of the gigs. The result was a positive buzz created around L.A. regarding the Beach Boys. This was the start of something good.

Carnegie Hall, New York, February 24, 1971

The Beach Boys appeared at New York's prestigious Carnegie Hall and showed they still had what it took. The show marked the beginning of a long road back to superstardom. Two shows were originally planned, but only one was performed as not enough tickets were sold for a second. By 1976, the Beach Boys were playing three SRO shows at the much-larger Madison Square Garden, an amazing comeback. From has-beens to one of the biggest-grossing tour acts on the planet in five years time, and the comeback really started with this Carnegie Hall gig. People who were there swear it was one of the Beach Boys' best shows ever. With Carl and Dennis peaking artistically and both in great physical shape, and with Mike, Al, and Bruce all nicely contributing as well, it is easy to believe it.

Fillmore East, New York, April 27, 1971

At the behest of manager Jack Rieley, the Beach Boys took a surprise guest spot at a Grateful Dead show at the Fillmore East concert hall. It was a roll of the dice, as the Beach Boys were not known for being popular with the Dead's loyal audience. But Jerry Garcia welcomed them perfectly by announcing to the semi-stunned crowd that the Beach Boys were "fellow Californians," which immediately reminded everyone of the common ground the bands shared. The music was a little sloppy as the two groups performed together, but everyone seemed to have fun. Then the Dead allowed the Beach Boys to perform "Good Vibrations" and "I Get Around" on their own, and the crowd reaction just got better. The Dead joined them again for a shared encore; and by the end the audience, which included Bob Dylan, was standing and cheering.

Wollman Skating Rink, Central Park, New York, July 2–3, 1971

Director John Moffitt captured exciting footage of the Beach Boys, in the prime of their performing careers, which was used in the TV special *Good Vibrations From Central Park*. Taped over two nights, with the group wearing the same clothes to give the illusion that it all happened in one, the special also included Ike and Tina Turner, Carly Simon, and Boz Scaggs—but it was the Beach Boys who stole the show with great performances of "Heroes and Villains," "Good Vibrations," and "Okie from Muskogee." The highlight, however, was when Dennis Wilson took the microphone for a soulful rendering of his *Sunflower* ballad "Forever," a truly unforgettable concert moment.

Madison Square Garden, New York, December 19, 1973

The 1972–1973 Beach Boys lineup that included guitarist Blondie Chaplin and drummer Ricky Fataar is the favorite of many hardcore Beach Boys fans. For that two-year stint, the band became one of the hottest concert-hall and arena attractions in the U.S. Although their popularity had seriously waned in the late '60s, several years of hard work and blown-away audiences began to turn the tide by late 1973. This Madison Square Garden concert was one of Blondie Chaplin's last with the Beach Boys. A backstage physical encounter with Mike Love's brother Steve ultimately led to Blondie's permanent departure.

The Beachago Tour, United States, May–July 1975

Thanks to four years of hard work and a little bit of luck, the Beach Boys were back on top of the world by 1975, when they teamed up with superstar group Chicago for this fondly remembered tour. The Beach Boys were frequently criticized in the 1960s for their deficiencies as performers; but by 1975, they had truly developed into an exciting live band. Frontman Mike Love danced around the stage in a gold- and silver-spangled jacket, while Dennis Wilson pounded out the beat with ferocious energy, baby brother Carl played mean licks on his guitar, and stoic Al Jardine kept the harmonies on track. With then-manager James William Guercio on bass and a five-piece horn section behind them, the Beach Boys really rocked! The encore performances featuring both bands onstage at once are still talked about with awe.

Midsummer Music, Wembley Stadium, London, U.K., June 21, 1975

The Beach Boys took a short break from the wildly successful Beachago Tour and flew to London to open for Elton John at Wembley Stadium. Unfortunately for Elton, the Beach Boys played what has been described as one the most well-received sets of their career, absolutely slaying the packed stadium with hit after hit after hit. By the time Elton took the stage, he had no chance of equaling what had just happened, and though he was at the height of his popularity, many fans left the venue during his set. The Beach Boys gained a reputation as headliners and nothing else, as no one wanted to follow them.

Oakland Coliseum, Oakland, California, July 2, 1976

As the Beach Boys hit a popularity peak by regularly selling out stadiums across the U.S. and releasing a hit single with "Rock and Roll Music," their 1976 summer tour needed one thing to make it even bigger . . . Brian Wilson. The reclusive Beach Boys leader hadn't been on stage performing with the boys since 1970, and that was brief. In truth he hadn't been a regular on stage since the end of 1964. It was on this sunny summer day in 1976 that Brian really came back. Several songs into the Beach Boys' set, he suddenly appeared behind a grand piano, playing along and smoking cigarettes as the band rocked out. Only some in the happy crowd of 50,000 plus realized the significance of the moment.

Central Park, New York, September 1, 1977

A free concert was given in New York's Central Park, drawing an estimated 150,000 fans. Few in the crowd knew of the tensions growing between members of the band. Although the concert came off well, prior to the flight out of New York the two battling factions within the band got into a

During his prime years, Dennis Wilson was often the fans' focal point during Beach Boys shows. His good looks and natural charisma made him easily the most popular of the Beach Boys with their female audience.   *Photo by Henry Diltz*

huge disagreement on the runway tarmac before boarding their separate planes. The Wilson faction (Dennis and Carl) and the Love/Jardine faction engaged in an ugly shouting match and nearly came to blows, with Brian in the middle being tugged at from both sides. To make things worse, it all happened in front of a *Rolling Stone* magazine reporter who spilled the entire story in the next issue.

Radio City Music Hall, New York, March 1, 1979

The group played a series of four nights at the famous Radio City Music Hall in New York to promote their new release *L.A. (Light Album)*. Despite the celebratory atmosphere surrounding the glitzy event, the Beach Boys were actually booed when they performed their new single, which was a full-blown disco arrangement of their 1967 song "Here Comes the Night." The disco song proved to be so unpopular that the band dropped it from their set within days. Brian only appeared with the band on the first night.

Knebworth Festival, Knebworth, U.K., June 21, 1980

The Beach Boys returned to the U.K. in 1980 for a short but memorable tour, capped by this one-off performance at the massive Knebworth Festival. Filmed for posterity, the concert featured all six Beach Boys, including Brian Wilson. While the performances pale in comparison to shows from the early 1970s, the Knebworth concert footage shows that the Beach Boys were still capable of putting on a great show in the midst of the personal turmoil that was engulfing many of its members. The footage has since taken on added emotional weight since it was the last time U.K. fans would get to see Dennis before his tragic death in 1983.

National Mall, Washington, D.C., July 4, 1980

Perhaps one of the most noteworthy concerts in Beach Boys history, the group drew over 500,000 fans to celebrate Independence Day in the nation's capitol. The performance was kind of sloppy, Brian was there but not in good shape, and Dennis was also showing major signs of deterioration. But the half million audience members were oblivious as the era of Beach Boys concerts that occurred on autopilot were in full swing. The minor detail of how well the band played became unimportant. All you needed was to put the words "Beach Boys" and "Fourth of July" together and everybody was happy no matter what. HBO filmed the event for a TV special.

Los Angeles County Fair, Pomona, California, September 27, 1983

This concert is significant because it was the last appearance by Dennis Wilson with the Beach Boys. The troubled drummer had been in and out of the band since 1979, and his antics at this show might have been the final straw. In three months, Dennis would be dead from drowning. The Beach Boys continued with great success, but they were never the same without Dennis, as he was undoubtedly the real Beach Boy.

Paramount Theater, New York, November 26, 1993

The Beach Boys performed a marathon 43-song concert in an effort to promote their thirtieth-anniversary CD box set, which had been released by Capitol earlier in the year. This tour included an "unplugged" set which has since become legendary in that it included material the band had rarely performed live, like "Vegetables." Fans who saw this tour say the Beach Boys were better rehearsed vocally than they had been in more than a decade.

Resorts Casino, Atlantic City, New Jersey, August 29, 1997

The end of another Beach Boys era occurred this night as Carl Wilson played his last show with the band. Battling cancer, he'd been sitting on a stool at many of the recent shows, unable to stand throughout the Beach Boys' long set. In September, David Marks returned to the Beach Boys to add some lost guitar chemistry, but the absence of Carl's voice and his immense presence was a massive blow to the band's credibility. The following February, Carl passed away. Al Jardine was forced out of the Beach Boys shortly thereafter, and formed his own band. The Beach Boys continued with Mike Love, Bruce Johnston, David Marks, and their backing band.

Sommerfest, Amberg, Germany, June 26, 1999

The Beach Boys played a series of concerts and outdoor festivals in Europe, including several monster shows in Germany. As a testament to their enduring presence, the band played to as many as 150,000 fans per show during this stretch, and one estimate gave this show's attendance as 400,000. Meanwhile, back in the U.S., Brian Wilson was in the midst of playing his first concerts as a solo act, and Al Jardine's "Family and Friends" band was also performing sporadically. When the Beach Boys returned from Europe, David Marks left the band again after his second less-than-two-year stretch in 36 years.

Ronald Reagan Presidential Library, Simi Valley, California, February 5, 2011

Alan Jardine rejoined Mike Love and Bruce Johnston's "Beach Boys" for the first time since 1998 at the Ronald Reagan 100th Birthday tribute concert.

ITINERARY
DECEMBER 6 - 20, 1998
AUSTRALIA

SUN.	DEC. 06	TRAVEL TO AUSTRALIA
MON.	DEC. 07	FLYING
TUE.	DEC. 08	ARRIVE and DAY OFF IN BRISBANE
WED.	DEC. 09	PLAY BRISBANE
THU.	DEC. 10	TRAVEL TO and DAY OFF IN MELBOURNE
FRI.	DEC. 11	PLAY MELBOURNE
SAT.	DEC. 12	TRAVEL TO and PLAY ADELAIDE
SUN.	DEC. 13	TRAVEL TO and DAY OFF IN SYDNEY
MON.	DEC. 14	DAY OFF IN SYDNEY
TUE.	DEC. 15	PLAY SYDNEY
WED.	DEC. 16	TRAVEL TO and PLAY CANBERRA
THU.	DEC. 17	TRAVEL TO and DAY OFF IN SYDNEY
FRI.	DEC. 18	PLAY NEWCASTLE
SAT.	DEC. 19	PLAY WOLLONGONG
SUN.	DEC. 20	TRAVEL HOME

The Beach Boys have successfully toured virtually every major concert market in the free world multiple times. Australia was one of the first countries outside of the U.S. where the group found chart success and widespread fame. They first toured Australia and New Zealand in 1964, and have returned there many times.

Brian Wilson was invited by the "Beach Boys" to this show and declined. David Marks was not invited. Jardine's presence added some great vocals to an otherwise rapidly aging front line. This was the first "Beach Boys" show with more than two actual Beach Boys since Marks performed with the band on their 2008 U.K. tour.

22

Break Away

Beach Boys Solo Albums

From the brilliant (Dennis Wilson—*Pacific Ocean Blue*) to the good (*Brian Wilson '88*) to the mediocre (*Carl Wilson*) to the bad (Bruce Johnston—*Going Public*) to the awful (Mike Love—*Looking Back With Love*), the Beach Boys have garnered very mixed reviews as solo artists. What follows is an overview of each group member's varied attempts at going it alone.

Bruce Johnston—*Going Public* (1977)

Bruce Johnston already had a successful career as a writer, producer, and studio musician long before he became one of the Beach Boys in 1965. He released his first single in 1959, and then his first solo albums *Surfers' Pajama Party* and *Surfin' Around the World* in 1963. In 1977, during his six-year hiatus from the Beach Boys, he released his *Going Public* LP. Much more was expected from Bruce, who had already won a "Song of the Year" Grammy award in 1976 for his composition "I Write the Songs," which had been turned into a mega-hit by Barry Manilow. But *Going Public* was mainly a collection of songs Bruce had written years earlier and that had been previously released in better versions than these. His dance version of "Pipeline" became something of a novelty that did quite well on the disco charts. Otherwise, this was not a great album, and Bruce has been candid in admitting it.

Dennis Wilson—*Pacific Ocean Blue* (1977)

Although the possibility of a Dennis Wilson solo LP had been mentioned as early as 1970, it blew many minds when Dennis's 1977 solo effort on Caribou Records turned out to be a virtual masterpiece of production meets emotion. *Pacific Ocean Blue* is the most progressive of all Beach Boys records other than *Pet Sounds* and *Smile*—and it shares similarities with both of them. *Pacific*

Ocean Blue is a fearless artistic statement, sometimes very sad, even tortured, but it also represents one last blissful wave of Beach Boys magic. Its songs range from expansive and rocking, like the epic "River Song," to raw love ballads like the brutally regretful "Thoughts of You." There is an impressive sonic palette that shows itself off on nearly every *Pacific Ocean Blue* track, giving proof that Dennis had become a talented and innovative producer.

Pacific Ocean Blue received excellent reviews from the rock press, including two stellar notices in *Rolling Stone* magazine. It also outsold the two Beach Boys LPs released in its wake, gaining nearly a quarter million in sales. Unfortunately for Dennis, it turned out to be a one-act play, as he was unable to pull together his planned follow-up *Bambu*. Rumors that Dennis was given an ultimatum by the other Beach Boys to either remain with the Beach Boys as their drummer, or further pursue his solo endeavors and be terminated, have been substantiated by a long list of insiders. From here, Dennis spiraled badly until his eventual drowning death in 1983.

Carl Wilson—*Carl Wilson* (1981)

The thought of a Carl Wilson solo LP at a time when the Beach Boys were becoming a parody of themselves seemed like a potentially wonderful thing. While the Beach Boys were churning out badly rehearsed performances of their hits at endless concerts and releasing no new material, Carl took a break from the band and concentrated on his own thing. Unfortunately, the resulting album turned out to be far less than it should have been. The eight songs were a collaboration between Carl and the late Myrna Smith, formerly a member of the Sweet Inspirations. Most of the material on Carl's debut LP is relatively forgettable, and its disappointing chart peak of #185 reflected that fact. One great exception is the track "Heaven," which has become a minor classic. However, *Carl Wilson* goes down as the weakest of the three debut solo LPs by each Wilson brother.

Mike Love—*Looking Back With Love* (1981)

Mike's solo LP was released only a few months after Carl's, and by comparison it made *Carl Wilson* look like a tour de force. *Looking Back With Love* is generally considered one of the worst train wrecks of all the Beach Boys solo LPs. Released on Boardwalk Records in October 1981, the label's head Neil Bogart died only months after the release of Mike's album, but rumors that hearing *Looking Back With Love* is what actually killed him are probably untrue. Mike only co-wrote one song on the LP, and despite having Brian guest on a cover of "Be My Baby," he could have used a mess of help to stand alone.

If the cover picturing Mike in a Dodgers cap and blue satin jacket doesn't turn your stomach, then you might actually be able to stand hearing *Looking Back With Love*. In a way it's a symbol of all that was squandered between *Holland* and the moment *Looking Back With Love* was released. Pretty much everything that was cool about the Beach Boys was history at this point. However bad it might be, Mike's solo album's standing might have actually improved with the subsequent releases of the Beach Boys' awful *Summer In Paradise* album and Brian's painfully spotty *Gettin' In Over My Head* CD.

Carl Wilson—*Youngblood* (1983)

Everyone figured that the second time would be the charm for Carl considering his first solo album was received with a generally lukewarm reaction. But to some *Youngblood* is even worse. Released on Caribou Records, and

produced by Jeff "Skunk" Baxter, it is a more ambitious effort than Carl's debut, but one with decidedly mixed results. There is a more up-tempo R&B and rock feel on many of the songs, but the collection somehow seems to be missing whatever that magical element is that makes Carl's output so great as one of the Beach Boys. A pop/funk single titled "What You Do to Me" was released as the album's single, and it reached #72 on the *Billboard* chart. This would be Carl's last attempt at a solo record.

Brian Wilson—*Brian Wilson* (1988)

Most fans were excited at the prospect of a Carl Wilson solo project, and he met the demand by releasing two albums apart from the Beach Boys. Unfortunately, neither record contained the expected magic from Carl, although there were fleeting flashes of brilliance, like his beautiful song "Heaven."

Released on Sire Records with much fanfare, *Brian Wilson* was initially touted as Brian's great return to form by many of his fans. The first solo LP by the genius who masterminded an iconic string of classic Beach Boys hits, everyone was waiting for this one. Upon release it received good reviews, but its commercial performance fell somewhat short of expectations. Reaching a decent #54 on the album chart, *Brian Wilson* did contain several great new songs. "Love and Mercy" became something of a signature song for Brian as a solo artist, and deservedly so. Its simple message and lovely melody were a spiritually affirming combination. Another winner was Brian's "Melt Away," with its heartbreaking yet hopeful message. The suite "Rio Grande" gave many Brian fans hope that he still had the ability to compose and create in his celebrated modular method of late 1966. While *Brian Wilson* easily stands as one his best solo efforts, it has lost some of its shine over time. The heavy influence of Dr. Eugene Landy in the creation of the album and the unfortunate late-'80s production style leaves *Brian Wilson* a few steps short of being a true classic.

Brian Wilson—*I Just Wasn't Made For These Times* (1995)

Producer Don Was celebrated the survival and renaissance of Brian Wilson with this CD and his black-and-white documentary of the same title. Brian performs a selection of his Beach Boys–era classics and a pair of solo tunes from his 1988 album. This was a very popular release with Brian's hardcore fans, and was a key to bringing some younger people into Brian's fan base. The CD did not chart in the U.S., but it did garner some good reviews and was considered a modest success.

Brian Wilson and Van Dyke Parks—*Orange Crate Art* (1995)

There was some confusion at first among Brian's fans regarding this CD. Many of them originally believed that Brian was more involved in this project than he really was. To be clear, *Orange Crate Art* is a Van Dyke Parks creation featuring Brian Wilson on vocals. Although it received very mixed reviews and failed to chart, it was hailed as a positive step for Brian.

Brian Wilson has had the most prolific solo career of any of the Beach Boys. Although his releases have been somewhat uneven, the fact that he's churned out more than ten solo albums is impressive. This show at Hollywood's Roxy Theatre was recorded and packaged into one of Brian's better CD releases.

Brian Wilson—*Imagination* (1998)

Released on Giant Records and distributed by Warner Music, *Imagination* was Brian's highest-profile release since his 1988 debut solo LP. On this CD Brian left the production duties to Joe Thomas, who was known for wearing many hats in the business including label head, film director, studio owner, and recording engineer. On *Imagination* Brian co-wrote four new songs with Thomas and several other collaborators. He also refurbished some older material from his Beach Boys days to fill out the lineup. The title track and single featured some of Brian's best-sounding vocals in many years. The record also featured the song "Lay Down Burden," which Brian dedicated to his late brother Carl. The main complaint about *Imagination* is the heavy-handed and somewhat sterile production by Thomas. The CD generally received positive reviews, but it failed to make much of a dent commercially, topping out at #88 on the U.S. *Billboard* album chart—from which it disappeared completely after only two weeks. It fared noticeably better in the U.K., reaching a respectable #30.

Brian Wilson—*Live at the Roxy Theatre* (2000)

It was quite an event when Brian and his excellent band performed on consecutive nights at the legendary Roxy Theatre on L.A.'s Sunset Strip in April 2000. The sense of celebration and awe that filled the room during those performances translates well on the *Brian Wilson—Live at the Roxy Theatre* two-disc set. This release was at first an Internet-only product that could be ordered through Brian's Website and was pressed on his own Brimel label. It became enough of a success that it was eventually picked up by the independent Oglio Records and distributed in retail stores.

The content of *Brian Wilson—Live at the Roxy* is basically another case of Brian covering the Beach Boys with a few additional odds and ends. However, what raises this to another level is the performance of Brian's incredible backing band, who make his music sparkle at every turn. To have been at these shows (I was) was to see Brian reclaim a piece of L.A., but not as a broken-down former genius, but instead as a renewed performer fronting one of the world's coolest bands.

Al Jardine—*Family and Friends Live in Las Vegas* (2001)

After engaging in a losing battle against Mike Love regarding issues surrounding Al's use of the name "Beach Boys Family and Friends" for his post–Beach Boys touring group, Al dropped the "Beach Boys" part of it and moved on. This CD release, although very limited in distribution, was a nice reflection of the quality performances his act could produce. Featuring a first-rate band with former Beach Boys ultra-pro sidemen like Billy Hinsche, Bobby Figueroa, and Ed Carter, not to mention Brian's daughters Carnie and Wendy on backing vocals, along with Al's sons Matt and Adam, what resulted was something of a Beach Boys extended-family reunion, and it sounded great. *Al Jardine—Family and Friends Live in Las Vegas* presents a good selection of Beach Boys classics performed by a band that certainly knows its way around the material. Al's vocals are first rate, and Matt's falsetto is impressive. Overall, a somewhat predictable, but nonetheless enjoyable, release.

Brian Wilson—*Pet Sounds Live* (2002)

Recorded in London in January 2002, *Pet Sounds Live* is exactly as billed. Brian and his amazing band perform the entire *Pet Sounds* album, beginning to end, and do an amazing job of it. But the problem is that such is little more than a novelty. It's never going to be better, or even as good, as the original LP, so why bother listening? If you were at one of the *Pet Sounds* shows it makes a nice souvenir of a memorable and important thing to witness. But as a CD for the average consumer, it's a bit of a square peg. The pattern well underway by this release is Brian (or his management) finding new ways to cover himself.

David Marks—*Something Funny Goin' On* (2003)

The former Beach Boys guitarist released this solo CD on his own Quiver Records, and it only received attention from a small number of hardcore fans. It features several strong original songs, but suffers from a less-than-flattering production and mix. One of the highlights is a guitar instrumental appropriately titled "The Legend," which shows off some of David's considerable skill as a musician.

Brian Wilson—*Gettin' In Over My Head* (2004)

Released in the midst of 2004's *Smile* tour frenzy, *Gettin' In Over My Head* is one of the weakest solo releases by any of the Beach Boys. Considering the pedigree of the project's guest artists, including Paul McCartney, Elton John, and Eric Clapton, the album falls flat due to Brian's weak vocals, an unfortunate production, and a general lack of cohesion. The CD features a posthumous vocal performance by Carl Wilson on the song "Soul Searchin'" and a co-lead vocal from Paul McCartney on the tune "A Friend Like You." Neither did enough to save this misguided effort, as the CD spent one week at #100 on the U.S. charts, and vanished.

Brian Wilson—*Brian Wilson Presents Smile* (2004)

This was the big bang of Beach Boys solo ventures, although it's hard to entirely separate it from the Beach Boys. After successfully premiering his newly "finished" *Smile* concept live in London earlier in the year, Brian and band set about recording the reconstructed version of the Beach Boys' long lost epic in April 2004. A mere 37 years after it was conceived and then abandoned, Brian and his team decided that tackling *Smile* was the logical step for him after performing *Pet Sounds*. Some said it was the only card left in his hand to play.

The upside is that no Beach Boys version of *Smile* had been released; therefore, the only competition or comparison to a new *Smile* would be the piles of bootleg recordings in varying audio quality, and always in an unfinished state, that circulated among the faithful. The downside is that those bootlegs had the Beach Boys' voices on them; and as fine as Brian's band is, they are no Beach Boys when it comes to vocals . . . nobody is.

The new *Brian Wilson Presents Smile* CD was a curious proposition. None of the original 1966 and 1967 session tapes would be used, but they were deftly aped by Brian's band to sound as close to the originals as possible. So what you have is Brian's band imitating elements of a 1967 project as best they could, and also giving pointers on how to assemble the pieces they are imitating so that it flows in a complete-sounding way that the aforementioned bootlegs do not. Original *Smile* lyricist Van Dyke Parks got involved to help spackle a few parts that had gaping holes, while Brian himself gave some key advice in how it all was supposed fit together. Mainly it was Wondermint Darian Sahanaja who did the impossible and managed to assemble a cohesive *Smile*-ish presentation in three movements. The final product was impressively compact and appealing. Hearing the *Smile* music in a complete form was a revelation. Brian's lost masterpiece really was a masterpiece, even if different people put the pieces together slightly differently, or not.

The critical and public reaction to *Brian Wilson Presents Smile* was unanimously positive. Brian won his first Grammy Award for Best Rock Instrumental Performance for the track "Mrs. O'Leary's Cow," which happened to be one of the original *Smile* elements that had haunted Brian the most. The CD also sold well, reaching #13 on the U.S. charts and #7 in the

U.K. For Brian, this was the commercial and critical peak of his somewhat spotty solo career, and truly something to be proud of.

Brian Wilson—*What I Really Want For Christmas* (2005)

A Brian Wilson Christmas album sounded like a better idea than it actually turned out to be. There is something unsettling about this release. Brian sounds stiff, over-Auto-Tuned, and the production isn't exactly stellar. The cover art is unimaginative, as are the entire contents of the CD. Bah humbug!

David Marks—*I Think About You Often* (2006)

Very few people are even aware of this fine David Marks release from late 2006. But in truth, it's one of the best Beach Boys solo albums and should be counted as such. David's sound rarely relies on anything that resembles the Beach Boys, although his Hawthorne accent and vocal textures at times eerily channel Dennis and Carl Wilson. The compositions and arrangements on this CD are uniquely David, sometimes in collaboration with his longtime friend Buzz Clifford, and with blues and jazz/rock elements weaved into the genre palette. The album includes an impressive number of highlights, including the lovely and nostalgic "Like 1969," with its effortlessly virtuoso guitar solo, and the wonderfully spacey "Light of the Spirit." *I Think About You Often* also benefits from the vocal contributions of Anna Montgomery, who backs David on the engaging rocker "Big Wave" as well as on the unapologetically morbid title track, which references the specter of death—a constantly looming companion in David's later life. The single element that keeps *I Think About You Often* in the upper echelon of Beach Boys solo work is David's fine guitar work, which never becomes self-absorbed or overdone, but does display a level of artistry that no other Beach Boy can claim on an instrument.

Dennis Wilson—*Pacific Ocean Blue: Legacy Edition/Bambu* (2008)

After being out-of-print for nearly two decades, Sony Records in conjunction with Jim Guercio's Caribou Records released a deluxe two-CD Legacy edition of Dennis's *Pacific Ocean Blue*. The package included 20 unreleased tracks, including a full disc showcasing Dennis's abandoned *Bambu* album, which was the planned follow-up to *Pacific Ocean Blue*. The remastered reissue, coupled with the newly mixed unreleased material, turned out to be a huge

"Pacific Ocean Blue"– the first solo album by Dennis Wilson.

On Caribou Records and Tapes.

According to most critics and fans, Dennis Wilson's lone solo LP, 1977's *Pacific Ocean Blue*, is the very best of any Beach Boys–related solo release. The Legacy Edition reissue, which also contained material slated for his unreleased *Bambu* album, was voted *Rolling Stone, Uncut,* and *MOJO* magazine's Reissue of the Year for 2008.

critical success, and also showed surprising commercial strength, giving Dennis a hit solo album 25 years after his death.

It's obvious that Dennis Wilson's music has impressive staying power, and that its appeal is independent of Brian Wilson and the Beach Boys. *Pacific Ocean Blue* did pretty damn good in 1977. It was reviewed well, and it sold decently. But as time passed, it only got better. Demand surpassed supply; and, by the '90s, used copies of the original *Pacific Ocean Blue* LP were selling for ten times the record's original retail price. Bootlegs of the *Bambu* sessions were also in great demand, and the cult of Dennis Wilson fans, many of whom were not fans of the Beach Boys, continued to grow.

Upon its release in June 2008, *Pacific Ocean Blue: Legacy Edition* sold better than expected, well over 120,000 units worldwide. It charted at #16 on the U.K. album chart, where it hadn't charted at all in 1977. In 2008, it also hit #8 on the *Billboard* catalog chart in the U.S. and #8 in Internet sales. It was chosen as the *Rolling Stone* magazine "Reissue of the Year," as well as the *MOJO* magazine "Reissue of the Year," and the *Uncut* magazine "Reissue of the Year." It was without a doubt one of the best-reviewed releases in all of the music business in 2008. Brian easily has the most historical importance and staying power of any member of the Beach Boys, but to think there is any question as to which Beach Boy is number two as an artist is to ignore the facts. Dennis Wilson, or the material he left behind, has carved out its own popularity niche that rivals Brian's, and easily surpasses all of the other Beach Boys' solo efforts.

Pacific Ocean Blue: Legacy Edition—Press Release

NEW YORK, June 25, 2008/PRNewswire—*Pacific Ocean Blue: Legacy Edition (Caribou/Epic/Legacy), the thirtieth-anniversary reissue of the long-out-of-print musical masterpiece from the Beach Boys' Dennis Wilson, is blowing up both in the States and worldwide following its U.S. release last Tuesday, June 17, 2008.*

Pacific Ocean Blue: Legacy Edition—a two-CD collection featuring the original album in its entirety as well as bonus tracks and the first official release of songs from Bambu, *Wilson's intended follow-up—was the #4 rock release for Amazon.com on the day of release. The album is already a top-seller in the U.K. and Europe, having debuted at #16 on the U.K. Album Chart, #67 in the Netherlands, #71 in Ireland, and rocketing to #5 in Norway. These feats are all the more remarkable considering that* Pacific Ocean Blue *was originally released more than 30 years ago and that these are current, not catalog charts.*

The release of Pacific Ocean Blue: Legacy Edition *has been a cause for celebration among fans and press alike. "The reissue's heart lies in tracks like 'River Song' and the rollicking 'What's Wrong'—two raw, emotional highlights that are as moody as anything Brian ever composed," wrote* Rolling Stone *in its four-star review of the album, while* MOJO *observed that "(Dennis) left behind* Pacific Ocean Blue *as his masterpiece, a soul-baring document of a disintegrating male psyche that is perfectly poised between pain and its transcendence." The* London Observer *called it "The holy grail for many-a rock fan," while the* London Guardian *labeled* Pacific Ocean Blue *a ". . . musical masterwork." Additionally, the Legacy Edition received 5-star reviews in the current editions of* Uncut *and* Record Collector.

Dennis Wilson's Pacific Ocean Blue *was the first solo album to be released by any of the Beach Boys, and has been out-of-print and unobtainable for more than a decade except as a pricey collector's item or bootleg. The deluxe Legacy Edition marks the occasion of its thirtieth anniversary, and the 25th anniversary of its creator's untimely death in 1983, at age 39.*

Brian Wilson—*That Lucky Old Sun* (2008)

Originally debuted in a series of concerts at Royal Festival Hall in London, *That Lucky Old Sun* is mainly a collaboration between Brian and his

Among the best of Brian Wilson's solo releases was 2008's *That Lucky Old Sun.* It stood out because unlike so many of Brian's releases, it consisted of newly written material, and because the sessions found Brian sounding confident and comfortable.

backing-band member Scott Bennett, with some assistance from Van Dyke Parks. The studio version was released in September 2008 and is one of Brian's very best solo works. One of the good things about *That Lucky Old Sun* is that Brian has finally become comfortable with his aging voice, and he uses it to better effect here. The themes are mostly nostalgia driven, and there is an air of bittersweet resignation that permeates many of the songs. The fact that Brian is allowed to express his humanity in a way that is fairly unforced compared to some of the solo material on his recent releases is refreshing.

The harmonic overtones of the Beach Boys seem to inhabit this CD like a friendly ghost. Brian can't really get away from his past, because what the Brian Wilson band does that is so great is uncannily re-create elements of the Beach Boys classic 1965–1966 sound. There have been cases of Brian attempting to artistically ditch the Beach Boys, but they always seem to find him because he cannot escape his own blood and soul. When Brian hits his target as a solo artist, there is no doubt that the sound is "Beach Boys" in one way or another. If you took the voice of every Beach Boy and inserted them into *That Lucky Old Sun* in their appropriate places, those voices would certainly not be out of place with the material. At his creative core, Brian writes for the spectrum that those voices inhabit.

That Lucky Old Sun became a relative success, gaining excellent reviews and selling decently. It charted at #21 in the U.S. and #37 in the U.K. With strong originals like "Midnight's Another Day," "Forever She'll Be My Surfer Girl," "Oxygen to the Brain," and "Southern California," it displays an overall quality that surpasses most of Brian's previous solo work. *That Lucky Old Sun* was described as "a musical love letter to his native Los Angeles" by *Rolling Stone* magazine; and for Brian and his band, the love they send out returns to them.

Al Jardine—*A Postcard From California* (2010)

Al's long-awaited solo CD didn't initially materialize as such, only being available as a digital download upon its release. *A Postcard From California* seemed to be in the works for an interminably long amount of time, with Al often setting and then changing its release date. When it finally was out it kind of hit the market with a whisper, on or near the same day Brian's Website began streaming a preview track from his much-anticipated Gershwin album.

The most impressive aspect of *A Postcard From California* is the long list of guest artists who pitched in to help Al. Among them are Neil Young, Steve Miller, David Crosby, Flea, David Marks, Brian Wilson, and Alec Baldwin. That sounds like a hell of a party! But for the most part the album is held down by the unimaginative arrangements, including an updated "Help Me, Rhonda" with Miller that makes one wonder why Al even bothered. As always Al's vocals are great, and at times his vocal gift overcomes the average material. There is nothing bad or embarrassing here; it's all fairly good, some of it slightly better than that. But the clean-living, regular-guy aesthetic that Al embodies makes for somewhat predictable music compared to a Brian or a Dennis, or even a David. When releasing a solo work, those comparisons are inevitably made; and although Al did a good enough job with *A Postcard From California*, it wasn't enough to change perceptions of him as a great vocalist with average musical chops.

Brian Wilson—*Brian Wilson Reimagines Gershwin* (2010)

There was a frenzied reaction among many of Brian's biggest fans when *Brian Wilson Reimagines Gershwin* was released on Walt Disney Records in August 2010. Many of them felt this was clearly Brian's best solo work, and that he'd finally hit a commercial homerun with this CD. One thing that stood out was Brian's improved vocal quality, which ran through the entire album. There were none of the inconsistent pitch and enunciation issues that plagued much of his earlier solo work. Instead *Brian Wilson Reimagines Gershwin* unveiled a confident and vocally facile Brian that hadn't been heard from in decades. This record truly delivers a series of first-rate vocal performances, and is a notable comeback in that sense.

The problem with *Brian Wilson Reimagines Gershwin* is that it's not very imaginative. The arrangements are very safe, offering no newly broken ground, and not even coming close. For anyone who is familiar with the string of legends who have tackled the Gershwin songbook prior to Brian, a vast amount of hallowed ground has already been covered. From Ella Fitzgerald to Nat King Cole to Nina Simone to Mel Tormé to Sarah Vaughan to Miles Davis to Frank Sinatra, it's all been done, and done as well as humanly possible. What seemed intriguing when it was announced that Brian would be recording an album of Gershwin covers was his potential to create uniquely offbeat and fresh-sounding musical and vocal arrangements of the material. I pictured *Smile* meets Gershwin. The CD's cover art did a better job of realizing that potential than Brian did.

His versions of "Summertime," "It Ain't Necessarily So," "'S Wonderful," "Love Is Here to Stay," and "Someone to Watch Over Me" are sung well, but are presented in a very straightforward way. If I'm going to listen to a "typical" Gershwin arrangement, I'd much rather hear Ella, Frank, or Sarah sing it than Brian. In the few cases where he changed things up a bit, like "They Can't Take That Away From Me"—which is arranged in a "Little Deuce Coupe/Saint Nick" style—and the Beach Boys/Spector-esque "I Got Rhythm," the changes are so derivative and predictable that it sounds like a parody of Beach Boys meet Gershwin.

The best moments on *Brian Wilson Reimagines Gershwin* are the gorgeous introductory harmonies built around a snippet of "Rhapsody in Blue," and the newly written Wilson/Gershwin composition "The Like In I Love You," which is extremely sugary but still tastes pretty darn good after multiple listens. In the end, critical reaction to the CD was mostly good, but not as consistently glowing as many of Brian's fans felt it deserved. In particular, some elements of the British press were very harsh in their assessment of Brian's Gershwin arrangements. The CD was a sales disappointment considering the initial hype and expectations, reaching #26 on the *Billboard* chart. The fact that it received not a single Grammy nomination was also a hard one to swallow for many Wilson-heads. One bright spot was its performance on the *Billboard* Jazz chart, where it hit the number-one position. All in all, *Brian Wilson Reimagines Gershwin* wasn't the giant success that many predicted it would be, but it still ranks as one of Brian's better solo releases due to his fine singing, and the generally pleasant listening experience it provides.

23

The Wilson Brothers

Spiritual Carpenters

I t is no mystery that Brian, Dennis, and Carl Wilson were not virtuoso instrumentalists. Carl was the best of the three, and that's because he worked very hard on developing his guitar-playing abilities until about 1965, when his job of being a Beach Boy and full-time vocalist diverted his attention from his former goal of being a great guitarist. His ability remained at an excellent but not exceptional level for the remainder of his life. Although Brian was a good keyboard player and a very decent bassist, and Dennis's ability on the drums was primitive but passionate (and while his keyboard abilities might have been just slightly better than Brian's), those instruments were not their forte. If you really think about it, the Wilsons' primary instrument was their ear. They were virtuoso at knowing what sounded right. And to take that idea further, perhaps it was the connection between those ears and their hearts that really made the product beyond virtuoso.

I think of Dennis, laboring on so many of those *Pacific Ocean Blue* tracks by himself. He didn't really play any instrument at a high level, but he crafted those tracks painstakingly. On many of them he plays all or nearly all of the instruments himself. They sound beautiful, even though he wasn't a great musician. It's his ears that were great. He found a way to make it magical. Carl too, with a track like "Feel Flows," which is really a jazz-flavored composition with veins of pop and funk. But labels didn't matter. Carl wasn't held back by the need to actually be a master of the genre that he was tackling. He probably didn't even think of it in those terms. Like Brian, he knew what sounded right . . . and more importantly what *felt* right. Because Carl was comparatively a novice at the jazz element, or at least primitive compared to a highly trained player, his music is put together in a very organic or nontraditional, and non-trained, way. Rules didn't matter, and the same held true for Brian. Even when he was using the best musicians in the business, he was approaching them as a complete renegade. He was incredibly inventive because the usual barriers didn't apply to him. Brian realized his vision by following his ears and his heart. That's why his music sounds like nothing else. The Wilson brothers were spiritual carpenters. They built their music not from the head, but from the soul.

Genius Meets Reality

Brian is among the greatest artists of our time. As a composer, arranger, and producer he is nearly unequaled in the history of pop. He could be the most original American artist ever. But there is a reality that is rarely articulated among his faithful supporters. You are completely fooling yourself if you think Brian Wilson would have "made it" without the Beach Boys as his vehicle to fame. The phenomenon of the Beach Boys gave Brian all of his cache; without it, no one would have cared who he was. The particular elements that gelled into the Beach Boys were essential to Brian finding his voice. Brian was an introvert. He needed the free-spirited Dennis for his connection to the culture. He needed the confidence of Mike to put his vision across. He needed Carl and Al and David to add their musicality and diverse influences to the musical palette.

If the Beach Boys had not pushed into a teen-friendly approach in 1962, they more than likely would never have been a hit. Brian wasn't the Beach Boy to drive their sound in an electric guitar–centric, self-contained-band direction. That credit goes to Carl and David. Brian was thinking Four Freshmen meets Phil Spector. Mike was thinking Coasters meet Jan and Dean. Together they were thinking Everly Brothers. Al was thinking Kingston Trio. But Carl and David were thinking Chuck Berry meets Dick Dale. And all the while Dennis was yelling about the holy trinity of surfing, cars, and girls. Brian took all of that and made it work. He not only made it work, he molded it into something that transcended all the rock music that came before. But alone he never would have found it.

Every element that made up the Beach Boys was crucial. Finding huge fame and all that power was a major long shot, and Brian isn't the only reason they pulled it off. He's the biggest reason, the most important reason. But genius doesn't exist in a vacuum. Without "Surfin' Safari," "Surfin' U.S.A.," "Little Deuce Coupe," "Surfer Girl," "Fun, Fun, Fun," and "I Get Around," there would never be *Pet Sounds* and "Good Vibrations." Without the foundation he'd built with his brothers and friends, Brian more than likely would have never had the chance to create his masterpieces.

Brian and Dennis—A Bad and Beautiful Combination

The conventional view is that, because Dennis's music was so good, Brian must have been behind the scenes pulling the strings. It couldn't possibly have been because Dennis himself was that good. How could Dennis have gone from nothing to material that is so deep and beautiful? Well, consider this: maybe one of the reasons Brian's stuff was so good is that he had a significant amount of help and influence from his brothers. I think Brian was truly inspired by Dennis and guided by Carl much of the time.

Dennis was working on his own music much earlier than 1968. It's just that no one was listening. There is evidence that Dennis was developing his own music as early as 1965, seriously writing songs in 1966, and beginning to record it in 1967. So it seems natural that his material released in 1968 would be relatively mature. Brian certainly influenced Dennis more than anyone, and helped him learn quite a bit. Brian was very engaged in helping Dennis write "Little Bird" and arrange "Forever." Carl helped Dennis even more, but influenced him less. That was Carl's role with both Brian and Dennis: to assist, support, facilitate, but also to lay back and let genius take its course. I'm certain it could be a frustrating, heartbreaking, and sometimes dangerous role to play. But Carl was there when it counted.

Brian and Dennis had one important thing in common. They had the same giant river of artistic and spiritual ideas flowing from another realm and straight into their heads. What came out of them was very different. Brian found a way to shape and craft that flow into something beautiful that everyone could relate to. Dennis just flung it out there; sometimes it was really sad, and scary, and sometimes it didn't make sense, or it was only bits of thoughts and sparks of ideas. He wasn't that concerned with making it palatable to the average person. Dennis was more concerned with it being real, truthful, and reflective of the absolute core of his inspiration. There is a lot of Brian in Dennis's music, but it has much more to do with Brian being his brother, and his musical hero, than with Brian physically helping Dennis make music.

The Cocaine Sessions

In 1980 and 1981, at the Venice Beach home of Dr. Garby Leon, a Harvard graduate and UCLA music faculty member who has since become a major consultant and story analyst in the film industry, a period of collaboration occurred between Brian and Dennis that is somewhat legendary in the story of the Beach Boys. Garby provided his Hammond organ and grand piano, as well as a pressure-free environment, for Dennis and Brian to work on their material together. He also ran tape on his home-recording equipment in an attempt to help the Wilsons capture what was developing. The Leon-recorded tapes are known to Beach Boys fans as the "cocaine sessions" or the "hamburger sessions." Rumors that Dennis was plying Brian with drugs and junk food is why this label has stuck. Regardless of the health issues that such a routine brings into question, there was by all accounts a definite creative spark occurring between the two troubled brothers. The demo recording of Brian's "Stevie" is the only song from this collaboration that was recorded in a proper studio, the session taking place at L.A.'s Sounds Good studio in January 1981. With Dennis and Garby handling the production chores, Dennis playing drums, and Brian playing everything else, "Stevie" was supposed to be just the beginning of a new creative wave with Dennis and Brian calling the creative shots. Instead it was the end.

The Beach Boys hierarchy and Brian's family pulled the financial plug on this collaboration when it was discovered that illicit substances were in full flow throughout the workday, every day. At one stage, Brian was reportedly found in a convulsive state after a cocaine overdose. Dennis subsequently had his face beaten into an unrecognizable pulp by Mike's brother Stan and his muscle-bound buddy Rocky Pamplin, whose resentment for Dennis ran

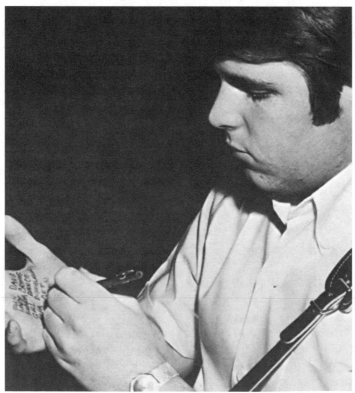

Carl was a tremendous support system for both Brian and Dennis during various periods of their development. His presence is felt, and heard, on the best work of each of his brothers.

extremely deep. Both Brian and Dennis had succumbed to major addictions during this period. And although "Stevie" was a far better track than anything the other Beach Boys were able to manage, it was decided that despite the excellent creative chemistry between Brian and Dennis that too much of another kind of chemistry was involved when they were together.

Left behind are many hours of work tapes recorded in Garby's home that reveal Brian and Dennis developing material far beyond the thin, bland songs that the other Beach Boys were submitting during this time. Among the "cocaine sessions" pieces are the darkly moving "Oh Lord" and a fascinating ballad titled "Bobby, Dale and Holly." Interestingly, the song "City Blues," which Brian refers to in a later interview as a song he "wrote with Dennis," does not list Dennis's name as a co-writer on Brian's 2004 solo album *Gettin' In Over My Head*. Evidence of its germination is on the Leon tapes. Several well-respected Beach Boys insiders confirm that some of "Rio Grande" from Brian's 1988 solo album was developed in this collaborative period as well. Other snippets of "Rio Grande" seem to exist in some of Dennis's earlier solo demos.

Brian has said in multiple interviews that this period, 1981 to 1982, is when he was the closest to Dennis. This is kind of scary considering that it was such an unhealthy time for both brothers. But according to those who were there, a genuine creative burst was underway between Dennis and Brian despite their lack of sobriety. They were unafraid to explore the darker, obsessive side of themselves, especially if it had the potential to lead to a more genuine self-expression through song. Simultaneously, Carl Wilson had become clean and sober and was working on his debut solo album, which ironically could have used a fine song like "Stevie" to raise it from its appointment with mediocrity.

The Wilson Brothers Album—What If?

There is enough residual evidence and anecdotes to support the theory that between 1977 and 1981, at least some thought was given to the prospect of a Wilson Brothers album project. In a sense *The Beach Boys Love You* hints at a Brian-led version of this concept. That album is one of the truly leftfield moments of Brian's career, showing his inventiveness and originality was still firmly in hand in the late 1970s. It was just a matter of him getting the right mix of support and freedom to be able to express his vision well.

Dennis and Carl also showed an ability to collaborate well with songs like "River Song" and "Rainbows," both of which were produced and sung by Dennis (with heavy Carl input). And then there is the *Bambu* material like "Baby Blue," "It's Not Too Late," and "Wild Situation," all featuring both

Talented but troubled Dennis began a fairly rapid deterioration beginning in late 1977, shortly after the release of his only solo LP. Within a few years his once expressive voice was virtually gone, and his substance-abuse problems had derailed his great potential as an artist.

Dennis and Carl's voices. "Angel Come Home" from *L.A. (Light Album)* is a good example of Carl contributing a song that Dennis could sing. If you take all of this and add in some of the "cocaine sessions" material, you may have something close to what a Wilson Brothers album would have been. There is no question it had the potential to be something very special. Let's dream a little.

The Wilson Brothers (produced by Brian, Dennis, and Carl)

"Rainbows" (written by Dennis, Carl, and Steve Kalinich; sung by Dennis)
"The Night Was So Young" (written by Brian; sung by Carl)
"Stevie" (written and sung by Brian)
"Angel Come Home" (written by Carl and G. Cushing-Murray; sung by Dennis)
"Wild Situation" (written by Dennis and Greg Jakobson; sung by Dennis)

"Baby Blue" (written by Dennis, Greg Jakobson, and Karen Lamm; sung by Carl and Dennis)

"I'll Bet He's Nice" (written by Brian; sung by Dennis, Brian, and Carl)

"It's Not Too Late" (written by Carli Munoz and Dennis; sung by Dennis and Carl)

"City Blues" (written by Brian and Dennis; sung by Brian)

"Oh Lord" (written by Brian and Dennis; sung by Brian)

"Bobby, Dale and Holly" (written by Brian and Dennis; sung by Brian and Dennis)

"I Wanna Pick You Up" (written by Brian; sung by Dennis and Brian)

"Rio Grande River Song" (written by Brian, Dennis, and Carl; sung by Brian and Dennis)

24

The Beach Boys On TV and Film

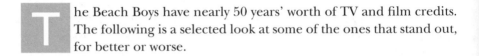

T he Beach Boys have nearly 50 years' worth of TV and film credits. The following is a selected look at some of the ones that stand out, for better or worse.

One Man's Challenge (1962)

This documentary film about the positive aspects of local teen-recreation centers is a great time capsule created by director Dale Smallin. The absolute highlight of the movie is the earliest performance footage of the Beach Boys. The group is seen performing "Surfin' Safari" in a clip that was filmed on July 28, 1962 at the Azusa Teen Club. In fact, it is the *only* known moving footage of the group in their classic Pendleton shirt phase featuring 14-year-old David Marks, a super-skinny Brian, and Mike Love with hair!

Pickwick Dance Party (Filmed on November 3, 1962)

This KTLA television show hosted by Bob Eubanks featured the Beach Boys performing their latest Capitol Records single, "Ten Little Indians." It is the only known live performance of the song, which suffered a very disappointing chart run.

The Red Skelton Show (September 24, 1963)

This appearance was the Beach Boys' first national exposure on television. Brian, Mike, Dennis, Carl, and David lip-synched to "Surfin' U.S.A." and the ballad "The Things We Did Last Summer." Aside from being their first national TV appearance, the show is mainly noteworthy for the horrible sailor outfits the boys were forced to wear.

The Steve Allen Show (March 12, 1964)

The Beach Boys performed "Surfin' U.S.A." and "Fun, Fun, Fun" live in front of a nonplussed audience of adults. There were no screaming girls and little energy in the room as the Beach Boys gamely played two up-tempo songs.

American Bandstand (March 14, 1964)

Once again the Beach Boys had trouble generating something positive on TV. Somehow they managed to get booked on an "all-Beatles" episode of Dick Clark's highly rated teen dance show. And to make it worse, they decided to lip-synch to "Don't Worry Baby" standing up, without their instruments. They look uncomfortable, to say the least. Carl Wilson later said that the group was devastated when they saw their segment air, noting that they'd made a big mistake by not holding their instruments during the performance. Considering that the band really did play all of the instruments on the hit version of "Don't Worry Baby," it seems odd that they chose to appear without them.

Closed-Circuit Concert (March 1964)

The group was filmed in a Burbank, California sound studio in front of a live audience. They performed ten songs with good energy, and the crowd rewarded them with a few screams and enthusiastic cheering. The footage was originally paired with the Beatles Washington, D.C. concert from February 1964, as well as a Lesley Gore set shot at the same Burbank location. The package was aired as a special closed-circuit broadcast in selected theaters around the U.S.

The Red Skelton Show (May 12, 1964)

The Beach Boys returned to television for their second appearance on Red Skelton's popular comedy/variety show. This time they mimed to their number-one hit "I Get Around," as well as singing "In My Room" with a string arrangement added.

The Ed Sullivan Show (September 27, 1964)

Appearing in a set decorated with several gleaming hot rods, the group turned in live performances of "I Get Around" and "Wendy." The audience energy was subdued compared to the Beatles recent Sullivan appearances, but when the camera found Dennis that momentarily changed as a number of girls let out screams for him. Carl makes a mistake during the guitar intro of "Wendy," but the band laughs it off and does a great job on the song.

The Girls on the Beach (Filmed in April 1964)

The Beach Boys never had their *A Hard Day's Night* style movie vehicle, but a few scenes from this 1965 Paramount release show what could have been: in particular, the segment of the boys performing "Little Honda" surrounded by a crowd of pretty girls. The energy between the group and the extras is fantastic, particularly Dennis, who is also given a couple of brief speaking lines early in the film.

The Monkey's Uncle (Filmed in June 1964)

Appearing in the opening sequence backing Annette Funicello, and performing the title song, this film didn't appear in theaters until August 1965, 14 months after the boys filmed their segment. Considering the way music culture evolved in that span, their *The Monkey's Uncle* performance only played into the perception of the Beach Boys as squares. Can you imagine seeing the Beatles in *Help!* a month earlier, and then seeing this? It's a cute clip in the context of its time, but the delay in its release turned it into an embarrassment for the Beach Boys.

The T.A.M.I. Show (Filmed on October 29, 1964)

This is the best example of the early Beach Boys on film. Filmed at the Santa Monica Civic Auditorium in front of a couple thousand local teenagers, this is truly one of rock history's best movies. An all-star bill including the Rolling Stones, the Supremes, James Brown, Chuck Berry, Marvin Gaye, Smokey Robinson and the Miracles, and hosts Jan and Dean make it a one-of-a-kind event. Even with all of that competition, the Beach Boys' highly charged four-song set is one of the absolute highlights of the film. It happens to occur at the apex of the group's 1960s popularity, and the audience is in a frenzy for them as soon as they hit the stage. Brian Wilson would soon be gone from the Beach Boys' live band, and this show only underlines that his presence added a tremendous balance to the Beach Boys as a live act. The real star, though, is Dennis, who is seen wildly assaulting his drums and eliciting waves of screams from the packed auditorium. Anyone who thinks

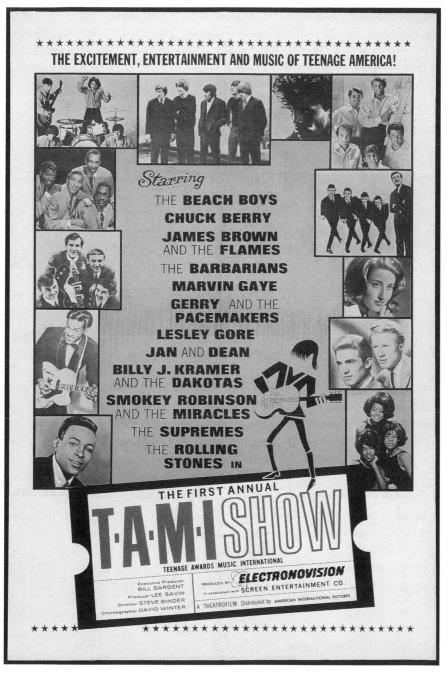

The Teenage Awards Music International concert filmed at the Santa Monica Civic Auditorium in October 1964 featured an eye-popping bill of future legends taking the stage one after the other. Among that vaunted list of rock aristocracy, the Beach Boys commanded the most money, being paid more than double what the Rolling Stones took in. At that moment in time, the Beach Boys' popularity was at its early peak, and their performance in this film is as electrifying as any in their history.

the Beach Boys were not an exciting live act in their early days needs to see this film. Although they appeared in the movie's initial 1965 run in theaters, later prints excised the Beach Boys' set. This was due to an ironclad clause in their original contract that made it too expensive to retain the material when the film was rereleased in theaters.

Ready ,Steady, Go! (Filmed on November 6, 1964)

The Beach Boys appeared live on this popular British TV show singing their biggest U.K. hit to date, "I Get Around," and their latest single "When I Grow Up (To Be a Man)." On the second song they stumble out of the gate and have to restart, but what an awesome recovery they make. It's incredible to hear the band performing such a complex song live, and in particular Brian's bass playing and the group harmonies are terrific. In the U.K. setting, it seems Mike is generating some of the loudest screams from the local birds.

Shindig! (Filmed on December 14, 1964)

On this special edition of America's top teen variety television show, the Beach Boys were the featured performers, playing five songs, plus an a cappella "We Three Kings of Orient Are." Host Jimmy O'Neil gives the group a particularly rousing introduction, calling them "America's number-one group"; and considering their massive popularity and chart placing on this date in time, he was not exaggerating one bit.

Shindig! (April 21, 1965)

Appearing for the second time on the popular TV show, the Beach Boys were still riding a big wave of popularity in the U.S. This episode opens with the group performing "Do You Wanna Dance?" Also performed in quick succession were "Fun, Fun, Fun," "Please Let Me Wonder," "Long Tall Texan," and "Help Me, Rhonda." A very diverse set, as Carl was the only Beach Boy who didn't have a lead-vocal showcase on this show.

The Andy Williams Show (Filmed on October 22, 1965)

The Beach Boys are looking a little silly in their striped shirts and white pants by this point, especially considering this TV show did not air until May 1966. Andy Williams joins the band on a version of "Little Honda" with the lyrics tweaked to "Little Cycle" so as not to upset any sponsors. It's a fairly embarrassing rendition no matter what the words. Overall, this is not one of their better television appearances.

The Jack Benny Hour (Filmed on October 23, 1965)

This TV appearance is a classic. The group performs "California Girls" and they thankfully ditch the striped shirts in favor of some colorful casual wear. They also participate in a comedy sketch with host Jack Benny and his guest Bob Hope. Back into the stripes they perform a hopping live version of "Barbara Ann" that almost makes the song sound cool.

The Beach Boys In London (Filmed in November 1966)

This 30-minute color film directed by Peter Whitehead, and produced by Andrew Loog Oldham's Immediate company, is a great document of the Beach Boys at the height of their popularity in Britain. The documentary is narrated by Marianne Faithfull and follows Carl, Dennis, Mike, Al, and Bruce from their arrival at Heathrow Airport to a press reception in London, and ultimately to their much-anticipated concert at the Hammersmith Odeon theater. It also includes a segment following Al and Dennis as they browse through several antique shops. The soundtrack includes "Good Vibrations" and a few *Pet Sounds* songs.

Inside Pop—The Rock Revolution (Filmed in December 1966)

This legendary CBS television documentary hosted by Leonard Bernstein features incredible live footage of Brian Wilson performing the song "Surf's Up" alone at a piano. By the time the special aired in April 1967, Brian's epic *Smile* project was coming unraveled. This is without a doubt one of the most important pieces of film having to do with the Beach Boys and their history.

UNICEF Benefit Concert (Filmed in December 1967)

This concert, filmed in Paris, was televised in Europe during the 1967 Christmas holiday. The Beach Boys are seen performing the ubiquitous "Barbara Ann," a lovely version of "God Only Knows," and a fantastic, harmonically robust rendition of "Oh Come All Ye Faithful" featuring Bruce at the piano with Mike, Dennis, Carl, and Al gathered around him. Their vocal performance on this traditional song is beautiful, even with the absence of Brian.

The Ed Sullivan Show (October 13, 1968)

The group appeared on Sullivan's long running Sunday night television variety show in white suits, performing their latest hit "Do It Again" and the two-year-old "Good Vibrations." Some sound and visual effects that don't work that well are added to the group's performance. This is a fair performance, but not a great one.

The Mike Douglas Show (April 1969)

Manson music for the masses. The Beach Boys appear on TV performing "I Can Hear Music" and Dennis and Charlie's "Never Learn Not to Love." Both songs are performed with live vocals over a prerecorded backing track, and both are very good visually. To see Dennis fronting the band on lead vocals is a treat, and he looks and sounds great. The fact that he's performing a spruced-up song written by a future mass murderer is a bit disconcerting. But this is some of the best footage of Dennis singing that exists. It's also great to see Carl performing "I Can Hear Music," which he of course sings beautifully.

The Mike Douglas Show (July 1969)

Following a European tour, the Beach Boys returned to the Douglas-hosted TV show, and performed both sides of their latest single. First "Break Away" was played with live vocals over a prerecorded backing track, followed by an interview touching on their recent travels in which Bruce dominates the conversation. Again with live vocals and prerecorded instruments, the rest of the group performs "Celebrate the News," while Carl pretends to play the drums. An interesting element is hearing Dennis and Mike trading vocal lines during the song's long fade.

Something Else (February 14, 1970)

The group appeared on the short-lived music show, hosted by comedian John Byner, miming to "Cotton Fields" under dark skies. Multiple camera set-ups make this an interesting segment. A fantasy sequence featuring all of the Beach Boys, separately with various girls, is built around the song "Good Vibrations."

Pop 2 (Filmed on December 8, 1970)

This eclectic French TV show featured a rare interview with the Beach Boys minus Bruce, interspersed with live concert segments of the full band filmed with a handheld camera that wandered around the stage. Both the visual perspective and the live sound are great. It's a revelation to see the band, especially in this rarely seen era, performing rarities like "Country Air" and "It's About Time" in front of a live audience. The show aired in Europe on April 17, 1971.

The David Frost Show (Filmed on March 1, 1971)

This is some of the best live footage of the Beach Boys just prior to Dennis's hand injury that kept him away from the drums for several years. Although Al mangles the lyrics to "Wouldn't It Be Nice," the group performs a lively version of the song. With their full brass section in tow, and several other auxiliary musicians including Ed Carter, Daryl Dragon, and Dennis Dragon, this appearance is a wonderful example of how the group sounded in concert circa early 1971. The group also performs "Cool, Cool Water" which is sung beautifully, especially by Carl.

The David Frost Show (Filmed on May 7, 1971)

The Beach Boys return to Frost's TV show, this time showcasing two Dennis Wilson songs and one *Smile* classic. They open with a full-band rendition of "Forever," and then follow that with a mini acoustic set featuring "Vegetables" and a great version of Dennis's "Lady." The interview segment mainly focuses on Dennis's role in the soon-to-be-released feature film *Two-Lane Blacktop*. Considering he is the focus of the interview *and* composer and singer of two of the three songs performed, this is probably the height of the brief post-*Sunflower* period when the Beach Boys seemed to be pushing Dennis as their frontman.

Good Vibrations From Central Park (Filmed on July 2, 1971)

This outdoor concert was captured for an NBC-TV special that aired on August 19, 1971. It is a fabulous document of the Beach Boys in transition. With Dennis now unable to play drums due to a severe hand injury, but prior to Ricky Fataar replacing him, the Beach Boys call upon Mike Kowalski to temporarily fill in on drums. The group performs a great version of "Heroes and Villains," and they also nicely pull off Mike's Merle Haggard showcase "Okie from Muskogee." Dennis sings a moving version of his "Forever" ballad, and then the band kick it into high gear for a rocking "It's About Time." The final song, "I Get Around," isn't quite as aesthetically satisfying as the rest, but the crowd goes nuts for it anyway.

Two-Lane Blacktop (July 1971)

This stands as the only example of one of the Beach Boys performing in a major acting role. Dennis Wilson was cast as the "Mechanic" in the existential muscle-car epic *Two-Lane Blacktop*, distributed by Universal Pictures. Costarring alongside James Taylor, Warren Oates, and Laurie Bird, Dennis does a fine job without relying on very much dialogue to develop his character. Instead it's the rugged visual aspect of the "Mechanic" that is intriguing, and shows that Dennis had an undeniable screen presence and major potential as a movie star. The film was not a commercial success in its theater run, but it reviewed quite well. In the years since its release *Two-Lane Blacktop*

Dennis pictured chatting with his *Two-Lane Blacktop* costar James Taylor. Considering the formidable musical talent the two of them shared, it seems sad that neither sang a single note during this film.

has become a favorite of serious film buffs who appreciate director Monte Hellman's lonely, stark vision, and the film's eye-catching cinematography. It has also become a cult favorite of car enthusiasts who feast on its rubber-burning action provided by a parade of vintage high-performance hot rods.

Old Grey Whistle Test (Filmed on May 16, 1972)

The Beach Boys appeared on the legendary British TV show singing "You Need a Mess of Help to Stand Alone." Their lineup for this performance includes former Flame members Blondie Chaplin and Ricky Fataar, as well as keyboardist Daryl Dragon.

Good Vibrations From London (June 28, 1972)

Filmed at London's outdoor Crystal Palace Bowl for this U.S.-aired TV special, the Beach Boys perform "Do It Again," a bloodcurdling take on "Wild Honey" with Blondie on lead vocals, and "Help Me, Rhonda" with Elton John sitting in on keyboards. The British audience gives the group its usual adulatory reaction despite being subjected to cold, rainy weather throughout the band's performance.

Dick Clark's New Year's Rockin' Eve (December 31, 1974)

Filmed a month prior to its New Years Eve TV broadcast, the Beach Boys are represented by only three members during this joint performance with the band Chicago. Mike Love, Carl Wilson, and Al Jardine perform as "the Beach Boys" and do a good job. But with no Brian as usual, no Dennis for unexplained reasons, and Bruce, Blondie, and Ricky having departed the band by this point, the group looks a little light on personnel. The tacky matching costumes they wore for this appearance don't help much, either.

It's OK (August 5, 1976)

This hour-long TV special devoted to the Beach Boys and sponsored by Dr Pepper came at the absolute height of the "Brian's Back" era. Produced by Lorne Michaels, with appearances by John Belushi, Dan Aykroyd, Van Dyke Parks, and Paul McCartney, it is a classic moment in the history of the Beach Boys. Featuring great interview segments interspersed with clips from the group's July 3, 1976 concert at a sold-out Anaheim Stadium, the Beach Boys are captured at peak of their second trip to the top of the rock-and-roll heap.

August 5, 2010
Flashback: The Beach Boys' *It's OK* Comeback Special Airs on NBC
by Howie Edelson

It was 34 years ago tonight (August 5, 1976) that the Beach Boys' NBC primetime special The Beach Boys: It's OK *premiered. The show, which was produced by* Saturday Night Live*'s executive producer Lorne Michaels, was based around the group's 15th anniversary, their new* 15 Big Ones *album, and the full-time return of Brian Wilson to the group, kicking off the legendary "Brian's Back" publicity campaign.*

The special included live performances filmed on July 3, 1976 at California's Anaheim Stadium in front of 55,000 fans, featuring the group's classic lineup: Mike Love, Dennis Wilson, Carl Wilson, and Al Jardine, with the long reclusive Brian behind the keyboards, playing only his second full concert in over six years.

The show's sketch in which Saturday Night Live*'s John Belushi and Dan Aykroyd pose as California Highway Patrolmen and force an overweight Brian out of bed to go surfing after issuing him a citation for failing to surf has gone on to become one of rock and roll's greatest comedic moments. Later that year, photographer Annie*

In the summer of 1976, the Beach Boys enjoyed their second commercial peak with a hit album, a hit single, a well-received NBC TV special, and unprecedented box-office success.

Leibovitz used a photo of the bathrobed Brian holding a surfboard for an iconic cover of Rolling Stone.

Beach Boys author, historian, and documentary producer Jon Stebbins, who wrote the definitive biographies on Dennis Wilson—The Real Beach Boy, *and David Marks*—The Lost Beach Boy, *explains that Mike Love's importance to the band's live shows should never be underestimated: "Mike's confidence standing onstage as a frontman is one of the really crucial things that he brought to the table. Without him, they woulda been screwed, man! They just did not have a personality in the band that could do what he did. And he did it well right from the start, and he got better and better and better at it. Until the point where then it became uncool to be that way. And it's sort of like he couldn't turn it off. Y'know, he was what he was."*

Peter Ames Carlin, the author of Catch a Wave: The Rise, Fall & Redemption of the Beach Boys' Brian Wilson, *says that no matter how far Brian tried to distance himself from the group, he always ended up returning: "Brian allowed himself to get dragged back into the Beach Boys, time after time, after time. If he didn't want do it, he wouldn't have done it, really. It's not necessarily the healthy decision, but I think it was the one that worked for him."*

Highlights in the special include Dennis Wilson acting as one of the judges of the Miss California beauty pageant, Dennis singing his signature "You Are So Beautiful" encore at the Anaheim show, and all three Wilson brothers harmonizing around the piano singing group chestnuts such as "I'm Bugged At My Old Man" and "Surfer Girl."

It's OK *also featured footage shot at Brian Wilson's 34th birthday party (June 20, 1976) held at brother Carl's Malibu home, with Paul and Linda McCartney and their kids all helping to present Wilson with his birthday cake.*

The title of the show was chosen to tie in with the band's then-current single, "It's OK." It was the follow up to their recent Top Five hit, a cover of Chuck Berry's "Rock and Roll Music," which earned the group their first Top Ten hit in nearly a decade. The footage from the It's OK *special has gone on to be featured in nearly every Beach Boys documentary since its network premiere. In 2005, the special was released on DVD as* The Beach Boys: Good Vibrations Tour.

Midnight Special (April 27, 1979)

The Beach Boys perform their classics "Surfin' U.S.A." and "Good Vibrations" as well as three songs from their current *L.A. (Light Album)*. The unfortunate disco rendition of "Here Comes the Night" is performed, plus "Angel Come Home" with an obviously deteriorating Dennis on lead vocals, and Al's recent U.K. hit "Lady Lynda." The Byrds' founder Roger McGuinn joins the boys for a raucous take of "Rock and Roll Music." This show is significant in that it's the last time Dennis was given a lead vocal during a Beach Boys TV appearance.

The Beach Boys In Concert (July 4, 1980)

HBO filmed this concert for television, and aired it several times in the early '80s. The band is seen performing in front of 500,000 fans at the National Mall in Washington, D.C. Brian is there, along with Mike, Carl, Dennis, Al, and Bruce. The concert is not one of their best, but compared to later shows it at least has the advantage of having a full complement of band members.

The Mike Douglas Show (December 10, 1980)

Marking their first *Mike Douglas Show* appearance in over a decade, the Beach Boys are seen performing live on Waikiki Beach in Hawaii. Brian is not part of the band's lineup, which includes Mike, Dennis, Carl, Al, and Bruce plus Bobby Figueroa, Mike Meros, and Ed Carter. The group gives a decent performance, and the visual appeal of seeing them set up in the sand with Diamond Head in the background is great. A notable moment occurs when Dennis informs Mike Douglas that this is the first time the Beach Boys have performed a concert on the beach!

The Beach Boys Twentieth Anniversary Special (Summer, 1981)

This TV show aired in syndication in various markets around the U.S. It includes interview segments and clips of the band's 1980 Knebworth concert, as well as several songs from the July 4, 1980 Washington, D.C. performance. This was the first official release of any of the Knebworth footage, which was finally released as a full concert on DVD in 2004.

Good Vibrations Over America (July 5, 1981)

This is the infamous live television concert broadcast from the docking site of the Queen Mary in Long Beach, California. What made this performance so dodgy is the fact that Carl Wilson was on hiatus from the band, and a wheezy Brian Wilson was asked to cover several of Carl's lead vocals. Not a good idea. Let's just say Brian's voice wasn't in the best of shape. The whole extravaganza was Mike's concept and production. He recruited Wolfman Jack to host the affair, which was also simulcast on FM radio. It goes down in history as one of the low points for the Beach Boys, especially since it was such a high-profile media event, and so many witnessed the train wreck the Beach Boys had become.

The Tonight Show (June 28, 1984)

The Beach Boys hadn't appeared on the legendary NBC-TV late-night talk show since the '60s. This episode unfortunately was missing star and host Johnny Carson, who was vacationing. His replacement, Joan Rivers, interviewed the group, including a newly svelte Brian, who had lost 100 pounds. Brian's behavior is typically odd. He rambles off something incoherent about Phil Spector; and at one point, he asks if Dr. Landy can join the panel—but no one responds. A significant amount of footage from an earlier Washington, D.C. concert is shown. In it there were several close-ups of Dennis, who had died only six months earlier, but neither the host nor any of the Beach Boys make any mention of him. The only music performed on the *Tonight Show* stage is a very lounge-spiked version of "Graduation Day" backed by the show's orchestra.

Ronald Reagan Inaugural Celebration (January 19, 1985)

The group was invited to perform at President Reagan's second inaugural festivities. The appearance is remembered for the beautiful a cappella performance of "Their Hearts Were Full of Spring" featuring a much-improved Brian singing the high harmony.

Live Aid (July 13, 1985)

This televised live-concert benefit for African famine relief took place on multiple stages in the U.S. and Europe. The Beach Boys were filmed performing a set in Philadelphia that included "Wouldn't It Be Nice," "California Girls," "Good Vibrations," "Help Me, Rhonda," and "Surfin' U.S.A."

Farm Aid (September 22, 1985)

The Beach Boys were featured among the acts performing for Willie Nelson's farm benefit, which took place at Memorial Stadium in Champaign, Illinois. The event was televised on the Nashville Network and raised millions.

The Beach Boys: An American Band (November 1985)

This film, directed by Malcolm Leo, was the first extensive documentary on the Beach Boys. It initially received a limited run in a handful of movie theaters across the U.S., grossing a modest $2,000,000. It quickly became available as a home VHS product, and for over a decade was considered the definitive film about the band. Leo has a habit of taking vintage clips and replacing their sound with music that didn't originally go with that particular footage. This ended up confusing fans for years as to the context and origins of certain parts of the film. However, with so much classic footage in it, *An American Band* is a revelation for anyone who loves the Beach Boys.

Endless Summer (Summer, 1989)

The group was briefly given its own television series in the summer of 1989. A total of 16 episodes aired, including segments filmed at a live concert in Costa Mesa, and classic unplugged campfire scenes filmed at Universal Studios that include a healthy-looking Brian, who is in very good spirits.

Summer Dreams (1990)

This 90-minute TV movie, based on Steven Gaines's book *Heroes and Villains*, centers around Bruce Greenwood's portrayal of the tragic Dennis Wilson. Although Greenwood does a decent job, the show is mainly remembered for the horrible fake beards and wigs worn by the actors.

I Just Wasn't Made For These Times (1993)

A documentary about Brian Wilson produced and directed by Don Was. It is built around Brian performing a selection of songs from his career, backed by a band put together by Was, plus interview segments with Tom Petty, David Crosby, and others.

Baywatch (Filmed in April 1995)

The Beach Boys episode of TV's *Baywatch* was significant because most of the show features the lineup of Mike, Brian, Carl, Al, and Bruce. But the live-concert portion of the episode, filmed on the Santa Monica Pier, is missing Carl and Brian, adding David Marks to the lineup with no explanation.

Home Improvement (January 14, 1997)

The group is featured in an episode, entitled "The Karate Kid Returns," of the popular TV series. They sing loose a cappella renditions of a few oldies, and interestingly their lineup for this show includes Al's son Matt, along with Mike, Carl, Bruce, and Al.

Endless Harmony (1998)

Alan Boyd directed this excellent documentary detailing the band's history and evolution. Upon its release, it essentially replaced Malcolm Leo's 1985 *American Band* as the definitive Beach Boys documentary.

Super Bowl XXXII Pregame Show (January 25, 1998)

Billed as "America's Band," a lineup including Mike Love, Bruce Johnston, David Marks, and Dean Torrence performed several Beach Boys hits as part of the Super Bowl extravaganza from Qualcomm Stadium in San Diego, California. Al Jardine was not invited to participate in this gig and only became aware of it after seeing it on TV.

The Beach Boys: An American Family (1999)

Actor and part-time Beach Boys sideman John Stamos produced this contro-versial two-part ABC TV miniseries dramatizing the band's history. Part One was met with a generally positive reaction from Beach Boys fans. However, Part Two, which ran with a disclaimer that appeared on screen, went off the deep end in its portrayal of Brian in his post-1965 days. He was shown as a blithering and incompetent fool who only achieved good things when Mike Love helped him. Needless to say, the fans and Brian's family were not happy. This miniseries is now thought of as a joke, and those who were involved in making it spend significant energy in distancing themselves from it.

What follows is my eyewitness account of a visit to the set during the produc-tion of *An American Family*.

On the Set of The Beach Boys: An American Family

It was one of those unforgettable events during an unforgettable time. It started when I spent an afternoon at former Beach Boys' photographer and Wilson insider Ed Roach's Santa Monica office. We met there with actor Nick Stabile, who was portraying Dennis in the ABC miniseries *The Beach Boys: An American Family*, which had just started shooting. Nick asked for some pointers regarding playing Dennis, and Ed and I obliged. A day or two later

Ed and I ran into the show's producer John Stamos at a Brian Wilson concert in Orange County. Stamos thanked us for giving Nick some help with his job of playing Dennis. He then invited us to visit the *American Family* "set" whenever we wanted. Ed got this look in his eye that signaled to me that this could be an excellent opportunity on several levels.

In the meantime, I helped my brother-in-law Felix get an audition for the part of one of Murry Wilson's Sunrays in the same miniseries. Felix did well at the audition and got the job. Ed and I decided it would be a good time to visit the set while Felix was filming his scenes.

Upon our arrival at the full-blown Hollywood set, located at the old United Western studios, we were immediately questioned by a group of security guards stationed outside. "We're guests of Mr. Stamos," said Ed. We were politely informed that Mr. Stamos was away from the set that day; and since they couldn't check it out with him, we couldn't go in. "Call him," Ed said as he walked past the security guys and onto the set. Once we got inside, it was too late to get rid of us. Everybody there either knew us, or wanted to know us, or were scared of us. Once they were all told it was Ed Roach (famous Beach Boys insider) and his friend who was writing a book about one of the Beach Boys, there was this constant energy of curiosity and fear trailing us everywhere we went. As if we were there to expose them. From that point until we left, our presence distracted all involved in the proceedings.

That was fine with Ed; he was there to have a good time, and I learned quickly what that look had been about at Brian's show. Ed had been on more than a few sets before, and he knew it was a virtual playground for "visitors" with producer's clearance like us, especially since our gracious host was nowhere to be found. Since Mr. Stamos couldn't check up on us his assistants and various stagehands, we were virtually at Ed's mercy. I followed him through several separated sections of the *American Family* set as we wandered freely. We visited a room portraying where much of *Pet Sounds* had been recorded, then we watched Felix shoot his Sunrays scene.

We explored further. We ran into somewhat horrified-looking friends who were working on the set. I shouldn't mention names, but I guess we gave them something to worry about because they turned even whiter than they are when they saw us coming. We may have had a drink or two that afternoon, I can't remember, but we weren't frothing at the mouth, or staggering, or belligerent. Everybody seemed concerned we might screw something up. Us? Well . . . at one point Ed *did* end up inside the frame of a 1963 scene being shot with surfer-shirted actors portraying Brian Wilson and Jan and Dean. Through the glass of the studio recording booth while mixing "Surf City" was the character of engineer Chuck Britz, and next to him was . . . 1999 Ed Roach with his shoulder-length hair and a big smile.

"Who is that guy in the booth?" yelled the director. "He's on camera! Can we get him out of there, pleeeese?"

People scuffled around the set, trying to please the director, but it had little effect on Ed. Sure, Ed's attire and hair length might not have been "period" for the 1963 scene, but since he was in the middle of telling the actor playing Chuck Britz about being in the studio with the *real* Brian Wilson, why should he move just cause they're shooting a little scene? When he finished his story, Ed stood up, walked out of the scene, and happily went down the hall to cause more mayhem.

Pretty soon we had a couple of nervous assistants, all of the Sunrays in full costume, and various members of the cast and crew following us around. We ran into Nick Stabile, who warmly welcomed us, and the other BB actors in full early-1960s Beach Boys hair and dress. It was surreal as hell to wander through a simulated Beach Boys world with no boundaries.

Then dinner was served. Myself, Ed, and the Sunrays were the first people to partake from the impressive spread of catered grub. According to Ed's gauge, this was an "all you can eat" affair, as confirmed by the sumptuous choice of lobster and other entrees. We were told had Stamos insisted upon the absolute top-tier L.A. caterers. Now we know where the budget went. We took a table to ourselves with the Sunrays. The rest of the production crew, soon seated at another table, were eyeing us nervously like we might be Manson family leftovers or something. They kept coming over, one by one, asking us if everything was okay. One production member was freaking out over our presence, saying he was gonna get fired because of us. Why? I told him, "Hey, man, we're guests of John Stamos, calm down!" Just because I was on my cell phone inviting *more* friends down to the set to join us, he got all bent out of shape. Then another crewmember came over and asked us if we were going to stay and eat. We looked up from our already half-eaten entrees and said, "Don't mind if we do." We went for seconds.

Soon the characters of Dennis Wilson and Bruce Johnston joined us at our table. And before long the show's director was there too. The rest of the crew were now looking over at us like we were the cool kids in school and they were the nerds. The director, Jeff Bleckner, proclaimed it was Ed who was the real deal, and that his production was basically just lightweight fiction loosely based on history. He was correct, but Ed barely slowed down from his onslaught on the eats to acknowledge him. And in a way Bleckner seemed almost apologetic, as if we had come down there specifically to kick his butt or something. We only wanted to accept Mr. Stamos's kind invitation. We came in peace.

I won't tell you how many helpings of lobster Ed consumed that evening. But wasn't it the Beach Boys and Dennis who taught Ed how to take advantage of first-class catering anyway? By eating so well, Ed was just allowing the great circle of rock and roll to flow forth in a balance and highly spiritual way. It was meant to be. And even though the miniseries would turn out to be artistically poor, Ed got to have fun, have a great meal, and cause some trouble. His old buddy Dennis would have appreciated that."

Beautiful Dreamer: Brian Wilson and the Story of Smile (2004)

This well-reviewed documentary directed by David Leaf includes interview segments with a long list of celebrities, including Elvis Costello, Paul McCartney, and George Martin. On one hand it is a very well-made and entertaining film; on the other hand it tends to perpetuate myths about the Beach Boys that are not entirely based in fact.

The Beach Boys: Wouldn't It Be Nice (January 9, 2005)

This 60-minute documentary directed by Matt O'Casey aired on BBC television. It features a breezy overview of the band's career with great new interview segments with Brian Wilson, Mike Love, Hal Blaine, Tony Asher, Van Dyke Parks, and many more. The highlight of the piece is the ending segment with Brian considering a question about a Beach Boys reunion.

The sad demise of Dennis Wilson is one rock history's most tragic falls. Pictured here in 1983 holding his son Gage, Dennis was in and out of the Beach Boys throughout the '80s due to his severe alcoholism.

Photo by Henry Diltz

1974: On the Road With the Beach Boys (2010)

This is a fascinating behind-the-scenes look at the Beach Boys touring regimen circa 1974. Directed by Billy Hinsche, who documented the band with his Portapak video camera while also playing guitar and keyboards in the touring lineup, this documentary comes from a true insider's point of view. Billy intersperses modern-day interview segments with many of the people who were there with him, like James Guercio, Ed Carter, Carli Munoz, and Bobby Figueroa.

Dennis Wilson: The Real Beach Boy (February 26, 2010)

This 60-minute documentary directed by Matt O' Casey is the first full-blown TV program to focus on Dennis. It premiered as part of the BBC "Legends" series and was a critical hit, receiving a Royal Television Society Award nomination for Best Documentary.

25

'Til I Die

Beach Boys Deaths

With each Beach Boys–related passing, something essential to the essence of their greatness disappears, and the band dies a little bit more with each one. The following is a reflection on the deaths of four members of the Wilson family.

Murry Wilson

The Beach Boys patriarch and first manager passed away from heart failure on June 4, 1973. He was only 55 years old, but had been in ill health for several years. For a long time he had been estranged from his wife Audree, and for a time was living with another woman. But in the months prior to his death, Audree had moved back in with Murry to care for him. He is buried at the Inglewood Park Cemetery, only a few miles from the site of the Wilsons' Hawthorne home, where a California State Landmark now stands in appreciation of the band he championed so relentlessly. Neither Brian nor Dennis attended his funeral.

Dennis Wilson

Severely alcoholic and homeless, Dennis Wilson tragically drowned in Marina del Rey on December 28, 1983. He was just 39 years old. Dennis was diving off the dock and into the slip where his beloved sailboat the Harmony had been moored prior to its 1981 repossession by the bank. Dennis was pulling discarded items from the marina floor that had been thrown from his boat years earlier. He was last seen bringing up a silver picture frame with a photo of himself and his former wife Karen Lamm pictured on their wedding day. He placed the frame on the dock and dove down again, this time never to return.

The official cause of death was ruled an accidental drowning. Dennis's blood-alcohol content was .28, and the water temperature was only 58 degrees. Dennis was afforded an honor usually reserved for military veterans, as the U.S. Coast Guard gave him an official sea burial. It was President

Reagan who made this possible at the request of Dennis's widow Shawn. The *New York Times* reported the following—

> Larry Speakes, the White House spokesman, said Mr. Wilson's family took Mr. Reagan up on a promise he made this summer when the Beach Boys visited the White House. The President said then that he would be glad to help the Beach Boys if they ever needed it.

This was a very sad end to a life that had been spiraling out of control for years.

Recording engineer Tom Murphy, who was trying to help a deteriorating Dennis finish his *Bambu* record during his last years, is emphatic that he'd had lost the ability to concentrate long enough to be productive in the studio. Murphy described it as awful thing to witness. Due to Dennis's severe alcoholism, there was no ability to focus on the work at hand for more than a few fleeting moments at a time. Just a few years earlier, during the *Pacific Ocean Blue* period, Dennis was known for leading marathon sessions, never losing his focus, and basically outlasting and outworking everyone around him. But by the early 1980s, getting any significant recording accomplished was impossible due to Dennis's constant substance abuse.

Dennis had written so much in the 1970s that he was still a virtual juke-box of snippets and motifs, and could sit down at a piano and play tons of things that were partial or being "developed," but there was no ability to follow through on anything. Murphy described Dennis as being like an Olympic cyclist who had won races just a few years prior. Dennis could still ride the bike, but he could never make it anywhere near the finish line during his last few years. The reasons for his freefall into addiction has been pored over by his loved ones for decades. His second wife Barbara relates, "He couldn't accept or love himself." She claims that Murry's parenting may have been responsible for Dennis's lack of self-worth. Dennis's third wife Karen Lamm basically claimed the same thing: "Dennis's biggest hang-up is that he never felt accepted by his father. He could never get past that." Most of his friends agree.

Dennis's 1968 connection to the Manson family only made it worse. After the horrific Tate/LaBianca murders in the summer of 1969, major guilt and shame was generated within Dennis, warranted or not. Dennis didn't relax, and didn't sleep well because he was constantly haunted by relentless inner turmoil, and in the long run that wore him down. At various points in his life, he got a little better: in 1970, when he was first with Barbara, and in 1974 and 1975, when he first was with Karen. But the darkness always returned, and always in a more severe form. Substances gave Dennis a brief break from obsessing about whatever that darkness and pain was . . . but of course they just created a larger problem, a deeper hole.

Living on the Harmony sailboat, and creating in the studio, were two outlets that were relatively healthy for Dennis. But once the boat had been repossessed and the studio was sold, he had no anchor. Instead he had more time on his hands and more opportunity to self-medicate his gnawing self-doubt, which eventually turned into a death spiral. The Beach Boys, and particularly Mike Love, had been fed up with Dennis's antics since the late 1970s. He was fired from, and rejoined, the band many times between 1979 and 1983. The Beach Boys' organization made a failed attempt to get him to detox and rehab, but he never stayed clean for longer than two days. With no other solutions left, they eventually cut off his money stream. Dennis spent his last days living on the streets. He had nothing left, except for his demons. The darkness was with him to the very end.

Brian's problems generate from a similar place. Both brothers were severely traumatized at an early age, and they were predisposed to addiction. They both were hardwired in a way that made them very fragile inside. Some of us have that built-in sense that everything is going to be okay, and we automatically like ourselves, and feel loved and secure at our core. It's what is known as a stable foundation. Brian and Dennis did not have that. In fact they both battled a giant deficiency in that area. They had massive self-doubt, tremendous insecurity, huge inner turmoil, and pain. Brian's morphed into huge fear and emotional paralysis, Dennis's morphed into self-destruction. Most people who knew Dennis say it's a miracle that he lasted until 39.

When Dennis drowned in December 1983, he'd become virtually homeless and disconnected from his band and family. Without him, the Beach Boys would continue as a successful act for decades, but to many fans they were never credible without Dennis.

DEPARTMENT OF TRANSPORTATION
UNITED STATES COAST GUARD   MAILING ADDRESS
COMMANDER (dpl)
ELEVENTH COAST GUARD DISTRICT
UNION BANK BLDG.
400 OCEANGATE
LONG BEACH, CA. 90822

09 January 1984

Regional Director
Environmental Protection Agency
Region IX Office
100 California Street
San Francisco, California 94111

Dear Sir:

Pursuant to Title 40 CFR, Part 229, the remains of DENNIS WILSON were
buried at sea by USCGC POINT JUDITH (WPB 82345) at 1711 local time (5:11 Pm)
04 January 1984, in location 33-53.9°N, 118-38.8°W. This position is
greater than three nautical miles from land and the water depth in
excess of 100 fathoms.

Sincerely,

J. F. STUMPFF
Commander, U. S. Coast Guard
Chief, Planning Staff
By direction of the District Commander

In January 1984, the Reagan Administration approved an official Coast Guard sea
burial for Dennis, which is rare for a civilian. In many ways Dennis and the Pacific
Ocean were always one in spirit, and this final act just made their dance eternal.

Audree Wilson

The self-described "Beach Boys' mom," Audree Wilson, passed away on
December 1, 1997 of heart and kidney failure. She was 79 years old. At the
time of her death, she had been admitted to intensive care at Cedars-Sinai
Medical Center on Beverly Boulevard in Los Angeles. Audree continues to
be greatly underrated as a musical influence on the Beach Boys, as it was
her boogie-woogie piano style that Brian and his brothers became enamored with a very young age. She was hugely supportive of her sons' musical
endeavors, but never used the high-pressure tactics of her husband Murry
to motivate them. Instead Audree gave them praise and a gentle nudge
forward. It was Audree who insisted that Dennis be included in Brian and
Carl's formative group—which evolved into the Beach Boys. There has been
speculation that Audree was an alcoholic, and that she also was complicit
in allowing her husband to physically abuse their children. But anyone who
personally knew Audree describes her as one of the kindest people in the

world. She was closer to, and maintained a much better relationship with, her sons than Murry. She also developed a close relationship with many of her nine grandchildren.

Carl Wilson

Barely two months after his mother Audree passed away, Carl Wilson succumbed to cancer on February 6, 1998. He'd been diagnosed with brain and lung cancer a year prior to his death, and fought the disease hard by undertaking chemotherapy treatments. Despite that he managed to continue touring with the Beach Boys until the end of August 1997, and many in the Beach Boys organization fully expected him to overcome his disease and return to the band. His passing was a deep blow to longtime fans of the band, as Carl represented a vocal standard that could never be duplicated. To many, the Beach Boys ended the day Carl died.

Unlike his brothers, Carl for the most part maintained an even presence and outwardly seemed to be the most normally adjusted of the Wilsons. He faced a period of heavy substance abuse in the late 1970s, but by the decade's end he had overcome that problem for good. One remaining vice that may have had a long-term consequence was his habit of smoking cigarettes, which lasted into the 1980s. Another factor that many believe contributed to Carl's eventual health problems was the stress that he so skillfully masked despite years of fretting over and coping with his two brothers' mental-health and substance-abuse issues. He was devastated by Dennis's death, and from there his relationship with Brian was at times shaky, including periods of estrangement.

In the late '80s, Carl and the Wilson family filed gross-negligence charges against Dr. Landy for his illegal use of psychotropic drugs on Brian and for his control of Brian's finances. A court-appointed conservator was appointed to oversee Brian's affairs, and eventually Landy was driven out. Many felt it was too late, and that permanent damage had already been done to Brian. Some pointed fingers at Carl for not reacting as swiftly as he could have. But Carl had for years made everyone else the priority and had acted as a stabilizer when things were threatening to fall apart. By the late '80s and '90s, he seemed to cede control of the Beach Boys to Mike, preferring to leave the battles of the past behind and to move forward in a somewhat passive role.

More than anything else, Carl will always be remembered for his beautiful voice. There was a quality in that instrument that matched the kind and centered essence of Carl the man. He is remembered as the Beach Boy who was the best mannered and the most consistently appreciative of the average fan. His loss is still felt with great sadness, while his voice still moves anyone who hears it.

Beach Boys Turmoil in the Aftermath of Carl's Death

The momentum that led to Al's 1998 departure was underway before Carl had to leave the touring Beach Boys due to the cancer that eventually killed him. Carl and Al were not at all in sync with each other regarding Mike's determination to change up some specific fundamental Beach Boys business matters. They ended up becoming "estranged" (Al's description) towards the end of Carl's life. They managed to patch it up before Carl passed away. But the reasons Al departed the Beach Boys in 1998 actually began as early as 1995 or 1996. David Marks was already playing occasional Beach Boys shows back then. He was not brought in to replace Carl, or at least not groomed or

With Carl Wilson too ill to tour, David Marks returned to a full-time position with the Beach Boys in 1997. In the aftermath of Carl's tragic death in 1998, a business disagreement between Mike Love and Al Jardine led to Al being virtually frozen out of the band. Therefore, the 1998 Beach Boys were down to three official members: David, Mike, and Bruce Johnston.

positioned to replace Carl. As it turned out , he actually did end up replacing Carl, but that was due to Carl's ill health and not to any specific strategy.

Carl's illness confused the process, and an adjustment was made. Al was never told why David was brought in, and didn't learn Dave's perspective on all of this until years later. In truth, Mike wanted the Beach Boys' concert productions and revenue stream set up in a certain way. Carl didn't resist Mike's proposed changes. Al did resist. Mike did it anyway. Subsequently Al was frozen out. Al was very surprised that Mike was able to pull it all off so smoothly. The fact that Carl became ill and passed away in the middle of all of this ended up putting all of the public's focus on that, and has distracted from the essence of the real story. David was kind of used as a pawn in Mike's game, and was really introduced as a potential sacrificial lamb as early as 1995. He didn't even realize it himself until much later.

David thought he was going to be playing *with* Carl once he rejoined the Beach Boys . . . not in place of him. This has been a tough one for Dave to live down, because a lot of fans assumed he was taking advantage of Carl's illness by suddenly jumping into the Beach Boys in 1997, just prior to Carl's death. David might have actually been there earlier if not for some serious legal troubles that resulted in a court case, imprisonment, and court-ordered post-incarceration program. By the time David was legally cleared to participate in the Beach Boys again, Carl was sick, and Mike and Al's disagreement over the group's business affairs was in full swing. If Carl had beaten the cancer, as many around the Beach Boys organization had assumed he would, and if he had rejoined the group, David believed he would have remained in the band alongside Carl. That's what he was hoping for.

26

Hang On To Your Ego

The Fun of Hating Mike Love

For a singer and lyricist who has had more hits and more success than nearly any living figure from the golden era of rock, Mike Love gets very little respect from many critics, journalists, and from the majority of Brian Wilson fans. Is it his fault, or is Mike a victim? The general perception of Mike Love as a bad guy might finally be changing a bit as of late. But he's got a long way to go before he loses the tag of being one of the most reviled figures in show business.

The reasons for the negative perceptions of Mike are many. They are rooted in something that is inherent. His manner, his way, and his outward personality are things that worked very well for the Beach Boys, but also created a backlash for Mike. He developed a playfully smart-aleck stage persona that relied on a somewhat aloof body language countered by stage patter that was purposely silly but rarely funny. As if he were too cool to actually be serious. That semi-cocky persona is one of the things that balanced Brian's stage fright. When Brian kicked loose and felt comfortable, he actually *was* naturally funny and more engaging than Mike, but it was hit-and-miss. Sometimes Brian froze. Mike has never frozen on stage in his life. His stage character inhabits him the minute he steps in front of people. He grins, nods his head, points to someone in the crowd, and from that moment he's both the frontman and the emcee. None of the Wilsons had the ability to take over the show on a nightly basis like Mike has for 50 years.

But a little bit of Mike goes a long way, and some tired of his act very quickly. Others couldn't get enough, and still consider him the quintessential frontman. I can see both sides. Beginning in the mid-'60s, Mike started taking some hits from certain quarters about his stage moves, his balding head, and his nasal voice. As the British Invasion types with Liverpool accents, lots of long hair, and mod clothes became the rage, a stripe-shirted, jerk-dancing, follicly challenged Mike looked a bit behind the times. He became something of a joke to many rock fans. And it got worse from there.

In 1967, while *Smile* was melting down, Mike was named as the culprit who most questioned Brian's recent creative direction and his approach to making records. Mike's infamous "don't fuck with the formula" comment may have been uttered in regard to *Pet Sounds*, but *Smile* is when Mike's crap truly hit the fan. From that point he was looked upon with suspicion and derision from many Brian supporters. Slowly this perception of Mike leaked into the press, and into the minds of fans. Coupled with his stage demeanor, these new rumors of Mike being anti-*Smile* slowly worked their way through the chain of insiders, press, and casual fans. Mike was beginning to be viewed as the bad guy.

More negative stories about Mike surfaced. He was accused of slapping his wife Suzanne in public, making her wear certain clothes, disallowing her to wear others, and barring her from smoking even if she wanted to. During their divorce proceedings, she was accused of being unstable and promiscuous. Mike also pursued the full custody rights of their children. Again Mike's image took serious blows, and again it only got worse.

We Gave Him Everything We Own Just to Sit at His Table

In the late 1960s, Mike threw himself into the study of Transcendental Meditation and the teachings of Maharishi Mahesh Yogi. He traveled to Rishikesh, India along with the Beatles to study at the Maharishi's mountain compound. When the Beatles had their fill and publically rejected the Maharishi, Mike went all in, convincing the Beach Boys to tour with the Maharishi as their intermission lecturer. The tour was a disaster. The Maharishi's public image was in tatters following the Beatles debacle. With their tour partially riding on the allure of the Maharishi, he became a sudden pariah, and the Beach Boys and Mike were left holding the bag. Mike was seen in some quarters as a poseur, trying to be hip, but really just a square in a white robe.

As the Beach Boys' popularity bottomed out in 1970, and their surf-and-hot-rod material was ridiculed by the acid generation, Mike updated his image, and to some he went too far. He was often seen in flowing robes, and even though the top of his head was relatively bald, he grew the rest as long as he could. He also grew out a Methuselah-esque beard, and looked similar to Robert Crumb's underground comic character Mr. Natural. At one point Mike went off the deep end from fasting and/or drinking too much fruit juice. There was some kind of institutional intervention causing Mike to miss some Beach Boys concerts. More fuel was added to the fire of Mike's detractors.

Mike's mid-1970s stage persona projected an incredibly flamboyant quality. He developed into a glitzy, prancing, whirling dervish of a frontman, and most concert audiences ate it up.

It's a Gas Gas Gas

By the mid-'70s, the Beach Boys were on the comeback trail, and Mike was a revitalized frontman. He adapted a flamboyant stage persona, borrowing dashes of Mick Jagger but retaining the smartass California attitude. His mode of dress continued to show about as much restraint as a gay pimp's. Truthfully he was a great entertainer during those days, and the Beach Boys' live shows certainly benefited from Mike's flashy ways. But at the same time he was also lobbying for a more retro sound and oldies-heavy song selection. In his mind, he was giving the fans what they wanted. Regardless of his intentions, it ended up hurting the band creatively, and also drove Mike further toward being the guy who was assigned blame for not being cool.

By the '80s Mike's battles with Dennis Wilson, on and off the stage, had taken their toll on both Beach Boys. Dennis had been the Beach Boy who took pleasure in standing up to Mike, with words and fists. He constantly needled and challenged Mike, while Mike demanded that Dennis put down the booze and drugs or get lost. Dennis got lost, completely, and died. From that time on there was no one to counter Mike's strength in band politics. Despite Carl's importance as a stage leader and as the "normal" Wilson brother, without Dennis around to physically enforce any anti-Mike sentiment, Mike pretty much had his way.

Mike pounded the ultimate nail into his own image coffin with his infamous Rock and Roll Hall of Fame acceptance speech in 1988. In front of an audience that included Bruce Springsteen, Bob Dylan, George Harrison, Mick Jagger, and a long list of other rock luminaries and press, Mike shared these words: *"The Beach Boys have continued to do, about, we did about 180 performances last year. I'd like to see the Mop Tops match that! I'd like to see Mick Jagger get out on this stage and do "I Get Around" versus "Jumpin' Jack Flash," any day now. And I'd like to see some people kick out the jams, and I challenge the Boss to get up on stage and jam."* As the other Beach Boys and the audience grew increasingly uncomfortable, Mike continued. *"I wanna see Billy Joel, see if he can still tickle ivories, lemme see. I know Mick Jagger won't be here tonight, he's gonna have to stay in England. But I'd like to see us in the Coliseum and he at Wembley Stadium because he's always been chickenshit to get on stage with the Beach Boys."*

The room was shocked. Carl Wilson was visibly embarrassed. Bob Dylan was heard saying, "I'm glad he didn't mention me." The rock press designated Mike as "Mr. Sour Grapes." No one could understand why, at the moment the Beach Boys were being honored for a career of making people happy, Mike decided to take potshots at his perceived rivals. It was a bizarre scene, and it had a devastating effect on Mike's image. Those who were already suspicious of him had public confirmation that he was petty and

conceited. For people who barely knew who Mike was, this was their introduction to him. From this point forward, the name Mike Love was ingrained
into the general public's mind as a controversial entity.

Sue City

Just as Mike's Rock and Roll Hall of Fame meltdown was fading from people's minds, he launched a cascade of high-profile lawsuits. In 1992, Mike
sued Brian to recover songwriting credits he had not been given for Beach
Boys songs to which he'd contributed lyrics. Later that same year, Mike
again sued Brian and the publishers of his autobiography for slander, libel,
and defamation of character. Love was awarded millions of dollars and the
restoration of more than 30 Beach Boys songwriting credits for the first suit.
For his second suit, Mike agreed to an out-of-court settlement that consisted
of a large cash payment of an undisclosed amount. Mike got the money,
but he also got the bad press for initiating these suits against Brian, who
was often described as defenseless and too mentally unstable to fight back.
That, of course, was ridiculous. Brian could afford lawyers just as competent
as Mike's. And Mike did deserve the majority of those songwriting credits.
Early on, Murry had purposely cut him out of the money loop by making
empty promises that Mike would be taken care of later. Later didn't come
until Mike sued Brian.

David Marks spent his last ten dollars on parking to testify in Mike's
behalf, not because he hated Brian or thought Mike was a genius, but
because he knew Mike had written lyrics to songs on the first four Beach
Boys LPs for which he was not credited. That was the truth. Brian shouldn't
be blamed for this, because those credits were the last thing on his mind.
Murry was the businessman. There was a pattern of Murry screwing the guys
whose name was not Wilson. Mike was first on that list. Mike did contribute
lyrics to a bunch of songs for which he wasn't credited on albums that sold
huge numbers. He tried to negotiate a settlement with Brian's management
and wasn't taken seriously. Mike was incredibly lucky to have a cousin named
Brian Wilson . . . but that doesn't erase the fact that he should have been
credited on the songs for which he wrote lyrics.

Mike's defensive posture is easier to understand if you go back to 1962
and look at the way he, and any outsider (Gary Usher, Al Jardine, David
Marks), were being systematically cut out of the Beach Boys pie by Murry,
and in very underhanded ways. Murry was constantly pressuring Brian to not
give Mike so many lead vocals, and to not to give him songwriting credits.
Brian resisted the advice as best he could. But when it came to business,
Murry usually got his way. That Mike would end up with a highly defensive,

There is something about Mike Love that gets under the skin of many people. In some ways he's been his own worst enemy, and in other ways he's been unjustly vilified. For sure, he's has been, and still is, a magnet for controversy.

and even aggressive stance regarding Brian, and his place in the Beach Boys, is an easy thing to understand. Instead of bending over and taking his screwing like Al did, or ejecting from the scene like David did, Mike hung in there and formulated an aggressive posture. He defended his ground and even invaded territory that wasn't rightly his. He's still doing it.

Mike is constantly calculating, and he'll never stop. It's got to be, because he's convinced on some level that if he shuts it off, he'll lose. Perhaps this is not something to admire. But it is understandable how Mike got there. There was friction and jealousy between he and the Wilsons from day one. Murry screwed him out of years of songwriting credits, and Mike probably took back more than he deserved. Regardless of whether he just took back what was rightfully his, or was overly greedy and took advantage of Brian, Mike was branded as one of the most litigious figures in show business. Mike's reaction was to keep suing people. In the late '90s, he sued Al Jardine for misuse of the Beach Boys name when Al tried to tour under the banner "Beach Boys Family and Friends." Mike won. Then Mike sued Brian and a British newspaper for misusing the Beach Boys' name and their image in a promotional CD that was included in the paper to promote *Brian Wilson Presents Smile.* Finally Mike's winning streak came to end. The lawsuit was not only thrown out of court on the grounds that it was without merit, but Mike was also charged with being liable for Brian's court costs.

September 18, 2007
Mike Love Ordered to Pay Brian Wilson Over $500,000

by Howie Edelson

Brian Wilson has won a victory against his cousin and Beach Boys cofounder Mike Love in their latest legal skirmish. According to Los Angeles Superior Court documents dated September 7, U.S. District Judge Audrey B. Collins ruled that Love is responsible to pay Wilson $518,000 in legal fees, with an additional $208,000 to his codefendants in his copyright-infringement suit against them.

The decision is the latest chapter in Love's prolonged lawsuit against Wilson due to a "freebie" CD that was briefly given out to British newspapers featuring Wilson's recent live versions of Beach Boys classics. Love's suit dealt with the specific fact that his image, along with the other Beach Boys', was used on the promotional CD.

In addition, Love was ordered to pay Wilson's codefendant and biographer David Leaf $59,000 in legal fees, and Sanctuary Records $149,264 for their respective defense fees. The legal fees of Wilson's co-manager Jean Sievers and her associated companies the Lippin Group and Soop, LLC are included in the $518,000 payout due Wilson.

In the decision, the court found that three of Love's claims against Wilson and his codefendants for copyright infringement "were groundless and unreasonable" and noted that the defendants were forced to defend themselves against "an over-pled complaint packed with a barrage of convoluted allegations."

Although Love can legally appeal the decision, he must first post a substantial bond, which would include the full $726,424, plus interest, to avoid Wilson and the other plaintiffs executing the Superior Court decision.

Love and Wilson, who are first cousins, have a long history battling each other in the courts. Love won a 1993 libel suit against Wilson for disparaging remarks made against him in Wilson's heavily ghostwritten autobiography, titled Wouldn't It Be Nice.

In 1994, Love sued and won half of Wilson's $10,000,000 settlement against music publishers Irving/Almo Music, who had purchased Wilson's pre-1969 songwriting catalogue. Wilson had alleged that at the time, his father Murry sold the catalogue without his permission.

As part of the ruling in his case against Wilson, Love was officially awarded co-credit for 39 songs, including "California Girls," "I Get Around," "Wouldn't It Be Nice," "Help Me, Rhonda," "Dance, Dance, Dance," "When I Grow Up (To Be a Man)," and many more.

Love, Wilson, Al Jardine, and the estate of the late Carl Wilson are still partners in the Beach Boys' corporation, Brother Records, Inc. (BRI).

Love, who tours with longtime bandmate Bruce Johnston, holds the exclusive right to tour under the Beach Boys name, with all the BRI partners receiving a percentage from Love's multimillion-dollar tour revenue.

Interview With Mike Love of the Beach Boys—April 5, 2010

by Howie Edelson

Mike Love, Not War

The Beach Boys will bring some welcome Californian sunshine to Castlebar this June. Edwin McGreal spoke to founding band member and music legend Mike Love last week. Mike Love is not your typical rock-and-roll star. No sordid tales of debauchery; very little evidence of skeletons in his closet; and, nearly 50 years after the Beach Boys were formed, he's still going strong, playing around 150 shows a year.

Love, now aged 69, is a very relaxed and positive person, which is not surprising when you listen to such upbeat songs as "Good Vibrations" and "I Get Around," summer anthems that have put a pep in the step of millions for over 40 years. And he and the Beach Boys will bring their sounds of summer to the TF Royal Theatre on June 26 (albeit minus Brian Wilson and Al Jardine).

So, still going strong all these years later, where does he get his energy?

"We don't burn the candle at both ends like we might have done in the early '60s," Love explained, speaking from his southern California base last week. "The Beach Boys are primarily a vocal group, we always emphasize our harmonies, and you can't sing those kind of harmonies if you're going to destroy yourself. I personally learned Transcendental Meditation [from renowned Indian guru Maharishi Mahesh Yogi, who taught many celebrities, including the Beatles]. I keep doing that every day, and it is profoundly relaxing and repairs a lot of wear and tear mentally, emotionally, and physically. It gives you a really nice outlet for stress rather than taking to the bottle or smoking a lot of pot or other drugs.

"People in my own family like my cousin Dennis [Wilson, founding member] became addicted to alcohol and various types of drugs, and he ended up drowning in 1983, long before he should have passed away. Then my cousin Carl [Wilson, founding member] passed away of lung cancer 12 years ago. But then, he started smoking when he was 13, so these lifestyle choices we make can have a tremendous impact on your health and well-being."

Musically, the '60s was a rollercoaster journey for the Beach Boys. There was the outstanding success of their totemic album Pet Sounds in 1966, but the release of "Good Vibrations" the same year is one Love looks back on with particular fondness. "I think, artistically, 'Good Vibrations' has to be right up there. It stands on its own. It is so unique. Also I wrote the words and I came up with the chorus—'I'm pickin' up good vibrations/she's giving me excitations.' It stands the test of time and is still an amazing song today; that is the song I was happiest to be involved with."

Subsequent decades didn't prove as successful, with the exception of "Kokomo" reaching number one in 1988. Love admits that Brian Wilson's well-publicized problems did play a part, but it wasn't all bad for the band to be minus their frontman. "Brian pretty much became a recluse for several years and he didn't take as dynamic a part in the production of our recordings. My cousin Carl played a bigger part, Bruce Johnston played a bigger part. Instead of Brian being 'the Stalin of the studio,' as I used to call him, it became a bit more democratic. I don't think it was reasonable that the [early success] would keep up forever, but the '60s did provide the foundation of our continued success to this day."

Moving to modern-day musicians, Love has no particular favourites, but he's exposed to the full gamut by his children. Some good, some not so good. "I unfortunately get exposed to some rap music from my 14-year-old daughter, but I also get exposed to Leona Lewis, Beyonce, and Alicia Keys; those are pleasant exposures. I don't think I'm obsessed with any new artist, but I'm not against them, either. I'm just as likely if I'm driving around to throw on the oldies channel just out of morbid curiosity to see if they're going to play a Beach Boys song," admitted Love, laughing at the thought.

Love hints that talks have taken place of a touring reunion with Brian Wilson and Al Jardine to mark the fiftieth anniversary of the band. For now, it is Love, together with longtime member Bruce Johnston and others who tour under the Beach Boys name—but the dynamic is the same, according to Love. "What we like to do every night is prove we can re-create those songs like they're meant to be sung. We have got nothing but compliments recently on how fantastic the show sounds. The special part [of touring] is recreating those songs and doing the absolute best job we can and seeing the audience join in and have a great time with us."

Still sending those good vibrations.

Beach Boys Versus Katy Perry? Mike Love Says No Way!

E! News 8/5/2010

Wish they all could be California girls? Only if they've properly cleared the publishing rights. Which Katy Perry apparently did not. Following a report that the Beach Boys' record company label is out to get a chunk of royalties from the bubbly summer anthem, one of the Boys exclusively tells E! News that the band feels nothing but good vibrations toward the girl-kissing songbird.

Take it away, Mike Love . . .

"The Beach Boys are definitely not suing Katy Perry; in fact, we are flattered that her fantastically successful song is bringing to mind to millions of people our 1965 recording of the Beach Boys' 'California Girls,'" says Love, who co-wrote the classic with Brian Wilson. "We think her song is great, and wish her all the success in the world."

It's safe to say the music publisher that controls the rights to the song doesn't feel exactly the same way. A spokesman for Rondor Music tells E! News that while the company doesn't intend on launching any litigation against Perry, it hopes that the creative team behind her hit do the right thing and give credit (and, it follows, royalties) where it's due. "In regard to the various rumors circulating, we would like to make it clear that there is no lawsuit against the writers or publishers of 'California Gurls.' We have established diminutive claims. It is up to the six writers and various publishers of 'California Gurls' to decide whether they honor the claim or not."

But the music publisher didn't stop there, and continued giving a real tsk-tsk to Perry & Co. "Using the words or melody in a new song taken from an original work is not appropriate under any circumstances, particularly one as well-know n and iconic as 'California Girls.' Rondor Music . . . is committed to protecting the rights of its artists and songwriters, and with the support of the writers, that is exactly what we are doing." Even if they're doing it without the cooperation of the artists they're protecting.

27

Love and Mercy

Brian Wilson's Perspective on Concert Tours

B rian Wilson released his first solo LP in 1988. But it wasn't until 1999 that he ventured forth on the solo career that many consider the crowning achievement of his life. And most surprisingly, Brian has been touring on a semi-regular basis, including many overseas appearances. For over a decade Brian's been doing exactly what everybody predicted he'd never be able to do: face the public. Is he doing it because he *wants* to, or because he's *told* to? From fearful recluse to fearful public figure, the somewhat mysterious evolution of Brian Wilson the performer continues to puzzle many of his fans. On one hand, they are delighted at the opportunity to cheer for their hero, and are honored to be in his presence. On the other hand, many feel they are witnessing Brian still stuck in the same hamster wheel that Murry forced him into all those years ago.

When asked in a recent interview what he disliked the most about touring, Brian replied that it was going on stage and performing. He didn't mind the long flights, the strange hotel rooms, the delays at airports, standing in line, fighting traffic, and being away from his home. No, none of that was as bad as performing for people. Upon hearing Brian say that, his "handler" quickly reminded Brian, through a fake smile, that he loves performing the shows. On cue Brian immediately took a U-turn, and agreed that he indeed loves the shows. So, could it be both? He fears taking the stage; but once he warms up, he enjoys himself? That seems plausible. But Brian began avoiding concert tours as early as 1963; and now, in 2011, he's still dreading the stage. When is enough enough? The man is 69 years old. Does he not deserve some peace?

It hasn't received very much attention from the majority of Beach Boys historians through the years, but Brian's first documented bout with stage fright, or avoidance of performing, came in April 1963, only one month after their *Surfin' U.S.A.* album was released. Founder member Al Jardine, who had left the group during its formative months, was rushed back into the fold as a part-time replacement for Brian. Then in June, when the group spent ten days performing in Hawaii, Brian again stayed home for unexplained reasons. Throughout the remainder of 1963, as the Beach Boys star rose and the demand for their personal appearances increased, Brian's participation in live performances was a hit-and-miss thing. Some nights the lineup would be Brian, Mike, Dennis, Carl, and David, while other nights Brian would opt out and Al would take his place.

Not until David left the Beach Boys in October 1963 was Brian's presence at Beach Boys shows routine, and then it only lasted until late 1964. Brian's father and Beach Boys manager Murry Wilson had long been advocating for Brian's 100-percent participation in Beach Boys shows, saying the fans deserved to see the same five guys who were on the album covers when they paid for a concert ticket. When David quit, it left no alternative for Brian but to play every show as the Beach Boys became the number-one band in America. At that point, Brian completely broke down from the stress and strain of being a full-time Beach Boy, and was never a consistent performer again. The pattern was near-complete withdrawal from public appearances between 1965 and 1976. Then a couple of years of being back in, and a few of being in and out, and then a decade of mostly being out. When he was there, it could be rough. Everyone was aware of his severe apprehension of being on stage. The evidence is overwhelming that Brian, at his core, prefers to not tour. I also think he's been cajoled and convinced time and time again that he needs to get out there. That he needs to face his fears. And the reasons for this have far more to do with perceived commerce, and cache, than they do with Brian being a great performer. He is not. He never was. He was a solid performer at his absolute peak in 1964, but for the most part he's been a reluctant and nonessential part of the live act.

And for latter-day Brian during his solo age, the commercial benefits of touring are less than assured. Since he travels to far corners with a very large band and sometimes a string section, but plays relatively small venues and only handfuls of dates at a time, the tours make little if any money. Several insiders have insisted to me that Brian's tours actually lose money. While evidence of his uneasiness in having to take the stage much of the time is clearly there, right on the surface, Brian has found a way to resign himself to the notion that this is his lot in life. I'm sure his dad's voice is still rattling around in his head. There are undoubtedly nights when he finds joy, and there are aspects of participating in the music that are unquestionably good for him. But none of that removes the fundamental truth that Brian Wilson fears the stage, or in his words, "hates" it.

So, if he hates it, and if the rumors are true that his tours actually lose money, why is he out there? Maybe it's the camaraderie of being among fellow musicians. He certainly has a great band backing him. Paul McCartney called Brian Wilson's band the "best in the business." That's high praise from a guy who spent a lot of time in the best band in the business, and who doesn't throw a lot of compliments around. And Paul is right. With Darian Sahanaja, Jeffrey Foskett, Scott Bennett, Nick Wonder, Probyn Gregory, Nelson Bragg, Taylor Mills, and the rest behind him, Brian is framed in the best possible light. It's almost as if they emit the perfect Brian Wilson sound, and Brian himself can either sing along, or just sit and enjoy it like the rest of us. His musical and vocal role within *his* band is not that important. He can be on, and it's great. He can be off, and it's great. But at the same time, it's all about Brian. The experience of seeing the master physically present while *his* notes, and *his* melodies, and *his* vocal-harmony arrangements are lovingly performed around him is a very spiritual thing. So as far as the hamster-wheel thing goes, he's locked in the coolest cage possible.

God Let Me Out of Here

But still there are times you can see the terror in his eyes. Brian sometimes experiences auditory hallucinations during the course of a concert. He has described them to more than one interviewer as "demons" screaming at him saying, "We're going to kill you." He has to try and ignore them, and sing over them. At one show in 2007, Brian, mid-set, laid down on the stage and was in a near-fetal position while the music around him was still playing. Al Jardine, who was guesting with Brian's band at that particular show, told me he found the incident highly disturbing. He said he wondered to himself if Brian should be performing at all. It was said that Brian was suffering from dehydration during that episode, but it conjured major speculation that all was far from well regarding Brian's state of mind while performing.

I was at a Hollywood Bowl concert in 2009 featuring Brian and the L.A. Philharmonic Orchestra. It was a sparkling and warm summer night, and it was fun. Brian did well. Then during the show's finale there was a fireworks display while the musicians were still playing. Brian looked utterly terrified, and I felt horrible for him. Later he said the sound of the fireworks exploding had hurt his ears. He seemed very shaken by all of the explosions and flashing lights while it was happening. But 20 minutes later, in the safety of the backstage area, he appeared fine. Crisis over.

Still, I could not get over the thought of him flinching as the explosions erupted overhead. The look in Brian's eyes kept running through my head. Why does Brian Wilson, who has given so much love to the world, have to be put through something that completely freaks him out? I enjoyed seeing him, like I always do, but I also felt bad for him, like I always do. Even back in

1976, when I was fortunate enough to see Brian and the Beach Boys perform on a sunny summer afternoon at the "Day on the Green" concert at which Brian made his bicentennial comeback, I felt bad for him. He looked out of place. He wasn't comfortable. That was 35 years ago. This man has been through hell.

Don't Worry Baby On Boards

But all it takes is a visit to Brian's official message board to read many of his fans assuring each other that Brian has overcome his fear, and that he loves to perform. If any alternate viewpoint is expressed, it is usually looked upon as alarmist pessimism. Brian is generally thought of among his faithful latter-day fans as some kind of cuddly old bear with an eccentric streak who has overcome his troubles and is happy happy happy! Even some of the most knowledgeable and longest-serving Brian fans will attest to the theory that Brian never does anything that Brian doesn't want to do. I have a hard time squaring that with the things I have witnessed as both an anonymous face in the audience, and as someone lucky enough to be backstage interacting with Brian and his band.

One incident in particular from 1999 still bothers me. That was when a friend and I witnessed Brian's "handlers" in a backstage room, during an intermission, screaming at him to do better on stage during the show's upcoming second half. Brian was cowering. He was being berated for not giving it his all. In a way, it was similar to angry parents scolding a child. It was a highly troubling thing to view, and still colors my perception of Brian and his situation.

There is a feeling that creeps up every time I see Brian in a performance situation, whether it's at a concert or on a TV show. I consistently get the sense that I'm seeing someone who really does not want to be there. He does his best. He has his good nights and days. But if he had complete control of his choices and was allowed to do as he pleases, without having to feel bad about letting someone down, or not doing what others insist is the best thing for him . . . I doubt he'd be performing in front of 17,000 people at the Hollywood Bowl with fireworks exploding over his head.

Took the Dive But Couldn't Swim

I am not be the first to suggest that Brian goes through life on autopilot. His copilot regularly takes over the controls or punches in new coordinates, and Brian goes that way. Murry did it, Landy did it, Carl did it—hell, even Dennis did it with a little Hamburger Helper. The last time Brian had absolute control over his compass direction and day-to-day activities was after Murry was fired in 1964. This resulted in an increasingly independent Brian who reeled off years of grand accomplishments, but also flirted with third-rail experimentations which led directly to the *Smile* meltdown and the subsequent decade of withdrawal and deterioration. So maybe Brian is better off with a copilot. Brian's present team of navigators has certainly increased his productivity. Eight solo albums in eleven years, and a few of them are very good. That would be an impressive run for an artist half Brian's age.

Today Brian trudges through concert tours, scary performances, slightly uncomfortable meet-and-greets with his fans, and various promotional activities that he can't get away from fast enough. In his heart of hearts, does he really want to be doing this? Probably not. But he's resigned to the reality that when he's taken the dive of complete independence, he's nearly drowned. If he wants to swim, he needs some floaties, like a wife, a manager, a direction, a plan, and a band of brothers—because his real ones are gone.

But still, I wonder, if Brian was a little more assertive, a little less remote controlled, would we be able to go see him in concert? And if not, what would Brian be doing instead? Maybe playing "Be My Baby" on his record player, or "Shortenin' Bread" on his piano. Or maybe eating a burger, drinking a beer, watching a baseball game, and wishing his brothers were still around to sing with him . . . in his room.

28

Wouldn't It Be Nice?

Reunions and the Current State of the Beach Boys' Legacy

The Beach Boys have been very successful at surviving in a business where long-term relevance is rare. They have also managed to mangle their legacy by selling out, confusing consumers, and dividing their fan base. Is there any chance we'll see them all together again making nice? The following is a selected overview of reunion rumors, and the Beach Boys' ongoing attempts at legacy repair.

Deep down, I am of the opinion that the Beach Boys died in December 1983—really before that, but I didn't know it yet. I held out hope until Dennis died. But, despite that pessimistic view, even today in 2011 there are enough of the original guys left that a band called the Beach Boys could legitimately record something new. I'm not saying I'd like it, but maybe I would. If Brian, Mike, Al, David, and Bruce want to do something, then they should. It won't be a possibility for much longer. Those guys have a connection that goes far deeper than lawsuits and cheerleaders and bad records and other embarrassing reasons as to why they are dead or should not try to resuscitate. They are the only guys in the world who can say they are original Beach Boys, who even with all the bad stuff thrown in were one of the greatest pop acts in history. If they want to add one last wheezing chapter to the story, I say go for it!

They'd get to laugh at Brian's unintentional jokes, and not laugh at Mike's intentional ones. They'd get to harmonize, and maybe not too well. If you were them, wouldn't you want to try it one more time just to see if the motor still turns over? They could be "Beach Boys" for a minute, or an hour, or a tour . . . and man, that must be a lot of fun. All the perfectly sensible reasons as to why they are finished, and shouldn't try to be anything anymore, doesn't take into account that these guys are really a just a dysfunctional family that could still show up for Thanksgiving dinner at the same table one more time, and perhaps they might enjoy the meal.

The Possibility of Mining the Archives for New Releases

Capitol/EMI has immediate financial problems that might sink that ship. The Beach Boys are the least of their worries. Brother Records Inc. has four voters who, from what I can tell, aren't all that interested in releasing rarities. Mike has said that putting out the unreleased stuff is "scraping the bottom of the barrel." Dennis's estate has no say. I doubt Brian ever thinks about it at all. Carl's kids don't seem very motivated, either. Al has spent years and years tweaking his own album, so he's probably not going to be much help with this one, either. Unless all of those entities are pointed in the same direction, nothing will happen.

Brother Records president Elliott Lott has been in the head position at BRI for a long time; he's an honorable person, managing to survive and maintain a status quo. It would seem logical that a relatively passive approach is the one being taken by most of these people. Therefore, nothing much will change as long as the cast remains the same. Money is a motivator, but there isn't much money in these type of rarities proposals. It takes someone, or a team of people, with crazy passion for the aesthetic potential of such a release to make it happen. But the people with real passion are essentially out of the power loop. The entire enterprise is shrinking, including the fan base. However, there is always potential for something to gel, because the music is just so damn good.

The Possibility of Finding Lost Material

Anything is possible. In June 2008, an article about me appeared in the *New Times*, California's Central Coast weekly entertainment newspaper. The article detailed my involvement in the just-released Dennis Wilson album *Pacific Ocean Blue: Legacy Edition*. A local singer/songwriter named Lance Robison saw the article and wrote an email to me mentioning that he had some old Beach Boys tapes that I might be interested in. Truthfully I took this with a giant grain of salt, thinking it wouldn't be anything unusual, but I did reply to the email just in case.

In my reply, I asked a few pertinent questions. My interest in this Lance Robison fellow grew exponentially upon his response. He answered that he'd had the tapes for about 40 years, they had Sea of Tunes written on them, the songs included "Don't Worry Baby," "Denny's Drums," and about four or five others. They'd never been copied. I emailed back, got his phone number, called him quick, and said to meet me at the Madonna Inn parking lot . . . and to bring the tapes!

When I drove up, Lance and his son opened the back of his Jeep, and there sat three tape boxes that looked exactly like they'd come right out of the pile on the cover of the Beach Boys album *Stack-o-Tracks*. One of them had a Western Recorders work sheet attached, with Chuck Britz's handwriting on it. It was dated January 1964. I opened one of the boxes; the tape was a half-inch wide and in pristine condition. These things looked like they hadn't been touched since 1964, and as I later learned they had only been played once in the four decades that Lance had them. He really hadn't paid any attention to them after his brother brought them home one day in approximately 1966 and sold them to him for 15 dollars. They were put on a shelf, brought out once in the 1980s just to sample what was on them at a friend's studio, and then put away again for 20-plus years. Lance says he tried to contact Brian Wilson through his management once, and the Beach Boys another time when they played locally, but their handlers told him that there wasn't any interest in his tapes. So on the shelf they stayed until he emailed me that day.

I immediately knew what Lance possessed was something that the Beach Boys did not have. These were the original multi-track reels of *Shut Down Volume 2* material. I was blown away that these had never been copied, destroyed, auctioned on eBay, or lost. Lance must be about the only person on earth who would have just kept them in a closet like a pair of shoes he never wore. My first reaction was to email Beach Boys archivist Alan Boyd the photos I had snapped of the tapes. My subject line to Alan read, "This is real." I was confident Alan would know what to do with them. I traveled to L.A. with Lance and the tapes. We listened to them in Mark Linett's studio, and they sounded so incredible that at least one of us was nearly brought to tears. Now we just had to find out how to get Lance to turn them over with no SWAT teams, no lawsuits, no threats . . . just . . . "What do you want, dude?"

As it turned out, Lance wanted to record a "real album" of some of the songs he had written over the same 40 years he'd had the tapes. His original material was great. Truthfully I fell in love with his music, and felt lucky to be involved with his project. The mojo of those old tapes must have rubbed some Wilson-vibe onto Lance's guitar strings, because he had some real gems in his arsenal. Mark Linett and Alan arranged for Lance to get a recording budget, and we all went into Mark's Your Place Or Mine studio and cut an album. This was Lance's big chance . . . his dream come true. He'd waited a long time; the tapes had waited a long time. They returned to their rightful home, and Lance's dream came true. In my opinion, things worked out fine.

In 2009, on their *Summer Love Songs* compilation, the Beach Boys released a newly mixed stereo version of "Don't Worry Baby"; and, for the first time, a true stereo version of "Why Do Fools Fall In Love" complete with its previously unheard original intro section. These versions were only made possible by the discovery of Lance's tapes.

Pictured is the box housing the original multi-track tape reel from the January 1964 sessions that produced the classic track "Don't Worry Baby." The tape was discovered along with two other lost *Shut Down Volume 2* multi-track reels in the possession of musician Lance Robison, who had stored them for over 40 years.

The Beach Boys' Own Feelings About a Reunion

August 4, 2009
Al Jardine Not Interested in a One-Off Beach Boys Reunion
by Howie Edelson

Al Jardine, who recently wrapped up a handful of solo shows with his Endless Summer Band, says that he's not up for any type of Beach Boys reunion shows without a long-term commitment attached. Jardine was forced out of the band in 1998 and not allowed any type of licensing agreement by the group's production company, Brother Records, Inc., to use the words "Beach Boys" when advertising his solo projects or shows.

With the Beach Boys' inner-band lawsuits seemingly all settled at the moment, Jardine was asked if he—like co-founder Mike Love—would be up for playing one or two concerts to be specially filmed and recorded featuring the surviving band members—Jardine, Love, Brian Wilson, David Marks, and Bruce Johnston. Jardine was adamant that a full-scale tour—rather than a TV special—would be needed to see him take the stage as a Beach Boy

THE BEACH BOYS

Summer Love Songs

ADVANCE

Previously unheard material exists in the Beach Boys' archives, and in some cases in the possession of fans. *Summer Love Songs*, released in 2009, contained the first stereo mix of the 1964 song "Why Do Fools Fall in Love," with a previously unheard intro section. This discovery was made possible by lost tapes that rested in a fan's closet for four decades.

again: "Of course, you don't have Carl Wilson there, which would be a big minus as far as I'm concerned. There's ways to do it—but again, that's like doing a one-off, isn't it? I wouldn't be interested in doing just a one-show deal like that. If you want to create an organization that goes out and works and produces a show that's of high value, of high quality—then you rehearse your ass off, make it the best you can, and you tour as a unit. You tour for a year. Like the Rolling Stones, they don't do one show for PBS, one show for . . . you do a tour. You either do it or don't do it. If it was going to be something like that it should be a worldwide tour; otherwise, no. I wouldn't be interested."

When pressed about the band regrouping in some way to commemorate their fiftieth anniversary in 2011, Jardine said: "I don't think it's going to happen. I find that a little annoying, to be honest with you [laughs], just a tad, it's so self-serving [laughs]. Y'know, had we made peace a lot sooner, these things need to matriculate, and they should happen and feel right—not because it's number '5-0.' I mean, that sounds so silly to me. 5-0, what does that mean? I mean, we're here now at 49, or 48, we should still be working. I mean, if we really wanted to work together, we'd work together now. But not to do it just for a . . . unless it were to be a continuation of the good will. If the good will were there—yeah."

In an exclusive interview back in 2006, Love and Johnston outlined their plans for a televised reunion with the surviving band members. Mike Love: "What I think is the right way to go about things is to do a PBS special at the Hollywood Bowl with some guests and maybe one at Wembley Stadium (in London) with a couple of guests like Paul McCartney. If he likes *Pet Sounds* so much, and if he likes "God Only Knows" so well—then have him sing it with us at Wembley Stadium, along with Elton John singing something, so on, and so forth. Maybe Eric Clapton will come out and do it for charity, do it for a really good cause, and then the same thing at the Hollywood Bowl, and that would be really cool." Bruce Johnston: "That would be the great reunion."

Brother Records, Inc. (BRI), was formed in 1967 and is owned and controlled by Brian Wilson, Mike Love, Al Jardine, and the estate of the late Carl Wilson. Shortly after cofounder Dennis Wilson's death in 1983, his estate sold his shares back to the band to repay loans.

Mike Love, who continues to tour with Bruce Johnston, was granted the exclusive license by BRI to tour under the Beach Boys name. Although he is the only partner in the group out on the road, Brian Wilson, Jardine, and Carl Wilson's estate receive a percentage from each Beach Boys tour.

Jardine's Endless Summer Band features former Beach Boys sidemen Ed Carter, Bobby Figueroa, Richie Cannata, and musical director Billy Hinsche. Also onboard are Jardine's sons Adam and Matt—who was also a Beach Boys sideman in the 1990s. For the most recent shows, co-founder David Marks was featured on lead guitar while sharing center stage with Jardine.

One of the highlights of the recent dates was after Jardine's set at New York City's B. B. King Blues Club on July 20, [where] most of the ensemble—including Jardine, his sons, Marks, Hinsche, and Figueroa—headed downtown to sit in at Cannata's weekly jam at the Bitter End. Jardine, sans guitar, again stood center stage with Marks, and sang lead on "Help Me, Rhonda" before moving stage right to bang on an unmiked upright piano during "Surfin' U.S.A." while Matt Jardine led the band on vocals with Marks handling the signature guitar runs.

Jardine is gearing up for the release of his long-delayed first solo album, called *A Postcard From California*. Apart from cameos by Brian Wilson and David Marks, the album also includes contributions from David Crosby, Stephen Stills, Neil Young, America, Flea, and Steve Miller. No release date has been announced for the set.

In a Way the Beach Boys Have Already Reunited—Twice

The Beach Boys' California State Landmark Celebration
My Hawthorne Experience

In 2005, the Beach Boys were given the high honor of having the location of their childhood home designated as a California State Historical Landmark. A large monument was erected near the former site of the Wilson and Marks homes in Hawthorne, California, on which the official landmark plaque is displayed. The homes themselves were razed in the 1980s to make room for the I-105 freeway, also known as the Century Freeway, which now looms above the remnants of the old neighborhood at West 119th Street in Hawthorne. The California State Historic Resources Commission, in a unanimous vote on August 6, 2004, granted the site's status as California State Historic Landmark No. 1041. A state-sanctioned unveiling ceremony was held on May 20, 2005 to make the Beach Boys an official part of the physical history of California.

Like many Beach Boys fans, I greatly anticipated the landmark ceremony and its surrounding events. As it turned out for me, the reality surpassed the fantasy. My wife Nadia and I were lucky enough to be the guests and companions of original Beach Boy David Marks and his wife Carrie throughout the weekend's activities. Sometimes being an author has its privileges, and in this case I was thrust into a virtual three-day Beach Boys' fan dream. I kept flashing back to being a seven-year-old in the early '60s, holding my treasured copy of the *Surfin' U.S.A.* LP. The Beach Boys are a major part of my fabric as an individual, no question. Whether that's good, bad, weird, obsessive, or whatever . . . I'm not really sure. But I know it's true.

Thursday, May 19—The Night Before

We met our hosts Dave and Carrie at their hotel near LAX airport. We also ran into Al Jardine, who was staying there as well. Phil Cooper from the U.K., who was assisting David and I with our *Lost Beach Boy* book project, and Beach Boys family member and classic sideman Billy Hinsche, met us in the lobby. From there we all drove to a reception at a restaurant named "Sticks and Steins." Included in the night's itinerary was a panel discussion and Q&A featuring David, Marilyn Wilson Rutherford, Beach Boys archivist Alan Boyd, Beach Boys promoter Fed Vail, and Beach Boys lyricist Stephen Kalinich.

Eventually, late arrival Harry Jarnagan joined us. Harry is a longtime Beach Boys fan, and was solely responsible for initiating the effort to have the Beach Boys recognized by the state of California. Also in attendance, and basically running the show, was the Wilsons' neighbor Paula Bondi-Springer, who was responsible for organizing the weekend's string of events. We all toasted Harry and Paula for the incredible work they had done in bringing this weekend to fruition.

The Sticks and Steins gathering was filled with Beach Boys fans from far and wide. One of them, Alan Cumming, had come all the way from Scotland to participate in the Beach Boys Landmark weekend. There were also fans from the U.K., Germany, Denmark, and Japan in attendance.

Friday, May 20—The Main Event

Friday was the big day. The Beach Boys would get their California State Historical Landmark; complete with an impressive monument built by Scott Wilson Construction. Scott is the son of the late Dennis Wilson.

On a typically sunny Southern California late morning, we arrived at the designated VIP parking lot near the Hawthorne Community Center. We immediately noticed a fleet of woodies, hot rods, and limos waiting to take family, friends, and guests to the nearby landmark site for the ceremony. Riding with us in our limo were Alan Boyd, former Brother Studio manager Trisha Campo, musician Adam Marsland, and our good friend Susan Lang. It didn't take long before we pulled up to the former site of the Wilson home at West 119th Street in Hawthorne. We stepped out of our car and walked a short ways to the event site.

Local residents had a variety of reactions as the procession of limousines drove up with all of the VIP guests in tow. They seemed curious, but resigned to accept the disruption of their normal routine, and pleased that this event would cement their neighborhood's place in popular culture. Undoubtedly their quiet community will see greater traffic now that it harbors a state-sanctioned landmark, one that yielded a genuine musical revolution.

Near the designated ceremony area was a temporary stage and many rows of seating. There was press everywhere, TV cameras, lots of security, and L.A. police. We entered a tented backstage area where Dave Marks and Brian Wilson greeted each other warmly. With arms around each other, Brian told Dave, "I always loved you," and Dave told Brian he loved him, too. It might sound corny, but if you were there it was hard to not get a little misty. In the air of the very neighborhood that generated an endless wave of harmony and interesting vibes, Dave and Brian undoubtedly had Carl and Dennis on their minds that day. I could hear them mentioning the late Wilson brothers to each other. I didn't want to disrespect their moment by eavesdropping, so I stepped away.

I was incredibly impressed by the warmness of the family element that this celebration projected. Billy Hinsche came by and introduced us to his mom. Al Jardine had his mom with him too. Wandering around the VIP area was more family like Marilyn Wilson Rutherford, her sister Diane Rovell, and Dennis's first wife Carole Wilson Bloom. And there were young Wilson kids everywhere. Dennis Wilson was represented with a full contingent of his offspring. We said hello to Scotty, Carl B., Michael, Gage, Chris, and Jennifer . . . all of Dennis's kids. Carl's boys Justin and Jonah were there too. Later we saw Brian's daughter Wendy toting her two young children around. It was like waking up in the middle of a silly Beach Boys dream . . . and you were there, and you were there, and . . . the place was packed with Wilsons. You could not turn around without bumping into one. There were many essential friends too like writer David Leaf and classic Beach Boys sidemen like Bobby Figueroa, Ed Carter, and Mike Meros. There were some of Brian's band members like Darian Sahanaja and Jeff Foskett present, as well as some old neighborhood regulars like Ron Swallow.

My wife and I sat down next to Carrie and David Marks: in the front row, right in front of the landmark monument and stage. Two seats down was David. Four seats down was . . . Brian freakin' Wilson! When Brian walked towards his seat, there was a wake of electricity following him. His "entourage" and fans clustered around him like a swarm of happy bees. Cameras flashed, people thrust forward. Everyone was jumping up and down, "There's Brian! Yowww!" He was the reason we were all there, when you really think about it. This was his day more than any anyone else's. As usual, Brian looked completely flustered by all the fuss, but resigned to it as well. Once he was in the safety of his chair, the gaggle of bees dissipated and he relaxed with his family. The *Surfin' U.S.A.* album fantasy popped into my thoughts again. I was eerily close to Brian Wilson, the genius behind it all. This was a very surreal moment for a fan that had never seriously dreamed of actually meeting his heroes. By this time I'd met them all, many times over. And now I was celebrating their history with them.

The site of the Wilsons' childhood home in Hawthorne was given its own California State Landmark designation in 2005. This was a huge honor, but one that was certainly earned. The Beach Boys were undoubtedly California's greatest promoters, and literally defined the world's perception of the Golden State through their music.

Former Beach Boys promoter Fred Vail kicked off the ceremony, filling an important role as the day's emcee. Vail is recognized by Beach Boys fans mainly for the sound of his voice at the very beginning of the 1964 *Beach Boys Concert* LP. It is Fred who famously announces "the fabulous Beach Boys" as they take the stage at the

Sacramento Memorial Coliseum. Since that LP has sold millions of copies, Fred's words have become an oft-heard and routinely mimicked part of Beach Boys lore.

Fred introduced some Hawthorne High students, who sang an a cappella song. This was a nice touch, drawing a connection between the current HHS kids and Brian and Al, who graduated from Hawthorne High way back in the 1960s. Dennis and Carl also attended Hawthorne High, although neither graduated. Somewhat predictably, Dennis was expelled in 1962 for getting in one too many fistfights, and Carl had to transfer to Hollywood Professional School in 1963 with the glare of Beach Boys fame becoming too intense for a public-school student.

As the current HHS kids sang somewhat shakily, I thought Brian might go up there and yell at them to get on pitch, but he didn't. He did seem a little irked at all the bad notes being hit. That must be torture for an ear like his. Brian then seemed to be soothed by the instrumental pieces performed by some other HHS students.

Next, Billy Hinsche's friends Tripsitter performed a nice a cappella number, and then Fred Vail talked some more. Beach Boys lyricist Stevie Kalinich read a nice poem; it was short but very sweet. When Vail resumed speaking, I watched Dave Marks burst into temporary tears at the mention of Dennis and Carl Wilson's names. You could feel DW and CW standing nearby silently watching. Their combined spirit hovered over the event all day.

The mayor of Hawthorne spoke next, and I was taken aback that during his prepared remarks he mentioned that the Beach Boys represented "clean" music with no drug influences. I guess he never listened to *Smiley Smile*. The mayor then came by our seats and presented Dave Marks with a key to the City of Hawthorne! He also presented one to Brian and one to Al. They were big gold plaques with large keys attached to them.

Finally the time came to unveil the landmark monument. With Dave and Brian on one end and Al on the other, the three men yanked off a light tarp that was covering the monument. In full view of everyone, the Beach Boys Landmark looked mighty impressive. It's very large, approximately twenty feet long, ten feet high, and five feet thick, and features individually inscribed bricks surrounding a sculptured image of six Beach Boys holding a surfboard. It's quite beautiful. Carl's, Dennis's, Brian's, Mike's, Al's, and David's names are highlighted by six individual bronze "45" record motifs. Bruce Johnston was not included on the Hawthorne monument, as he was not a part of the era of the band connected to this historical site, whereas each of the others either lived here and/or rehearsed here, and essentially created the early Beach Boys sound here. By the time Bruce joined the group in 1965, the Wilsons no longer lived at the address, and the 119th Street era had passed.

The monument is adorned with an official California State Landmark plaque explaining who the Beach Boys were and why they are so important to the history of California. To be honored with one of these is a HUGE compliment. In essence, California was saying "thank you" to its most effective promoters.

Fred Vail talked some more, succeeded by David Marks himself taking the stage with guitar in hand. Billy Hinsche, and Dennis's grandson Matt Wilson, joined him on keyboards and guitar, respectively. They performed one of Dennis's songs from *Pacific Ocean Blue* called "You and I." It's a classic soft jazz ballad. Dave finger-flicked and tip-twisted off two amazing guitar solos. The crowd seemed very appreciative of Dave's effort, and gave him a warm ovation.

Carl and Dennis's son's band In Bloom were up next. Justin and Carl B. Wilson each play their father's primary instrument, while their friend Mario Tucker plays the bass. In Bloom is very non–Beach Boys in their sound and format. But watching Carl and Dennis's boys perform with obvious synergy and joy is a powerful experience. They could have taken the easy and obvious route by emulating their father's or the Beach Boys' sound. I've heard each of them sing their father's material, and Carl B. and Justin's individual voices are very close to Denny's and Carl's. But instead of revisiting the past, In Bloom has chosen to take things in an entirely different direction; and for that, I have great respect for them. It's your thing . . . do what you wanna do.

Landmark organizer Harry Jarnagan spoke about what it took to make the idea of a state-sanctioned Beach Boys tribute become a reality. Although his speech was less than entertaining, Harry deserved some stage time. It was his sweat that initiated and pushed the landmark through the petitioning process. Paula Bondi-Springer spoke after Jarnagan. The L.A. sun pounded down on the crowd. The day was growing long.

Then came Al Jardine. After initially refusing to sing a song, he then (under a sheen of faux reluctance) vocalized along with the tune that gave its name to his new children's book, *Sloop John B: A Pirate's Tale*, as it played over the facility's sound system. Beach Boys karaoke, a very hip concept.

Finally, Brian Wilson and an all-acoustic version of his group topped off the afternoon. Brian just looked so dang happy that day. With a very intimate quality they sang "Surfer Girl" and "In My Room." It was casual and beautiful. Brian then thanked the audience for coming and told everyone to have a great day. It was easy to tell there was love in his heart and peace in his mind . . . and every word he said was meant for you, you, you, you, you, you, you . . .

After Brian left the stage, and the event had officially ended, the crowd lingered around the wonderful gleaming monument. They mingled with each other, chatting, embracing, taking photos, and examining the individual bricks, which were engraved with dedications, messages, names, and initials. My name is on there with other names like Wilson, Jardine, Marks, Kalinich, Parks, Groseclose, Leaf, Marotta, and initials like CW and DW. As the crowd thinned out, CW and DW stayed behind, hovering above. If you get the chance, go visit the landmark . . . they'll always be there.

We retreated to the VIP tent area, where we encountered Jeffrey Foskett standing with Brian and his wife Melinda. Dave Marks and Brian embraced again, and Dave thanked Brian for, well . . . everything. That's how I remember him putting it. Next up was the official reception and dinner.

Our limo deposited us back at the Hawthorne Community Center. Inside was an amazing scene: a huge hall with decorated tables, a big stage on one end, food on one side, booze on the other. Faux flower leis and Beach Boys sunglasses were passed out, and the joint was really rockin'. A Beach Boys tribute band named the Beach Toys held the stage with their 1965 Beach Boys time-capsule routine. It must have been surreal for Brian Wilson to witness that.

We sat with Carl and Dave's old guitar teacher John Maus. He turned into John Walker of the Walker Brothers somewhere along the line, but to Dave he's still Johnny Maus. Also at our table was record producer Danny Moore, who's written hit songs like "Shambala" and "My Maria." Dave used to play guitar on his sessions. Former Beach Boys sideman Adrian Baker stopped by to say hello. He told me about how Dennis Wilson used to play piano for him in the early 1980s, and how at first he just thought it was drunken nonsense until he realized it was genius, and it was just pouring out of old Dennis like magical light.

Sitting nearby were Taylor Mills and Scott Bennett from Brian's band. Brian himself was sitting on the other side of us. Also in attendance were Eddy Medora of the Sunrays and his cute wife, a 1960s TV personality who had appeared on *My Favorite Martian*. Domenic Priore came over with Mark London and hung out at our table for a while. Domenic pointed out that the "Band Without A Name," an outfit for which Dave Marks was briefly a guitarist and vocalist in 1966, had performed at teen dances in this very room nearly 40 years prior.

Midway through the party, Adam Marsland's band—featuring Evie Sands on guitar and vocals and Alan Boyd on keyboards—took the stage. They played all kinds of great music from the later-period Beach Boys LPs. Probyn Gregory, from Brian's group, sat in for a couple of tunes with Alan and

Adam's band. Then he came by our table to say hello. He's a great musician and a mellow cat. Our bands played crappy clubs together in the early 1980s around L.A. Who would've have known we'd end up in this freaky Beach Boys dream?

After many fun-filled hours at the fantastic Hawthorne reception party, we ended up at the hotel lounge again. We gathered to eat some more, and watch highlights of the landmark ceremony on the local TV newscasts. There were Dave, Brian, and Al on TV! Coverage was everywhere. I started thinking about the *Surfin' U.S.A.* LP in my house in the 1960s again. How did I get "here"?

Nadia and I retreated to Hollywood for a little sleep. We needed to rise and shine for a Malibu beach party in the morning. All the fun was starting to wear us out.

Saturday, May 21—Beach Party and David Marks in Concert

Morning came fast, and we peeled our weary bodies out of bed, threw on some shorts, and headed to Malibu. It was a long but gorgeous drive up the Pacific Coast. Upon arriving we paid a quick visit to the Paradise Cove beach party, then headed directly back to Hollywood.

As afternoon turned to evening, we headed out for the David Marks All-Star Beach Band concert in Anaheim, near Disneyland. It was held in a nice modern venue that looked very comfortable and seemed like it would be acoustically perfect for the show. The place was packed with Beach Boys extended-family types and fans. Outside we saw Buzz Clifford of "Baby Sittin' Boogie" fame, who is Dave Marks's lifelong friend and collaborator. Buzz was chatting with Bill Trenkle, the original bassist from Dave and the Marksmen.

Backstage, Bobby Figueroa and Billy Hinsche were getting ready for the show. Ed Carter was practicing unplugged bass runs as Matt Jardine was bouncing around being affable. Dave was on the phone trying to track down guitarist Phil Bardowell, who hadn't shown up yet. John Maus was tuning up his white Stratocaster. There were several opening acts, including Tripsitter, whom everybody seemed to enjoy. Finally Bardowell came in the door with moments to spare. It was time for Dave and the boys to hit the stage.

Fred Vail climbed on stage and introduced the band to the large audience. Fred was everywhere that weekend: at the bar greeting fans, at the ceremony talking all day, in our limo telling stories, and now in Anaheim announcing Dave's group.

Dave's band kicked into a series of surf, hot-rod, and oldies rock hits. They sounded great, despite the venue's never-ending technical difficulties.

The monitors were screwing up, some of the microphones were bad, and the sound crew looked overmatched, but still the band kicked the problems aside and burned rubber through the night. Dave played lead guitar and sang. Billy Hinsche was on keyboards and vocals. Matt Jardine handled vocals and percussion. Bobby Figueroa was on drums and vocals. Ed Carter played bass and sang a little. Phil Bardowell played guitar and sang a lot. Mike Meros fingered the Hammond B3 and other assorted keyboards. This is a great band, and they conveyed a genuine sense of fun as they played. The joint was really hopping throughout their long set.

Dave invited some cool guest performers to join the proceedings. One was Eddie Bertrand from Eddie and the Showmen, who did his surf-rock-meets-LSD-meltdown act. We didn't know whether to applaud or to call the paramedics. He's a very trippy guy, and he wandered around the stage with his guitar feeding back and echoing up a storm, looking to be in some kind of hallucinogenic trance as he played. The audience went bananas for him, giving him the longest standing ovation of the night. Not to be outdone was John Maus, who grabbed his Fender Stratocaster, and with the help of his wife Cynthia on keyboards, slayed the audience with two great Ray Charles tunes. Other guests included Buzz Clifford and Eddie Medora of the Sunrays. Sweet young Charlotte Cooper graced the stage at one point, singing "Don't Worry Baby" in her pure style. Then a load of cheerleaders poured onto stage and kicked and grinned and shook their pom-poms as the band tore through "Be True To Your School."

After the concert, we all adjourned to a VIP party at a local restaurant. There they had more food and kegs of beer. A good sampling of all of the names I've mentioned in this chapter were there for one final landmark-weekend hurrah. I greatly enjoyed hanging out with Dave Marks for three days; and toward the end of the evening, I mentioned to him that I was carrying my subliminal copy of *Surfin' U.S.A.* He couldn't actually see it, but he understood what I meant.

It was pushing two AM, and we were all hungry again. It's hard to find food in Anaheim that late. Stevie Kalinich and I both insisted we would not stop searching until we were eating, so we continued cruising the boulevards looking for an OPEN sign. Somehow while combing the streets of Anaheim, it came to our attention that the latest edition of the *L.A. Times* newspaper featured a great article about the landmark ceremony and it featured a photo that nearly all of us were in. Phil Cooper decided to buy up every copy we could get our hands on. We ended up sitting in a parking lot with two huge blazing electric signs towering over us. There we sat reading our pile of papers. Then Dave Marks pointed out something interesting. The sign on our right read DENNY'S. The sign on our left read CARL'S.

It was a surreal ending to a surreal weekend, and I kept wondering how I'd traveled from holding that LP when I was a kid to "here." It doesn't really matter, I guess. But it sure was fun.

June 13, 2006
At the Capitol Records Tower Rooftop—the Beach Boys Reunion

I'm the kind of fan who on a purely aesthetic level wishes the Beach Boys' name had been retired when Dennis Wilson died. Of course the band has done many worthy things since that day in December 1983. They have had many sold-out tours; had a single hit number one and a compilation CD go double platinum; been inducted into the Rock and Roll Hall of Fame; and been honored with a lifetime Grammy award. They've had their share of latter-day success, but part of me didn't want to know about it. In short, to me the Beach Boys stopped feeling like "the Beach Boys" sometime around 1980. I'm a grumpy old fan who really wants to remember them as five stripe-shirted Californians with Fender guitars and no lawyers. When I rode the elevator to the Capitol rooftop on June 13, 2006, the last thing I ever expected to see was the Beach Boys.

On the rooftop of the historic Capitol Records Tower in Hollywood, Brian Wilson, Mike Love, Al Jardine, David Marks, and Bruce Johnston of the Beach Boys were together again. For the first time in a very long time, the five guys standing and interacting in front of the press actually looked like "the Beach Boys."

I stepped off the elevator and mingled with the tight group of press who'd been invited there that day. Security was heavy. Only a few "civilians" were allowed to witness this. Everybody who was there had to get clearance from Capitol; and, believe me, those clearances were very difficult to come by. It was organized as an intimate, semiprivate award presentation, a new product announcement for the fortieth-anniversary *Pet Sounds* and "Good Vibrations" releases, and a nicely hyped photo-op for the press. There were no more than 50 people on the roof. The very first things I noticed when I got up there were the handsome double-platinum awards for the *Sounds of Summer* CD that were laid out for the various individuals. When I eyed Dennis and Carl's awards, it struck me as a very sad thing that they'd never see or hold them. So much of each man went into those songs, and because of that they are a huge part of why the Beach Boys' music is still selling. But they weren't here. Looking across glorious warm L.A. from that bird's-eye Hollywood perch, I flashed on how much Dennis would have enjoyed the sun . . . and the moment. But his award sat there alone, staring back at me, reflecting the L.A. sunshine he loved so much.

Then, to My Utter Surprise, the Beach Boys Showed Up

It wasn't Brian Wilson, the celebrated solo artist, or Mike Love, on his endless tour, or Al Jardine, the scorned former bandmate, or Bruce Johnston, insisting the touring act is not a mirage, or David Marks, an important, yet almost entirely uncredited element of the original Beach Boys. It wasn't five men from separate lives uncomfortably resigned to being near each other for a few minutes. No. This time it was something else.

Instead of five individuals with entourages entering from different sides of the stage à la 1979, on June 13, 2006 they arrived as a "group." They embraced, they laughed, they interacted, they celebrated, and they worked the press as a unit. I'm telling you, they looked like the Beach Boys! The chemistry was there, and it was good. They supported each other and they seemed . . . harmonious. I was standing two feet from Mike and Brian and watched in awe at just how much they were enjoying each other's company. Uncomfortable? Not in the least. Brian was cracking everybody up with his funny banter. His sense of humor was the most dynamic element of the entire event. Mike smiled and told me, "Everybody is on their best behavior today, and this is the way it should always be."

With David there, the group dynamic seemed somewhat altered . . . nudged towards something closer to family. The personalities were transferred back to a time before they were famous. They were the kids in the neighborhood again, the same ones who showed up at that same Hollywood building 44 years ago in their T-shirts, cut-offs, and thongs. They remembered recording there, and how all the adults in suits looked at them like five Pendleton-clad aliens from Planet Surf. There are only so many Beach Boys; it's an inside thing, an exclusive club. The joy they were feeling wasn't from the awards being presented to them, or the press clamoring for them, or the announcement of more product to enrich them. The pure joy for

Mike Love and Brian Wilson reunite on the Capitol Records rooftop in 2006. Any future Beach Boys reunion hinges on whether these two extremely successful men are motivated to bury their differences and reach a musical compromise.

these guys was the simple act of being together. And as skeptical as I am, I must say, it truly moved me.

As the group was posing for an endless string of photographs and answering all the questions thrown their way, I discreetly slipped something out of my bag. The night before I'd pasted a couple of old headshots of Carl and Dennis onto cardboard and brought them along . . . just in case. I asked David to pose with them, which he was kind enough to do. And then to my amazement, he strolled over to his old friend Mike and showed him the photos. Then Al came over to have a look, too. Before I knew it, the press was snapping away at them holding photos of the two departed Wilsons. My sadness was long gone. On a sunny L.A. day, the Beach Boys were together again.

Will it happen again? Will they re-form? Will they record? Will they tour? I don't know; and in a way, it doesn't really matter. What I saw on the Capitol Records rooftop that day was a true reunion of spirit and of good vibrations. It was simply a beautiful thing to witness.

And the Legacy Bombardment Continues

March 2010—Press Release
Music Legends the Beach Boys to Perform With Special Guest John Stamos on the Season Premiere of *Dancing With the Stars: The Results Show*, Tuesday, March 30, on ABC

Hollywood, California—On the season premiere of *Dancing With the Stars: The Results Show*, the first couple of the season is eliminated. Grammy Lifetime Achievement Award® recipients the Beach Boys take to the stage, and, in an uplifting Macy's "Stars of Dance" performance, Haitian dancers honor victims of the Haiti earthquake when *Dancing With the Stars: The Results Show* premieres in its new time period, TUESDAY, MARCH 30 (8:00–9:00 PM, ET), on the ABC Television Network.

Often called "America's Band," the Beach Boys will perform a medley of their hits "California Girls," "Kokomo," and "Fun, Fun, Fun." Honorary band member John Stamos (*ER*, *Full House*) will sit in with the band on guitar and drums. In 2011, the Beach Boys will celebrate their fiftieth anniversary. For nearly five decades they have recorded and performed the music that has become the world's favorite soundtrack to summer. Inducted into the Rock and Roll Hall of Fame in 1988, and winners of NARAS' Lifetime Achievement Grammy Award, the Beach Boys are an American institution that is iconic around the world. They will be accompanied on the stage by professional *Dancing With the Stars* dancers Louis Van Amstel, Anna

Trebunskya, Maksim Chmerkovskiy, Cheryl Burke, Damian Whitewood, and Ashly Costa. The Beach Boys are led by original band member Mike Love and longtime performer Bruce Johnston, along with Christian Love, Scott Totten, Randell Kirsch, John Cowsill, and Tim Bonhomme.

Dancing With the Stars is the U.S. version of the international smash hit series *Strictly Come Dancing*. This version is produced by BBC Worldwide Productions.

For the latest Beach Boys news and to access the band's tour dates, please visit the official Website: www.thebeachboys.com

29

A Thing or Two

Influences, Instruments, and Locations

Some Beach Boys odds and ends, meant to help fill out their big picture, are listed in the pages ahead. Who were their musical heroes? What brand and model instruments did they play? Where did they live? There are more answers to those questions than you can imagine, and some of them are here.

The Beach Boys' Musical Influences

The following is a selected list of artists whose music influenced Brian, Carl, Dennis, Mike, Al, David, and Bruce—and in turn, the Beach Boys.

Brian

Four Freshmen, George Gershwin, Elvis Presley, the Everly Brothers, Phil Spector, Jan and Dean, the Beatles, Randy Newman

Carl

Chuck Berry, Dick Dale, Duane Eddy, Brian Wilson, the Beatles, Stevie Wonder, the Miracles

Dennis

Dion, Brian Wilson, the Beatles, Beethoven, Wagner, Marvin Gaye

Mike

The Coasters, the Olympics, Chuck Berry, Elvis Presley, the Everly Brothers

Al

The Kingston Trio, the Limeliters, Leadbelly, Peter, Paul and Mary, Bob Dylan

David

Dick Dale, Duane Eddy, B. B. King, Chuck Berry, the Beatles, Eric Clapton

Bruce

Nelson Riddle, Frank Sinatra, Little Richard, Brian Wilson

Beach Boys Equipment

No Surfboards, No Guitars, and No 409s

When Dave Marks's parents gave him a Sears Silvertone acoustic guitar for Christmas in 1957, he was immediately able to interact musically with his neighbor Carl Wilson. Murry had purchased a Kay hollow-body electric for Carl around the same time. Dave soon upgraded to a Carvin electric guitar that he bought from his and Carl's guitar teacher, John Maus, in 1959. The earliest incarnation of the pre–Beach Boys playing electric guitars together emerged sometime in 1959. By the time the Beach Boys had signed a recording contract with Capitol Records, Carl and David were playing matching 1962 sunburst Fender Stratocasters, which they used on the earliest Beach Boys recordings for Capitol. Brian also went Fender with his 1962 sunburst Precision bass.

The Beach Boys continued to only use Fender guitars and amplifiers for their first several years. They are pictured on the iconic 1964 *Beach Boys Concert* LP with 100 percent Fender gear. People often asked the group if Fender sponsored them, or if they had signed an endorsement deal and were compensated with free equipment. The answer is no. David Marks's famous quote is, "We got nothing for free. No surfboards, no guitars, and no 409s." The first time the band strayed from Fender equipment was in August 1964, when Carl switched to a Rickenbacker 12-string after seeing George Harrison's instrument in the Beatles film *A Hard Day's Night*. From that point the Beach Boys began to mix in different brands with their signature Fender gear. Finally, in 1966, Fender began featuring the Beach Boys in some of their ads. By the 1970s the Beach Boys were more often seen playing Gibsons than Fenders, although Fender maintained a presence in their growing equipment arsenal.

The following is a selected list of some of the equipment the Beach Boys used on stage and in the studio during the 1960s and 1970s.

Brian Wilson

Bass
    Fender Precision—Sunburst
    Fender Precision—Olympic White

Amplifier
    Fender Bassman

Keyboards
    Hammond C3 Organ
    Baldwin Organ
    Grand Piano

Carl Wilson

Guitars
    Kay single cutaway acoustic—with pick-up added
    Fender Stratocaster—Sunburst
    Fender Jaguar—Olympic White
    Rickenbacker 360/12—Fireglo
    Rickenbacker 360/DBV64
    Fender Electric XII—Olympic White
    Guild Starfire IV
    Fender Telecaster—Natural with Bigsby Tremolo
    Gibson ES-335 Custom—Blonde with Bigsby Tremolo
    Fender Stratocaster—Olympic White
    Epiphone 360 Riviera 12-string—Tobacco Sunburst with Gibson neck

Bass
    Hofner Copy

Amplifiers
    Fender Dual Showman—Blonde with Outboard Spring Reverb Unit
    Fender Bandmaster
    Fender Bassman
    Fender Twin Reverb
    Fender Dual Showman—Black

Al Jardine

Guitars
>Fender Stratocaster—Olympic White
>Fender Stratocaster—Red
>Gibson Les Paul—Black
>Fender Electric XII—Sunburst
>Epiphone Casino
>Gibson ES—335
>Gibson Les Paul Junior

Bass
>Stand-Up—model unknown
>Fender Precision—Sunburst
>Fender Precision—Olympic White

Amplifiers
>Fender Showman—Blonde with Outboard Spring Reverb Unit
>Fender Dual Showman
>Fender Bassman

David Marks

Guitars
>Silvertone F-Hole Acoustic—Blue and White
>Fender Stratocaster—Sunburst
>Fender Jaguar—Red

Amplifiers
>Fender Bandmaster
>Fender Showman—Blonde with Outboard Spring Reverb Unit

Dennis Wilson

Drums
>Gretsch—Gold Sparkle Finish
>Camco—Miscellaneous Custom Finishes
>Ludwig
>Rogers
>Slingerland
>Zickos—Clear
>Yamaha—Black

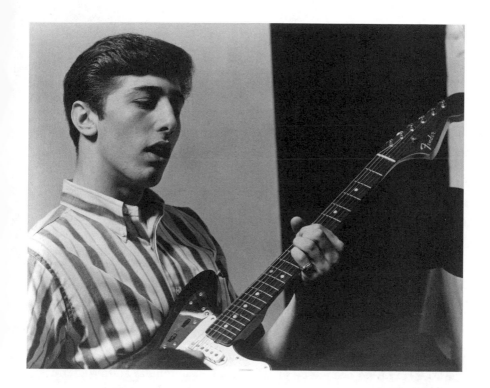

Bruce Johnston

Bass
    Fender Precision—Olympic White
    Fender Precision—Blue
    Hofner Copy

Keyboards
    Hammond C3 Organ
    Farfisa Organ
    Wurlitzer EP-110 Electric Piano

Blondie Chaplin

Guitars
    Gibson Les Paul—Goldtop Gibson
    Les Paul Junior
Bass
    Fender Precision—Sunburst

Locations

Below is a selected list of some of the Beach Boys' residences and other significant locations in their history. All of them are in Los Angeles unless noted otherwise.

- 8012 South Harvard Boulevard—The Wilsons' first home, and where Murry, Audree, Brian, and Dennis lived prior to Carl's birth.
- 4969 East Firestone Boulevard, Southgate—The location of the A.B.L.E. Machinery Company, which was Murry Wilson's business. Brian, Dennis, and Carl sometimes worked there on weekends, helping their father clean the equipment.
- 1882 West Washington Boulevard, 2438 South Grand Avenue, 3301 East 14th Street (last location)—Locations of Love Sheet Metal, Mike's father's business.
- 3701 West 119th Street, Hawthorne—The Wilson family home from 1944 to 1965. Murry and the group used this as the Beach Boys' business address, and also used the converted garage as a rehearsal studio for many years. The location was demolished in the mid-1980s to make room for the 105 Freeway.
- Corner of Mount Vernon and Fairway, View Park, Baldwin Hills—The Love Family home and the site of Love/Wilson holiday gatherings during the 1950s. Brian immortalized the location in his *Holland* album fairytale.
- 11901 Almertens Place, Inglewood—David Marks's family home, 1957–1966, located directly across the street from the Wilson home.
- Corner of La Brea Boulevard and West Washington Boulevard—Site of the gas station that Mike worked at circa 1961.
- 2511 Mayberry Street—Home of Hite and Dorinda Morgan, where the first Beach Boys demos were recorded in September 1961.
- 10212 Sixth Avenue, Inglewood—The second Love family home following Milton Love's bankruptcy, circa 1962.
- 16636 Yukon, Torrance—Al's home 1962.
- 5642½ Aldama Street, Highland Park—Mike and Frances's home, 1962–1963.
- Crenshaw Park Apartments, 10800 Crenshaw Boulevard—Brian and Bob Norberg's apartment, approximately 1963.
- 616 Sierra Bonita Drive, Crenshaw district—The home of the Rovell family, where Brian and his brothers spent much of their time throughout 1963 and 1964.
- 7235 Hollywood Blvd, Hollywood—Brian's apartment circa 1964.
- 600 Hyde Park Avenue, Inglewood—Dennis's apartment circa 1964.
- 228 119th Place, Manhattan Beach—Al's apartment circa 1964.

- 1448 North Laurel Way, Beverly Hills—Brian and Marilyn's home from 1965 to early 1967.
- 124 West Hillsdale, Inglewood—Dennis's townhouse circa 1965.
- 9171 Wilshire Boulevard—Carl's apartment circa 1965.
- 4012 Neon Drive Manhattan Beach—Mike and Suzanne's home circa 1965.
- 2600 Benedict Canyon—Dennis and Carole's home from 1965 to 1967.
- 116 Montana Avenue, #9, Santa Monica—Bruce's apartment circa 1965.
- 1902 Coldwater Canyon—Carl and Annie's home from late 1966 until the 1970s.
- 1215 Coldwater Canyon—Mike and Suzanne's home from 1966 to 1967.
- 10452 Bellagio Road, Bel Air—Brian and Marilyn's home from early 1967 to 1979. This location is where the Beach Boys recorded much of their music between 1967 and 1971.
- 1820 Westridge, Brentwood—Al's home circa 1967.
- Beresford Apartments, 7231 Franklin Avenue, Hollywood—David Marks owned this apartment building, which was managed by his parents from 1967 to 1971. It was lost due to nonpayment of property taxes.
- 14400 West Sunset Blvd, Pacific Palisades—Dennis's home circa 1968, where Charles Manson and his followers were live-in guests. This sprawling log-cabin-style home was the former hunting lodge of Will Rogers.
- 4449 Coldwater Canyon, Beverly Hills—Bruce's home circa 1969.
- 1454 Fifth Street, Santa Monica—Site of Brother Studio, where the Beach Boys recorded from 1974 to 1978.
- Slip C-1100, Marquesa Way, Marina Del Rey—Where Dennis berthed his sailboat the Harmony, on which he lived periodically between 1974 and 1980. This is also the site of Dennis's drowning death in 1983.
- 32184 Broad Beach Road, Malibu—Dennis and Karen's home in 1976.
- 101 Mesa Lane, Santa Barbara—Mike's home in the late 1970s to 1980s.
- Crest Streets, Coldwater Canyon—Christine McVie's home, where Dennis periodically lived circa 1979–1980.

30

Best of the Beach Boys

All-Time Song and Album Lists

From Different Countries and Different Time Periods
(Courtesy of Joost van Gisbergen)

Songs/Singles

Rolling Stone Magazine's 500 Greatest Songs of All Time (United States, 2004)
Based on votes by 172 musicians, critics, and music-industry figures.
    "Good Vibrations" (#6)
    "God Only Knows" (#25)
    "California Girls" (#71)
    "Don't Worry Baby" (#176)
    "In My Room" (#209)
    "Caroline, No" (#210)
    "Sloop John B" (#271)

Radio 2's Top 2000 (The Netherlands, 2010)
Based on votes by almost 2,000,000 of the radio station's listeners.
    "God Only Knows" (#20)
    "Good Vibrations" (#105)
    "Sloop John B" (#318)
    "Tears in the Morning" (#618)
    "I Can Hear Music" (#1078)
    "Wouldn't It Be Nice" (#1136)
    "California Girls" (#1248)
    "Then I Kissed Her" (#1515)
    "Heroes and Villains" (#1902)
    "I Get Around" (#1920)
    "Barbara Ann" (#1941)

Radio 10 Gold's 4000 (The Netherlands, 2010)
Based on votes by the radio station's listeners.
    "Sloop John B" (#28)
    "Good Vibrations" (#70)
    "God Only Knows" (#114)
    "Barbara Ann" (#568)
    "I Can Hear Music" (#972)
    "Break Away" (#1172)
    "Do It Again" (#1192)
    "Kokomo" (#1515)
    "Tears in the Morning" (#1900)
    "Bluebirds Over the Mountain" (#2079)
    "Help Me, Rhonda" (#2370)
    "Wouldn't It Be Nice" (#2526)
    "Cotton Fields" (#2818)
    "California Girls" (#3027)
    "Darlin'" (#3279)
    "I Get Around" (#3722)
    "Sail On Sailor" (#3945)

Q104.3's All-Time Top 1043 (United States, 2010)
    "Good Vibrations" (#188)
    "I Get Around" (#620)
    "God Only Knows" (#836)

Joe-FM's Hitarchief Top 2000 (Belgium, 2010)
    "Good Vibrations" (#251)
    "Sloop John B" (#503)
    "California Girls" (#828)
    "I Can Hear Music" (#1898)

Aloha People & Music's
Perfect Pop Song Top 20
(The Netherlands, 2004)
Based on votes by 85 famous
Dutch musicians.
    "God Only Knows" (#1)
    "Good Vibrations" (#18)

MOJO Magazine's Readers' All-Time Top 100 Singles (U.K., 1997)
   "Good Vibrations" (#3)
   "God Only Knows" (#12)

MOJO Magazine's Writers & Staff's All-Time Top 100 Singles (U.K., 2000)
   "God Only Knows" (#13)

MOJO Magazine's Artists, Producers, & Music-Industry Personalities' All-Time Top 100 Singles (U.K., 1997)
   "Good Vibrations" (#1)
   "Don't Worry Baby" (#11)
   "God Only Knows" (#28)

NME Magazine's Writers' Top 100 Singles of All Time (U.K., 1976)
   "I Get Around"/"Don't Worry Baby" (#3)
   "Good Vibrations" (#8)
   "California Girls" (#30)
   "God Only Knows" (#97)

NME Magazine's Writers' Top 150 Singles of All Time (U.K., 1987)
   "Good Vibrations" (#28)

NME Magazine's Greatest Singles of All Time (U.K., 2002)
   "Good Vibrations" (#13)
   "God Only Knows" (#59)

NME Magazine's Readers' All-Time Top 100 Singles (U.K., 1976)
   "Good Vibrations" (#11)
   "I Get Around" (#39)
   "God Only Knows" (#52)
   "California Girls" (#85)

Spin Magazine's 100 Greatest Singles of All Time (United States, 1989)
   "Don't Worry Baby" (#11)

Q Magazine's Readers' Top 100 Singles of All Time (U.K., 1999)
   "Good Vibrations" (#11)
   "God Only Knows" (#43)

Q Magazine's 100 Greatest Songs of All Time (U.K., 2006)
"Good Vibrations" (#21)
"God Only Knows" (#36)

Highest-rated songs on cabinessence.net—Top 10
Based on votes by visitors of the Website.
"God Only Knows" (9.65)
"Wouldn't It Be Nice" (9.57)
"I Get Around" (9.57)
"Please Let Me Wonder" (9.48)
"Good Vibrations" (9.47)
"This Whole World" (9.42)
"She Knows Me Too Well" (9.37)
"Caroline, No" (9.36)
"Surf's Up" (9.36)
"California Girls" (9.35)

Highest-charting songs on US charts—Top 10
"Kokomo" (#1, 1 week at #1, chart run of 28 weeks)
"I Get Around" (#1, 2 weeks at #1, chart run of 15 weeks)
"Help Me, Rhonda" (#1, 2 weeks at #1, chart run of 14 weeks)
"Good Vibrations" (#1, 1 week at #1, chart run of 14 weeks)
"Barbara Ann" (#2, chart run of 11 weeks)
"Surfin' U.S.A." (#3, chart run of 25 weeks)
"California Girls" (#3, chart run of 11 weeks)
"Sloop John B" (#3, chart run of 11 weeks)
"Rock & Roll Music" (#5, chart run of 17 weeks)
"Fun, Fun, Fun" (#5, chart run of 11 weeks)

Highest-charting songs on U.K. charts—Top 10
"Good Vibrations" (#1, 2 weeks at #1, chart run of 13 weeks)
"Do It Again" (#1, 1 week at #1, chart run of 14 weeks)
"Sloop John B" (#2, chart run of 15 weeks)
"God Only Knows" (#2, chart run of 14 weeks)
"Barbara Ann" (#3, chart run of 10 weeks)
"Cotton Fields" (#5, chart run of 17 weeks)
"Then I Kissed Her" (#5, chart run of 11 weeks)
"Break Away" (#6, chart run of 11 weeks)
"Lady Lynda" (#6, chart run of 11 weeks)
"I Get Around" (#7, chart run of 13 weeks)

Highest-charting songs on Dutch charts—Top 10
   "Sloop John B" (#1, chart run of 20 weeks)
   "Then I Kissed Her" (#2, chart run of 13 weeks)
   "Good Vibrations" (#4, chart run of 14 weeks)
   "Do It Again" (#5, chart run of 14 weeks)
   "Kokomo" (#6, chart run of 10 weeks)
   "Tears in the Morning" (#6, chart run of 9 weeks)
   "I Can Hear Music" (#6, chart run of 7 weeks)
   "Bluebirds Over the Mountain" (#9, chart run of 6 weeks)
   "God Only Knows" (#11, chart run of 8 weeks)
   "Wipeout" (#11, chart run of 8 weeks)

Highest-charting songs on German charts—Top 10
   "Sloop John B" (#1)
   "Barbara Ann" (#2)
   "Do It Again" (#4)
   "Kokomo" (#7)
   "Good Vibrations" (#8)
   "Help Me, Rhonda" (#10)
   "I Can Hear Music" (#13)
   "Break Away" (#29)
   "Cotton Fields" (#29)
   "California Girls" (#30)

Highest-charting songs on Australian charts—Top 10
   "Do It Again" (#1)
   "Cotton Fields" (#1)
   "Kokomo" (#1)
   "Wouldn't It Be Nice" (#2)
   "Good Vibrations" (#2)
   "Fun, Fun, Fun" (#6)
   "Surfer Girl" (#8)
   "Surfin' U.S.A." (#9)
   "Wild Honey" (#10)
   "Heroes and Villains" (#11)

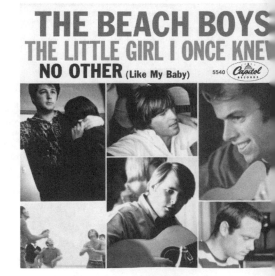

Highest-charting songs on Swedish charts—Top 10
  "Surfin' Safari" (#1)
  "Barbara Ann" (#2)
  "Cotton Fields" (#2)
  "Good Vibrations" (#3)
  "Sloop John B" (#4)
  "Then I Kissed Her" (#4)
  "Help Me, Rhonda" (#7)
  "Heroes and Villains" (#7)
  "Ten Little Indians" (#8)
  "Surfin' U.S.A." (#8)
  "Do It Again" (#8)

Highest-charting songs on Norwegian charts
  "Barbara Ann" (#1)
  "Sloop John B" (#1)
  "Cotton Fields" (#1)
  "Good Vibrations" (#2)
  "Do It Again" (#5)
  "God Only Knows" (#6)
  "Then I Kissed Her" (#10)

Songs included in the book *1001 Songs You Must Hear Before You Die*
  "God Only Knows"
  "Good Vibrations"
  "Surf's Up"

Songs included in the Rock and Roll Hall of Fame's 500 Songs That Shaped Rock and Roll
  "California Girls"
  "Don't Worry Baby"
  "God Only Knows"
  "Good Vibrations"
  "Surfin' U.S.A."

Albums

www.BestEverAlbums.com
Overall Chart (2010)
Overall ranking for the best albums in history as determined by their aggregate positions in over 2,100 different greatest-album charts on BestEverAlbums.com.

>   *Pet Sounds* (#11)
>   *Sunflower* (#670)
>   *Surf's Up* (#1042)
>   *Smiley Smile* (#1688)
>   *The Pet Sounds Sessions* (#1854)
>   *The Beach Boys Today!* (#2062)
>   *Wild Honey* (#2100)
>   *Golden Greats* (#3728)
>   *Friends* (#3827)
>   *The Platinum Collection* (#4934)
>   *Endless Summer* (#5265)
>   *Beach Boys' Party!* (#7938)
>   *20/20* (#8317)

Rolling Stone Magazine's 500 Greatest Albums of All Time (United States, 2003)
Based on votes by 273 rock musicians, critics, and industry figures, each of whom submitted a list of 50 albums.

>   *Pet Sounds* (#2)
>   *The Beach Boys Today!* (#267)
>   *Sunflower* (#376)

Radio Caroline's Staff's Top 500 (U.K., 2010)

>   *Pet Sounds* (#20)
>   *Holland* (#85)
>   *Smiley Smile* (#298)

MOJO Magazine's Writers & Staff's 100 Greatest Albums Ever Made (U.K., 1995)

>   *Pet Sounds* (#1)

MOJO Magazine's Reader's 100 Greatest Albums Ever Made (U.K., 1996)

>   *Pet Sounds* (#2)
>   *Surf's Up* (#75)

NME Magazine's Writers' All-Time Top 100 (U.K., 1974)

>   *Pet Sounds* (#3)
>   *Smiley Smile* (#62)

Best of the Beach Boys Vol. 1 (#83)
Surf's Up (#96)

NME Magazine's Writers' All-Time Top 100 (U.K., 1985)
   Pet Sounds (#20)
   Best of the Beach Boys (#95)

NME Magazine's Writers' All-Time Top 100 (U.K., 1993)
   Pet Sounds (#1)
   Surf's Up (#46)

NME Magazine's 100 Best Albums (U.K., 2003)
   Pet Sounds (#3)
   Surf's Up (#100)

Q Magazine's Readers' 100 Greatest Albums Ever (U.K., 1998)
   Pet Sounds (#31)

Q Magazine's Readers' 100 Greatest Albums Ever (U.K., 2003)
   Pet Sounds (#99)

Q Magazine's Readers' 100 Greatest Albums Ever (U.K., 2006)
   Pet Sounds (#18)

The *Times'* 100 Best Albums of All Time (U.K., 1993)
   Pet Sounds (#1)

VH1's Top 100 Albums (U.S., 2001)
   Pet Sounds (#3)

Highest-charting albums on U.S. charts—Top 10
   Endless Summer (#1, 1 week at #1, chart run of 150 weeks)
   Beach Boys Concert (#1, 4 weeks at #1, chart run of 62 weeks)
   Surfin' U.S.A. (#2, chart run of 65 weeks)
   Summer Days (And Summer Nights!!) (#2, chart run of 33 weeks)
   The Beach Boys Today! (#4, chart run of 50 weeks)
   All Summer Long (#4, chart run of 49 weeks)
   Little Deuce Coupe (#4, chart run of 46 weeks)
   Beach Boys' Party! (#6, chart run of 24 weeks)
   Surfer Girl (#7, chart run of 50 weeks)
   Spirit of America (#7, chart run of 43 weeks)

Highest-charting albums on U.K. charts—Top 10
  20 Golden Hits (#1, 10 weeks at #1, chart run of 76 weeks)
  Best of the Beach Boys (#2, chart run of 140 weeks)
  Pet Sounds (#2, chart run of 39 weeks)
  Summer Dreams: 28 Classic Tracks (#2, chart run of 27 weeks)
  Best of the Beach Boys Vol. 2 (#3, chart run of 39 weeks)
  Beach Boys' Party! (#3, chart run of 14 weeks)
  20/20 (#3, chart run of 9 weeks)
  Summer Days (And Summer Nights!!) (#4, chart run of 22 weeks)
  Greatest Hits (#5, chart run of 22 weeks)
  The Beach Boys Today! (#6, chart run of 24 weeks)

Highest-charting solo albums on US charts—Top 5
  Brian Wilson Presents Smile (#13)
  Brian Wilson: *That Lucky Old Sun* (#21)
  Brian Wilson Reimagines Gershwin (#26)
  Brian Wilson (self-titled) (#54)
  Brian Wilson: *Imagination* (#88)

Highest-charting solo albums on U.K. charts—Top 5
  Brian Wilson Presents Smile (#7)
  Dennis Wilson: *Pacific Ocean Blue—Legacy Edition* (#16)
  Brian Wilson: *Imagination* (#30)
  Brian Wilson: *That Lucky Old Sun* (#37)
  Brian Wilson: *Gettin' In Over My Head* (#53)

Highest-charting albums on Dutch charts—Top 10
No album charts before 1969
  The Definite Album (#8, chart run of 13 weeks)
  Beach Boys' Best: 40 All-Time Greatest Hits (#9, chart run of 12 weeks)
  Holland (#11, chart run of 6 weeks)
  20 Greatest Hits (#16, chart run of 10 weeks)
  L.A. (Light Album) (#22, chart run of 7 weeks)
  California Gold (#23, chart run of 13 weeks)
  15 Big Ones (#23, chart run of 9 weeks)
  The Beach Boys Love You (#29, chart run of 6 weeks)
  Sunflower (#30, chart run of 12 weeks)
  The Platinum Collection (#33, chart run of 7 weeks)

Highest-charting albums on Australian charts—Top 10
  Beach Boys Concert (#3)
  The Very Best of the Beach Boys (#8)
  Summer Dreams: 28 Classic Tracks (#10)
  15 Big Ones (#17)
  Endless Summer (#23)
  Still Cruisin' (#24)
  20 Golden Greats (#26)
  The Beach Boys In Concert (#29)
  Surf's Up (#32)
  Holland (#37)

Best-rated albums in the book *The New Rolling Stone Album Guide*
  Pet Sounds (5 stars)
  Sunflower (5 stars)
  The Pet Sounds Sessions (5 stars)
  Surfer Girl (4 stars)
  The Beach Boys Today! (4 stars)
  Wild Honey (4 stars)
  Friends (4 stars)
  20/20 (4 stars)
  The Beach Boys Love You (4 stars)
  Good Vibrations: Thirty Years of the Beach Boys (4 stars)

Best-rated albums in the book *All Music Guide, Fourth Edition*
  Greatest Hits, Vol. 1 (5 stars + marked as "essential recording" and "first
      purchase")
  Pet Sounds (5 stars + marked as "essential recording")
  Endless Summer (5 stars + marked as "essential recording")
  Good Vibrations: Thirty Years of the Beach Boys (5 stars + marked as "essential
      recording")
  Greatest Hits, Vol. 2 (5 stars + marked as "essential recording")
  The Beach Boys Today! (5 stars)
  Sunflower (5 stars)
  Surfin' U.S.A. (4 stars)
  Summer Days (And Summer Nights!!) (4 stars)
  Beach Boys' Party! (4 stars)
  Smiley Smile (4 stars)
  Wild Honey (4 stars)

Surf's Up (4 stars)
The Beach Boys Love You (4 stars)
Endless Harmony (4 stars)
Greatest Hits, Vol. 3: Best of the Brother Years (4 stars)

Best-rated albums in the book *The Virgin Encyclopedia of Popular Music*
Pet Sounds (5 stars)
Sunflower (5 stars)
Surf's Up (5 stars)
Endless Summer (5 stars)
Good Vibrations: Thirty Years of the Beach Boys (5 stars)
The Pet Sounds Sessions (5 stars)
Greatest Hits, Vol. 1: 20 Good Vibrations (5 stars)
Shut Down Volume 2 (4 stars)
All Summer Long (4 stars)
The Beach Boys Today! (4 stars)
Summer Days (And Summer Nights!!) (4 stars)
Smiley Smile (4 stars)
Friends (4 stars)
Holland (4 stars)
Spirit of America (4 stars)
Made in U.S.A. (4 stars)
Summer Dreams (4 stars)
Endless Harmony (4 stars)
Greatest Hits, Vol. 2: 20 More Good Vibrations (4 stars)
Greatest Hits, Vol. 3: Best of the Brother Years (4 stars)

Albums included in the book *1001 Albums You Must Hear Before You Die*
The Beach Boys Today!
Pet Sounds
Surf's Up

Bibliography

Books

Bacon, Tony and Paul Day. *The Fender Book: A Complete History of Fender Electric Guitars*. San Francisco: GPI Books, 1992.

Badman, Keith. *The Beach Boys: The Definitive Diary of America's Greatest Band on Stage and in the Studio*. San Francisco: Backbeat, 2004.

Carlin, Peter Ames. *Catch a Wave: The Rise, Fall & Redemption of the Beach Boys' Brian Wilson*. Rodale, 2006.

Chidester, Brian and Domenic Priore. *Pop Surf Culture*. Santa Monica Press, 2008.

Chidester, Brian and Domenic Priore. *Dumb Angel Gazette No. 4: All Summer Long*. Neptune Kingdom's Press, 2005.

Clark, Alan. *The Beach Boys: The Early Years*. The National Rock and Roll Archives, 1993.

Crenshaw, Marshall. *Hollywood Rock: A Guide to Rock' 'n' Roll in the Movies*. Harper Perennial, 1994.

Doe, Andrew and John Tobler. *The Complete Guide to the Music of the Beach Boys*. London: Omnibus, 1997.

Elliott, Brad. *Surf's Up: The Beach Boys on Record, 1961–1981*. Ann Arbor: Popular Culture, Ink, 1991.

Gaines, Steven. *Heroes and Villains: The True Story of the Beach Boys*. New York: New American Library, 1986.

Kubernick, Harvey. *Canyon of Dreams*. New York: Sterling, 2009.

Leaf, David. *The Beach Boys and the California Myth*. New York: Grosset, 1978.

McParland, Stephen J. *Smile, Sun, Sand & Pet Sounds*. California Music, 1999.

McParland, Stephen J. *It's Party Time*. PTB Productions, 1992.

Priore, Domenic. *Riot on Sunset Strip: Rock and Roll's Last Stand in Hollywood*. London: Jawbone, 2007.

Priore, Domenic. *Look! Listen! Vibrate! Smile!* Surfin' Colours Productions, 1988.

Selvin, Joel. *Monterey Pop*. San Francisco: Chronicle Books, 1992.

Whitburn, Joel. *The Billboard Book of Top 40 Albums*. Rev. ed. New York: Billboard, 1991.

Whitburn, Joel. *The Billboard Book of Top 40 Singles*. 8th ed. New York: Billboard, 2004.

White, Timothy. *The Nearest Faraway Place: Brian Wilson, the Beach Boys, and the Southern California Experience*. New York: Holt, 1994.

Articles

Beard, David. Various. *Endless Summer Quarterly*. 2000–2011

Crowe, Jerry. "Back to the Beach." *Los Angeles Times*. October 11, 1997.

Doe, Andrew. "In the Beginning . . ." Bellagio 10452 Website. 2002.

Hinsche, Billy. "Al Jardine: Rock and Roll Music." *Guitar One*. November 2001.

Hinsche, Billy. "Carl Wilson: The Lost Interview." *Guitar One*. November 2001.

Isadore, Jim. "Beach Boys: Rocket to Stardom on Surfboard Safari." *Centinela Sunday Press*. September 2, 1962.

Little, William. "The Day the Music Died." *The Times*. March 16, 2005.

Sharp, Ken. "Alan Jardine: A Beach Boy Still Riding the Waves." *Goldmine*. July 28, 2000.

Websites and Other Media

www.beachboysarchives.com

Bellagio 10452—www.esquarterly.com/bellagio

California Saga—www.mountvernonandfairway.de/main.htm

Eric Aniversario's Beach Boys Set-List Archive—members.tripod.com/~fun_fun_fun/setlists.html

Internet Movie Database—www.imdb.com

www.smileysmile.net

Elmer Marks's Beach Boys tour journals, 1963

Index

Grateful acknowledgment is made to the following for permission to use both published and unpublished materials:

The Independent: Obituary of Eugene Landy, Psychotherapist to Brian Wilson, by Peter Ames Carlin (April 1, 2006) Used by permission.

Gene Sculatti: "Meeting the Reclusive Brian". Used by permission.

Howie Edelson: "Flashback: The Beach Boys' "It's O.K." comeback special airs on NBC"; "Mike Love Ordered to Pay Brian Wilson Over $500,000"; "Mike Love of The Beach Boys, April 5, 2010"; "Al Jardine Not Interested In A One-Off Beach Boys Reunion". Used by permission.

The author also expresses gratitude to the following for quoted materials:

E! News: "Beach Boys Versus Katy Perry? Mike Love Says No Way!" (August 5, 2010)

Billboard.com: Beach Boys' Lost *Smile* Album to See Release in 2011, by Ed Christman (March 11, 2011).

Jay Jones: "Music Legends The Beach Boys To Perform With Special Guest John Stamos On The Season Premiere Of *Dancing with the Stars, the Results Show,* Tuesday, March 30, on ABC." (Press release)

Capitol/EMI: "The Beach Boys' Legendary *Smile* Album Sessions To Be Released This Year By Capitol/EMI." March 14, 2011. (Press release)

Sony Entertainment: "Pacific Ocean Blue:Legacy Edition", New York, June 25, 2008. (Press Release)

Every reasonable effort has been made to contact copyright holders and secure permissions. Omissions can be remedied in future editions.